WATERWAYS GUIDE 5

North West & the Pennines

Collins

Also available:

◯ Collins NICHOLSON
Waterways guides and map

1   Grand Union, Oxford & the South East

2   Severn, Avon & Birmingham

3   Birmingham & the Heart of England

4   Four Counties & the Welsh Canals

6   Nottingham, York & the North East

7   River Thames & the Southern Waterways

Inland Waterways Map of Great Britain

Published by Nicholson
An imprint of HarperCollins*Publishers*
Westerhill Road, Bishopbriggs,
Glasgow G64 2QT

www.harpercollins.co.uk
www.bartholomewmaps.com

River Thames Guide first published by Nicholson 1969
Waterways guides 1 South, 2 Midlands and 3 North first published by Nicholson 1971
This edition first published by Nicholson and Ordnance Survey 1997
New edition published by Nicholson 2000, 2003, 2006, 2009
Reprinted 2006, 2007, 2009, 2010

Researched and written by Jonathan Mosse, Judith Pile and David Lobban.
Designed by Bob Vickers.
Editorial and project management Cicely Frew.

The publishers gratefully acknowledge the assistance given by British Waterways and
their staff in the preparation of this guide.

Grateful thanks is also due to the Environment Agency
and members of the Inland Waterways Association.

All photographs reproduced by kind permission of Derek Pratt Photography, apart from:
Shutterstock p27–45 Paul Reid, p68 Andrei Nekrassov, p69–84 Kevin Eaves, p76 (green woodpecker) Borislav Borisov,
p92 Andrew Barker, p153 (great tit) Marcin Perkowski, p184 Alan Scheer, p200 Karel Gallas; Paul Huggins p34, 42, 72, 76
(grey heron).

Wending their quiet way through town and country, the inland navigations of Britain offer boaters, walkers and cyclists a unique insight into a fascinating, but once almost lost, world. When built this was the province of the boatmen and their families, who lived a mainly itinerant lifestyle: often colourful, to our eyes picturesque but, for them, remarkably harsh. Transporting the nation's goods during the late 1700s and early 1800s, negotiating locks, traversing aqueducts and passing through long narrow tunnels, canals were the arteries of trade during the initial part of the industrial revolution.

Then the railways came: the waterways were eclipsed in a remarkably short time by a faster and more flexible transport system, and a steady decline began. In a desperate fight for survival canal tolls were cut, crews toiled for longer hours and worked the boats with their whole family living aboard. Canal companies merged, totally uneconomic waterways were abandoned, some were modernised but it was all to no avail. Large scale commercial carrying on inland waterways had reached the finale of its short life.

At the end of World War II a few enthusiasts roamed this hidden world and harboured a vision of what it could become: a living transport museum which stretched the length and breadth of the country; a place where people could spend their leisure time and, on just a few of the wider waterways, a still modestly viable transport system.

The restoration struggle began and, from modest beginnings, Britain's inland waterways are now seen as an irreplaceable part of the fabric of the nation. Long abandoned waterways, once seen as an eyesore and a danger, are recognised for the valuable contribution they make to our quality of life, and restoration schemes are integrating them back into the network. Let us hope that the country's network of inland waterways continues to be cherished and well-used, maintained and developed as we move through the 21st century.

If you would like to comment on any aspect of the guides, please write to Nicholson Waterways Guides, Collins Geo, Westerhill Road, Bishopbriggs, Glasgow G64 2QT or email nicholson@harpercollins.co.uk.

❚ CONTENTS

The Waterways of Britain

Kingston upon Hull

R Humber

Lincoln

Fossdyke & Witham Navigations

Kyme Eau

South Kyme • Boston

King's Lynn

Wisbech

R Nene

Peterborough

R Bure

R Yare

R Great Ouse

R Waveney

R Great Ouse

R Cam

Cambridge

Bishop's Stortford

River Stort

Chelmer & Blackwater Navigation

Hertford

Hemel Hempstead

Chelmsford • Maldon

Watford

River Lee

Slough

London

R Thames

River Wey

Guildford

Godalming

River Medway

Chatham

Maidstone

Tonbridge

Dover

Brighton

English Channel

KEY

Waterways featured in this guide

Unnavigable section

Waterways featured in:

Guide 1

Guide 2

Guide 3

Guide 4

Guide 6

Guide 7

The Inland Waterways Map of Great Britain covers the canal and river navigations of England, Scotland and Wales.

GENERAL INFORMATION FOR WATERWAYS USERS

INTRODUCTION

Boaters, walkers, fishermen, cyclists and gongoozlers (on-lookers) all share in the enjoyment of our quite amazing waterway heritage. British Waterways and the Environment Agency, along with other navigation authorities, are empowered to develop, maintain and control this resource. It is to this end that a series of guides, codes, and regulations have come into existence over the years, evolving to match a burgeoning – and occasionally conflicting – demand. Set out in this section are key points as they relate to everyone wishing to enjoy the waterways.

The *Boater's Handbook* is available from all navigation authorities and can be downloaded from www.aina.org.uk. It contains a complete range of safety information, boat-handling know-how, warning symbols and illustrations.

BRITISH WATERWAYS

British Waterways (BW) cares for 2,200 miles of the country's canals and rivers. *The Waterways Code* gives advice and guidance to visitors on how to enjoy the inland waterways safely. It, and the *Boater's Handbook*, are available from the Customer Service Centre or from www.waterscape.com/downloads. BW Customer Service Centre is staffed Mon–Fri, 08.00–18.00, Sat 09.00–13.00. The helpful staff will answer general enquiries and provide information about boat licensing, boating holidays and activities on the waterways. They can be contacted on 0845 6715530; enquiries@britishwaterways.co.uk; British Waterways Customer Service Centre, 64 Clarendon Road, Watford WD17 1DA. Visit www.waterscape.com for up-to-date information on almost every aspect of the inland waterways, from news and events to moorings.

Emergency Helpline Available from BW outside normal office hours on weekdays and throughout weekends. For emergency help, or to report something dangerous, such as serious damage to structures or water escaping, call 0800 47 999 47.

ENVIRONMENT AGENCY

The Environment Agency (EA) manages around 600 miles of the country's rivers. For general enquiries or to obtain a copy of the *Boater's Handbook*, contact EA Customer Services on 08708 506 506; enquiries@environment-agency.gov.uk. To find out about their work nationally (or to download a copy of the *Handbook)* and for lots of other useful information, visit www.environment-agency.gov.uk.

Incident Hotline The EA maintain an Incident Hotline. To report damage or danger to the natural environment, damage to structures or water escaping, telephone 0800 80 70 60.

LICENSING – BOATS

The majority of the navigations covered in the Nicholson guides are controlled by BW and are managed on a day-to-day basis by local Waterway Offices (you will find details of these in the introductions to each waterway). All craft using the inland waterways must be licenced and charges are based on the dimensions of the craft. In a few cases, these include reciprocal agreements with other waterway authorities (as indicated in the text). BW and the EA offer an optional Gold Licence which covers unlimited navigation on the waterways of both authorities. Permits for permanent mooring on BW waterways are issued by BW.

Contact the BW Boat Licensing Team on 0845 6715530; www.britishwaterways.co.uk/licenseit; British Waterways Boat Licensing, PO Box 162, Leeds LS9 1AX.

BOAT SAFETY SCHEME

BW and the EA operate the Boat Safety Scheme – boat construction standards and regular tests required by all licence holders on BW and EA waterways. A Boat Safety Certificate (for new boats, a Declaration of Conformity), is necessary to obtain a craft licence. BW also requires proof of insurance for Third Party Liability for a minimum of £1,000,000 for powered boats. The scheme is gradually being adopted by other waterway authorities. Contact details are: 01923 201278; www.boatsafetyscheme.com; Boat Safety

Scheme, 64 Clarendon Road, Watford, Herts WD17 1DA. The website offers useful advice on preventing fires and avoiding carbon monoxide poisoning.

TRAINING

The Royal Yachting Association (RYA) runs one and two day courses leading to the Inland Waters Helmsman's Certificate, specifically designed for novices and experienced boaters wishing to cruise the inland waterways. For details of RYA schools, telephone 0845 345 0384 or visit www.rya.org.uk. The practical course notes are available to buy. Contact your local boat clubs, too. The National Community Boats Association (NCBA) run courses on boat-handling and safety on the water. Telephone 0845 0510649 or visit www.national-cba.co.uk.

LICENSING – CYCLISTS

Not all towpaths are open to cyclists. Maps on www.waterscape.com show the stretches of towpath open to cyclists, and local offices can supply more information. A cycle permit is usually required. For further information and to obtain a permit, contact BW Customer Services or visit www.waterscape.com.

TOWPATHS

Few, if any, artificial cuts or canals in this country are without an intact towpath accessible to the walker at least and the Thames is the only river in the country with a designated National Trail along its path from source to sea. However, on some other river navigations, towpaths have on occasion fallen into disuse or, sometimes, been lost to erosion. The indication of a towpath in this guide does not necessarily imply a public right of way or mean that a right to cycle along it exists. Horse riding and motorcycling are forbidden on all towpaths.

INDIVIDUAL WATERWAY GUIDES

No national guide can cover the minutiae of detail concerning every waterway, and some BW Waterway Managers produce guides to specific navigations under their charge. Copies of individual guides (where available) can be obtained from the relevant BW Waterway Office or downloaded from www.waterscape.com/boatersguides. Please note that times – such as operating times of bridges and locks – do change year by year and from winter to summer.

STOPPAGES

BW and the EA both publish winter stoppage programmes which are sent out to all licence holders, boatyards and hire companies. Inevitably, emergencies occur necessitating the unexpected closure of a waterway, perhaps during the peak season. You can check for stoppages on individual waterways between specific dates on www.waterscape.com/stoppages, lockside noticeboards or by telephoning 01923 201401; for stoppages and river conditions on EA waters, visit www.environment-agency.gov.uk.

NAVIGATION AUTHORITIES AND WATERWAYS SOCIETIES

Most inland navigations are managed by BW or the EA, but there are several other navigation authorities. For details of these, contact the Association of Inland Navigation Authorities on 0113 243 3125 or visit www.aina.org.uk. The boater, conditioned perhaps by the uniformity of our national road network, should be sensitive to the need to observe different codes and operating practices.

BW is a public corporation, responsible to the Department for Environment, Food and Rural Affairs in England and Wales, and is linked with an ombudsman. BW has a comprehensive complaints procedure and a free explanatory leaflet is available from Customer Services. Problems and complaints should be addressed to the local Waterway Manager in the first instance. For more information, visit their website.

The EA is the national body, sponsored by the Department for Environment, Food and Rural Affairs, to manage the quality of air, land and water in England and Wales. For more information, visit its website.

The Inland Waterways Association (IWA) campaigns for the use, maintenance and restoration of Britain's inland waterways, through branches all over the country. For more information, contact them on 01494 783453; iwa@waterways.org.uk; www.waterways.org.uk; The Inland Waterways Association, Island House, Moor Road, Chesham HP5 1WA. Their website has a huge amount of information of interest to boaters, including comprehensive details of the many and varied waterways societies.

STARTING OUT

Extensive information and advice on booking a boating holiday is available from the Inland Waterways Association, www.visitthames.co.uk and www.waterscape.com. Please book a waterway holiday from a licensed operator – only in this way can you be sure that you have proper insurance cover, service and support during your holiday. It is illegal for private boat owners to hire out their craft. If you are hiring a holiday craft for the first time, the boatyard will brief you thoroughly. Take notes, follow their instructions and don't be afraid to ask if there is anything you do not understand. BW have produced a short DVD giving basic information on using a boat safely. Copies are available from BW Customer Services (charge).

PLACES TO VISIT ALONG THE WAY

This guide contains a wealth of information, not just about the canals and rivers and navigating on them, but also on the visitor attractions and places to eat and drink close to the waterways. Opening and closing times, and other details often change; establishments close and new ones open. If you are making special plans to eat in a particular pub, or visit a certain museum it is always advisable to check in advance.

MORE INFORMATION

An internet search will reveal many websites on the inland waterways. Those listed below are just a small sample:

National Community Boats Association is a national charity and training provider, supporting community boat projects and encouraging more people to access the inland waterways. Telephone 0845 0510649; www.national-cba.co.uk.

National Association of Boat Owners is dedicated to promoting the interests of private boaters on Britain's canals and rivers. Visit www.nabo.org.uk.

www.canalplan.org.uk is an online journey-planner and gazetteer for the inland waterways.

www.canals.com is a valuable source of information on anything related to cruising the canals, with loads of links to canal and waterways related websites.

www.saveourwaterways.org is the website of Save Our Waterways, a campaign which embraces all waterways users and is dedicated to securing the long-term future of the inland waterways.

www.ukcanals.net lists services and useful information for all waterways users.

GENERAL CRUISING NOTES

Most canals and rivers are saucer shaped, being deepest at the middle. Few canals have more than 3-4ft of water and many have much less. Keep to the centre of the channel except on bends, where the deepest water is on the outside of the bend. When you meet another boat, keep to the right, slow down and aim to miss the approaching craft by a couple of yards. If you meet a loaded commercial boat keep right out of the way and be prepared to follow his instructions. Do not assume that you should pass on the right. If you meet a boat being towed from the bank, pass it on the outside. When overtaking, keep the other boat on your right side.

Some BW and EA facilities are operated by pre-paid cards, obtainable from BW and EA regional and local waterways offices, lock keepers and boatyards. Weekend visitors should purchase cards in advance. A handcuff/anti-vandal key is commonly used on locks where vandalism is a problem. A watermate/sanitary key opens sanitary stations, waterpoints and some bridges and locks. Both keys and pre-paid cards can be obtained via BW Customer Service Centre.

Safety

Boating is a safe pastime. However, it makes sense to take simple safety precautions, particularly if you have children aboard.

- Never drink and drive a boat – it may travel slowly, but it weighs many tons.
- Be careful with naked flames and never leave the boat with the hob or oven lit. Familiarise yourself and your crew with the location and operation of the fire extinguishers.
- Never block ventilation grills. Boats are enclosed spaces and levels of carbon monoxide can build up from faulty appliances or just from using the cooker.

- Be careful along the bank and around locks. Slipping from the bank might only give you a cold-water soaking, but falling from the side of, or into a lock is more dangerous. Beware of slippery or rough ground.
- Remember that fingers and toes are precious! If a major collision is imminent, never try to fend off with your hands or feet; and always keep hands and arms inside the boat.
- Weil's disease is a particularly dangerous infection present in water which can attack the central nervous system and major organs. It is caused by bacteria entering the bloodstream through cuts and broken skin, and the eyes, nose and mouth. The flu-like symptoms occur two-four weeks after exposure. Always wash your hands thoroughly after contact with the water. Visit www.leptospirosis.org for details.

Speed

There is a general speed limit of 4 mph on most BW canals. There is no need to go any faster – the faster you go, the bigger a wave the boat creates: if your wash is breaking against the bank, causing large waves or throwing moored boats around, slow down. Slow down also when passing engineering works and anglers; when there is a lot of floating rubbish on the water (try to drift over obvious obstructions in neutral); when approaching blind corners, narrow bridges and junctions.

Mooring

Generally you may moor where you wish on BW property, as long as you are *not causing an obstruction*. Do not moor in a winding hole or junction, the approaches to a lock or tunnel, or at a water point or sanitary station. Your boat should carry metal mooring stakes, and these should be driven firmly into the ground with a mallet if there are no mooring rings. Do not stretch mooring lines across the towpath and take account of anyone who may walk past. Always consider the security of your boat when there is no one aboard. On tideways and commercial waterways it is advisable to moor only at recognised sites, and allow for any rise or fall of the tide.

Bridges

On narrow canals slow down well in advance and aim to miss one side (usually the towpath side) by about 9 inches. *Keep everyone inboard when passing under bridges and ensure there is nothing on the roof of the boat that will hit the bridge.* If a boat is coming the other way, that nearest to the bridge has priority. Take special care with moveable structures – the crew member operating the bridge should be strong and heavy enough to hold it steady as the boat passes through.

Going aground

You can sometimes go aground if the water level on a canal has dropped or you are on a particularly shallow stretch. If it does happen, try reversing *gently*, or pushing off with the boat hook. Another method is to get your crew to rock the boat from side to side using the boat hook, or move all crew to the end opposite to that which is aground. Or, have all crew leave the boat, except the helmsman, and it will often float off quite easily.

Tunnels

Again, ensure that everyone is inboard. Make sure the tunnel is clear before you enter, and use your headlight. Follow any instructions given on notice boards by the entrance.

Fuel

Hire craft usually carry fuel sufficient for the rental period.

Water

It is advisable to top up daily.

Lavatories

Hire craft usually have pump out toilets. Have these emptied *before* things become critical. Keep the receipt and your boatyard will usually reimburse you. The Green Blue, an organisation providing environmental advice for boating and watersports, has produced a series of maps locating pump out facilities within the UK. Visit www.thegreenblue.org.uk/youandyourboat for these and other advice.

Boatyards

Hire fleets are usually turned around on a Saturday, making this a bad time to call in for services.

VHF Radio

The IWA recommends that all pleasure craft navigating the larger waterways used by freight carrying vessels, or any tidal navigation, should carry marine-band VHF radio and have a qualified radio operator on board. In some cases the navigation authority requires craft to carry radio and maintain a listening watch. Two examples of this are for boats on the tidal River Ouse wishing to enter Goole Docks and the Aire & Calder Navigation, and for boats on the tidal Thames, over 45ft, navigating between Teddington Lock and Limehouse Basin. VHF radio users must have a current operator's certificate. The training is not expensive and will present no problem to the average inland waterways boater. Contact the RYA (see Training) for details.

PLANNING A CRUISE

Don't try to go too far too fast. Go slowly, don't be too ambitious, and enjoy the experience. Mileages indicated on the maps are for guidance only. A *rough* calculation of time taken to cover the ground is the lock-miles system:

Add the number of *miles* to the number of *locks* on your proposed journey, and divide the resulting figure by three. This will give you an approximate guide to the number of *hours* your travel will take.

TIDAL WATERWAYS

The typical steel narrow boat found on the inland waterways is totally unsuitable for cruising on tidal estuaries. However, the adventurous will inevitably wish to add additional 'ring cruises' to the more predictable circuits of inland Britain. Passage is possible in most estuaries if careful consideration is given to the key factors of weather conditions, tides, crew experience, the condition of the boat and its equipment and, perhaps of overriding importance, the need to take expert advice. In many cases it will be prudent to employ the skilled services of a local pilot. Within the text, where inland navigations connect with a tidal waterway, details are given of sources of advice and pilotage. It is also essential to inform your insurance company of your intention to navigate on tidal waterways as they may very well have special requirements or wish to levy an additional premium. This guide is to the inland waterways of Britain and therefore recognizes that tideways – and especially estuaries – require a different approach and many additional skills. We do not hesitate to draw the boater's attention to the appropriate source material.

LOCKS AND THEIR USE

A lock is a simple and ingenious device for transporting your craft from one water level to another. When both sets of gates are closed it may be filled or emptied using gates, or ground paddles, at the top or bottom of the lock. These are operated with a windlass.

If a lock is empty, or 'set' for you, the crew open the gates and you drive the boat in. If the lock is full of water, the crew should check first to see if any boat is waiting or coming in the other direction. If a boat is in sight, you must let them through first: do not empty or 'turn' the lock against them. This is not only discourteous, and against the rules, but wastes precious water.

In the diagrams the *plan* shows how the gates point uphill, the water pressure forcing them together. Water is flooding into the lock through the underground culverts that are operated by the ground paddles: when the lock is 'full', the top gates (on the left of the drawing) can be opened. One may imagine a boat entering, the crew closing the gates and paddles after it.

In the *elevation*, the bottom paddles have been raised (opened) so that the lock empties. A boat will, of course, float down with the water. When the lock is 'empty' the bottom gates can be opened and the descending boat can leave.

Remember that when going *up* a lock, a boat should be tied up to prevent it being thrown about by the the rush of incoming water; but when going *down* a lock, a boat should never be tied up or it will be left high and dry.

- Make safety your prime concern. *Keep a close eye on young children.*
- Always take your time, and do not leap about.
- Never open the paddles at one end without ensuring those at the other end are closed.
- Keep to the landward side of the balance beam when opening and closing gates.

Ground paddles open. Water fills the chamber through the culverts.

Gate paddles closed, retaining water in the lock chamber.

A plan of a lock filling.

Ground paddles closed preventing water from the upper level filling the chamber.

Gate paddles open. Water flows from the chamber to the lower level.

An elevation of a lock emptying.

Crew prepares to open ground paddles after lower gates and paddles have been closed by departing crew.

Boat leaves lock to lower level – crew begins to close lower gates and then to close gate paddles so the chamber may refill.

Boat waiting to enter from upper level after chamber has been refilled.

Lock gate with paddle mechanism.

- Never leave your windlass slotted onto the paddle spindle – it will be dangerous should anything slip.
- Keep your boat away from the top and bottom gates to prevent it getting caught on the gate or the lock cill.
- Never drop the paddles – always wind them down.

- Be wary of fierce *top gate* paddles, especially in wide locks. Operate them slowly, and close them if there is *any* adverse effect.
- Always follow the navigation authority's instructions, where given on notices or by their staff.

Salterhebble Locks, Calder & Hebble Navigation (see page 52)

MAXIMUM DIMENSIONS

River Lock to tail of Leeds Lock
Length: 141' 0"
Beam: 17' 9"
Headroom: 11' 9"
Draught: 7' 7"

Leeds Lock to Castleford
Length: 200' 0"
Beam: 20' 0"
Headroom: 11' 9"
Draught: 8' 2"

Castleford to Wakefield
Length: 141' 0"
Beam: 17' 9"
Headroom: 11' 10"
Draught: 7' 7"

MANAGER

0113 281 6800;
enquiries.yorkshire@britishwaterways.co.uk

MILEAGE

LEEDS to
Castleford: 10 miles, 5 locks
Wakefield: 17½ miles, 10 locks including Fall Ing

SAFETY NOTES

BW produce an excellent set of *Cruising Notes* for pleasure boaters using this navigation, obtainable by contacting the Waterway Unit Manager's office above, or downloadable from www.waterscape.com/boatersguides. This is both a commercial waterway and one developed from a river navigation: both pose their own disciplines highlighted in the notes.
Each lock on the waterway has a set of traffic lights both upstream and downstream of the lock chamber. The purpose of these lights is to convey instructions and advice to approaching craft.

Red light
Stop and moor up on the lock approach. The lock is currently in use.

Amber light *(between the red and green lights)*
The lock keeper is not on duty. You will need to self-operate.

Green light
Proceed into lock.

Red & green lights together
The lock is available for use. The lock keeper will prepare and operate the lock for you.

Flashing red light
Flood conditions – unsafe for navigation.

Most lock approach moorings are immediately upstream and downstream of the lock chamber. However, **please note:**

1 Knostrop Lock downstream approach mooring is located alongside the lock bulnose.

2 Locks at Leeds, Lemonroyd, Castleford, Woodnook and Broadreach allow access to river sections of the navigation. For interpretation of river level gauge boards *see* Safety Notes in the introduction to the Calder & Hebble Navigation on page 46.

3 There is a safe haven mooring immediately upstream of Lemonroyd Lock.

All locks between Leeds and Wakefield (except Fall Ing Lock) are equipped with VHF Marine Band Radio. They monitor and operate on channel 74. In an emergency non-VHF users contact the manager's office or out of office hours telephone 0800 47 999 47. Mobile phone users telephone 01384 215785.

The River Aire was first made navigable to Leeds in 1700, and rapidly became a great commercial success, taking coal out of the Yorkshire coalfield and bringing back raw wool, corn and agricultural produce. Improvements were then made to the difficult lower reaches, with first Selby and later Goole becoming Yorkshire's principal inland port. The opening of the New Junction Canal in 1905 further secured its suitability for commercial traffic, which until recently amounted to some 2 million tonnes a year, mainly coal, sand and petroleum. With the completion of coal extraction at the St Aidens opencast site, together with the unacceptably high sulphur content of the material from Kellingley colliery, coal carrying has suddenly drawn to a halt. However, petroleum tonnages are on the increase while the quantities of sand and gravel carried by barge to Lafarge's Whitwood terminal look to be extremely healthy.

Leeds

The great Aire & Calder
Navigation joins the Leeds &
Liverpool Canal at River Lock, in the
centre of Leeds by the City's station.
The area above the lock has undergone
extensive redevelopment, effectively
separating the waterway from the railway.
Heading east, the waterway passes under three
substantial bridges, generally hemmed in by tall
buildings and warehouses with much new building and
development, particularly housing. Industry predominates
below Leeds Lock, although the lock itself is quite handsomely
situated – overlooked by tall Victorian warehouses and the Royal
Armouries Museum. Keep right to avoid the weir at Leeds Lock. Boaters
should take the centre channel at Knostrop Flood Lock, through the gates
which are usually open (they are closed when the river level rises after
prolonged heavy rain, effectively closing the navigation), avoiding the river and a
weir to the left, and the disused basin of Leeds Oil Terminal to the right. Passing the
old bonded warehouses and container terminal the navigation enters an artificial channel,
with the River Aire to the north, which is to persist for a little over 7 miles until the river is
rejoined below Lemonroyd Lock. Beyond the Thwaite Mills Industrial Museum a no-man's-land of
closed collieries and landscaped spoil heaps is entered. Below the museum boaters should brace
themselves for loud detonations emanating from a factory on the south bank of the navigation.
These are caused by the destructive testing of gas bottles. The towpath is diverted at Fishpond Lock,
a lonely outpost, to avoid a small wooded area now maintained as a local nature reserve.

WALKING & CYCLING
The towpath from Leeds to Mickletown is now part of the Trans Pennine Trail (National Cycle Route 67) and is
well used by walkers and cyclists alike. There are two excellent interpretation boards between Victoria and
Crown Point Bridges – entitled 'Eye on the Aire' – depicting local activity in times gone by.

NAVIGATIONAL NOTES

1 All the locks on the Aire & Calder operate mechanically. Lock keepers move from lock to lock, primarily to operate them for commercial traffic. They will assist boaters through locks whenever possible but all locks can now be self-operated. Obey the traffic light signals.

2 Remember that this is a river navigation. Many of the locks are accompanied by large weirs, so keep a sharp lookout for the signs which direct you safely into the locks.

3 When the river level rises after prolonged heavy rain, the flood gates will be closed. Pleasure craft should stay put until they are advised by a lock keeper that it is safe to proceed.

4 This is a commercial waterway, used by 600-tonne tankers and large sand carrying barges. Keep a lookout for them, and give them a clear passage. Moor carefully, using bollards or fixed rings rather than mooring stakes, since the wash from these craft can be substantial.

BOAT TRIPS

Kirkstall Flyboat Canal Wharf, Holbeck, Leeds LS11 5PS (0113 245 6195) is a restaurant boat seating up to 52 persons. Licensed bar and food available.
Leeds City Cruisers (0845 388 4901; www.leedscitycruisers.co.uk). Waterbus service, trips along the Aire and Calder, private hire and dining cruises from Clarence Dock (LS10 1LE), aboard the *Black Prince*.

Boatyards

Ⓑ **Clarence Dock Leeds** Armouries Drive, Leeds LS10 1LE (01977 554351). Beside the Royal Armouries Museum. 🛁 🚰 ⚓ Overnight mooring, long-term mooring, pump out, showers, toilets, disabled facilities.

17

Leeds

W. Yorks. All services. A vast industrial city that was a wool centre in the Middle Ages and has continued to grow to prosperity under the textile and clothing trades; indeed Marks & Spencer started business here with a stall in the market. Montague Burton also became established in the city, building what was to become, by 1921, the largest clothing factory in the world. However the last few years have brought substantial changes, with old industries being replaced by new, and the atmosphere is one of growth and prosperity. The great town hall in Victoria Square (walk north from Victoria Bridge and turn left at Great George Street) stands as a magnificent monument to Victorian civic pride. It was designed by Cuthbert Brodrick and opened in 1858. Looking at the Corinthian columns on all sides and the clock tower some 255ft high, it is hard to believe that Brodrick was only 29 years old when he submitted his plans. As a measure of this man's self-confidence, note that he also designed the organ, installed in 1859, which itself weighs almost 70 tonnes, has 6,500 pipes and stands 50ft high. The light and airy Corn Exchange (north of Leeds Bridge along Call Lane and now a shopping arcade) built in 1861 is also Brodrick's work. Always the cultural centre of Yorkshire, the city hosts an international concert season and an international piano competition. It has several splendid theatres, including The Grand in Briggate, modelled on La Scala, Milan; the City Varieties, the oldest surviving music hall in the country; and the Leeds Playhouse Repertory Theatre. Also impressive is the way, perhaps unique in the development of northern industrial towns, that contemporary and Victorian buildings stand harmoniously side by side. There are several splendid parks and rich museums, and excellent shopping facilities, including the ornate Victorian Queens and County arcades. Headingley, the home of Yorkshire cricket and a test match venue, attracts an enthusiastic following in the area, and of course the city's association with football and rugby teams is known worldwide. Boaters should try to spend a day here if they possibly can – there are good moorings on the Leeds & Liverpool Canal by Office Lock, or above Leeds Lock. *See also* page 135 (Leeds & Liverpool Canal) for information on Leeds Industrial Museum and Abbey House Museum.

Metro. The area is well served by an excellent, cheap bus and train service which offers a variety of Day Rover tickets. Telephone 0113 245 7676 or visit www.wymetro.com for details.

Tourist Information Centre The Arcade, Leeds City Station, Leeds LS1 4DT (0113 242 5242; www. leeds.gov.uk). The usual mine of information concerning places to visit and accommodation. *Open Mon–Sat 09.00–17.30 and Sun 10.00– 16.00.*

Henry Moore Institute 74 The Headrow, Leeds LS1 3AH (0113 246 7467; www.henry-moore-fdn.co.uk). Walk north from Victoria Bridge. Award-winning institute housing four galleries showing temporary sculpture exhibitions of all periods and nationalities. Shop. *Open daily 10.00–17.30 (Wed until 21.00).* Information line 0113 234 3158. Free.

City Art Gallery The Headrow, Leeds LS1 3AA (0113 247 8248; www.leeds.gov.uk/artgallery). Fine collections of paintings, watercolours, sculpture and 20th-C British Art. Collections include Victorian paintings, British watercolours, French Post-Impressionist paintings and British sculpture. *Open Mon–Sat 10.00–17.00 (Wed 20.00) and Sun 13.00–17.00.* Disabled facilities. Free.

Leeds-Settle-Carlisle Line From Leeds City Station LS1 4DT (www.settle-carlisle.co.uk). The 70 miles from Settle to Carlisle is said to be one of the most memorable rail journeys in the world, so this would make an excellent day trip away from the boat. There is a *daily* passenger service between Leeds and Carlisle with no need to book. *Every Sat and Sun, May–Oct* there are free guided walks from trains on the line. Coach tours around the Yorkshire Dales also connect. Details from leaflets at the station or Tourist Information Centre.

Middleton Railway The Station, Moor Road, Hunslet, Leeds LS10 2JQ (0113 271 0320; www.middletonrailway.org.uk). Built in 1758 to link Leeds with the Middleton Colliery, this is considered to be the world's oldest railway. It operates at *weekends Easter-end of year* from the industrial suburb of Hunslet, where steam engines were once built. Charge.

Royal Armouries Armouries Drive, Leeds LS10 1LT (0113 220 1916; www.armouries.org.uk). Beside Leeds Lock with moorings in Clarence Dock, adjacent to the complex. The emphasis is on participation in this massive, interactive museum reputed to be Britain's largest post-war leisure development. Five themed galleries unfold stories of weapons, battles, tournaments, falconry and the Wild West. See, touch, smell and handle before retiring to watch the skills of an armourer or experience the tranquillity of a Japanese tea garden. *Open daily 10.00–17.00. Closed 24–25 Dec.* Two cafés and a bistro. Charge.

Thackray Museum 141 Beckett Street, Leeds LS9 7LN (0113 244 4343; www.thackraymuseum.org). A hands-on experience covering the history of medicine from Victorian times to the present day. This award-winning museum introduces you to Sherlock Bones and his tour of the Giant Gut, allows you to experience surgery without anaesthetics in 'Pain, Pus and Blood' and lets you assist Mrs Hirst with her 12th child. A truly participative establishment. Shop and café. *Open Tue–Sat and B Hol Mon 10.00–17.00. Last admission 15.00 – but allow 3 hours for your visit.* Bus Nos 4, 4C, 22, 42, 50, 50A, 88. Information hotline 0113 245 7084. Charge.

Leeds Town Hall The Headrow, Leeds LS1 3AD (0113 247 7989; www.leedsconcertseason.com). Built in 1858, Queen Victoria performed the official opening. Today it is a venue for concerts of all types of music and light entertainment.

Leeds Corn Exchange 42 Call Lane, Leeds LS1 6DT (0113 234 0363; www.cornx.net) A Grade 1 listed Victorian building, restored to its original splendour. There are plans to turn the building into a focus for food, with a restaurant and food and drink retailers, as well as cookware and kitchen appliances.

The Grand Theatre 46 New Briggate, Leeds LS1 6NZ (0113 222 6222; www.leedsgrandtheatre. com) Theatre and opera house, showing ballet as well as all types of shows. Also workshops and special events.

The City Varieties Music Hall Swan Street, Leeds LS1 6LW (0845644 1881; www.tickets. cityvarieties.co.uk) Pantomime and all kinds of variety shows in a grade II listed building where variety shows have been held since 1865.

Headingley Carnegie Stadium Leeds LS6 3BU (0870 429 6774; www.yorkshireccc.com). Home to theYorkshire County Cricket Club since 1891.

Thwaite Mills Watermill Thwaite Lane, Stourton, Leeds LS10 1RP (0870 121 4901; www.leeds.gov.uk/thwaiteMills). A canalside flint and china stone-grinding mill built in 1872 and powered by two waterwheels until 1975, when they were washed away, bringing closure a year later. Visitors are able to see the working conditions in the mill, as well as a Marshall engine and various artefacts. *Open Tue–Sun 10.00–17.00.* Charge.

Tropical World and Roundhay Park Roundhay, Leeds LS8 1DF (0113 266 1850; www.roundhaypark.org.uk). A wide selection of buses from the city centre serves this tropical paradise featuring butterflies, exotic blooms and colourful fish. This is also one of Europe's largest parks, with woodland walks, scented gardens (including National Collections), canal gardens, waterfalls and a ruined castle. *Open 10.00–18.00 (16.00 in winter) daily except Christmas.* Charge.

● Woodlesford
W. Yorks. PO, tel, stores, garage, station. Good moorings above the lock and nearby pubs make this a popular stopping place for boaters. There is a very popular bird hide adjacent to the canal. The supermarket (0113 282 4119) here is *open daily 04.30-21.00.*

Pubs and Restaurants

A fine city such as Leeds has many pubs and restaurants. The following is a selection of those fairly close to the navigation.

✕♀ Hansa's Gujarati Vegetarian Restaurant 72–74 North Street, Leeds LS2 7PN (0113 244 4408; www.hansasrestaurant.com). Worth seeking out for excellent, home-cooked dishes with an Indian flavour. A unique establishment serving Indian vegetarian cuisine from the State of Gujarat in a split-level restaurant with an elegant, homely atmosphere. *Open Mon–Sat E and Sun L.* Families warmly welcomed.

✕♀ River Plate 36-8 The Calls, Leeds LS2 7EW (0113 391 2792; www.riverplate.co.uk). Argentinian restaurant and bar. Outside seating. Regular food and drink offers. *Open Mon–Sat 17.00-23.00, Thu–Sat also 12.00-15.00. Bar open until midnight.*

✕♀ Olive Press Canal Wharf, Water Lane, Leeds LS11 5PS (0113 244 6611; www.heathcotes.co.uk). Italian favourites, including pasta and pizza. Children had the opportunity to make their own pizza. *Open from 11.30 (12.00 Sun).*

● Grove Back Row, Leeds LS11 5PL (0113 243 9254). South of Victoria Bridge. Small traditional ale house dispensing an excellent selection of real ales (four regulars and four rotating guests) and inexpensive bar snacks *L (not Sat).* Home-made steak pie and hot beef and onion rolls are specialities. Children welcome *until 21.00;* dogs at all hours. Folk *Fri* and live music *regularly.* Outside seating.

● Adelphi Hunslet Road, Leeds LS10 1JQ (0113 245 6377; www.theadelphi.co.uk). South of Leeds Bridge. A superbly restored and very grand Victorian pub, with lots of etched glass and mahogany. Listed inside and out. Real ale and food *L and E Mon–Sun.* Children welcome; dogs in taproom only. Outside seating. Regular quiz nights; comedy club *last Mon of every month.*

● ✕ Whitelock's Turk's Head Yard, Briggate, Leeds LS1 6HB (0113 245 3950). North of Leeds Bridge. An unspoilt Edwardian pub, one of the first buildings to have electricity. Reputedly the oldest pub in the city (its first licence was granted in 1715) and described by John Betjeman as 'the very heart of Leeds', this hostelry serves up to eight real ales and has a floral-hung beer garden set in an alleyway. Excellent, freshly prepared traditional English food is available, both in the bar and restaurant, *L and E, daily (all day in the bar).* Children welcome in restaurant.

● Duck & Drake Kirkgate, Leeds LS2 7DR (0113 246 5806). North of Crown Point Bridge, near the church. Simply decorated pub with an open fire and a choice of real ales. Bar snacks available *L only.* Beer garden. Live music *weekends.* No children.

● Palace Kirkgate, Leeds LS2 7DJ (0113 244 5882). Straightforward, no-frills pub dispensing 12 changing real ales, *open all day.* Food is available daily *11.30-19.00.* Children welcome *at mealtimes;* dogs *other than at mealtimes.* Quiz *Mon and Wed.* Outside seating and pub games.

● Viaduct 11 Lower Bridgate, Leeds LS1 6ER (0113 245 4863). Long, narrow pub featuring a selection of milds together with other real ales. Excellent disabled facilities. This pub is the official home of Leeds United supporters and serves food *all day (until 16.00 on Sun).* Children welcome *until 16.00.* Pub games and large screen TV. Disco *Fri and Sat.*

● Two Pointers Church Street, Woodlesford, Leeds LS26 8RE (0113 282 3124). Up the hill from the lock. A smart and friendly village pub. Real ale. Outside seating. Dogs welcome. *Occasional* entertainment. Patio.

● White Hart Church Street, Woodlesford, Leeds LS26 8RD (0113 282 2205). Just past The Two Pointers. A snug and comfy real ale pub.

Castleford

The navigation continues along its straight course with the River Aire just to the north, its meanderings having endowed it with a series of oxbow lakes. All around are the remains of disused coal workings, some landscaped into smooth grassy banks, others a gaunt pale grey. At Woodlesford a path up from the lock leads to *two pubs, a post office, and shops.*

NAVIGATIONAL NOTES

1 Boaters must on *no account* take the river course towards the weir at Castleford Junction. Make sure you are clear about where to go *before* you get there.
2 The Lafarge sand and gravel wharf is at Whitwood, just below the old Fairies Hill Lock, and receives regular barge deliveries. Watch out for large craft manoeuvring in this area.

WALKING & CYCLING

It is possible – during the summer months – for pedestrians to follow a path on the north side of the navigation, from Caroline Bridge to Castleford, with waymarked deviations around the lake near Woodend and through Allerton Bywater. Otherwise see notes on page 23.

There is also a *supermarket and off-licence*. Just before Fleet Bridge an arm branches off to the north. A disused lock here once used to connect with the river. Enclosed within the arm is an oil terminal – notice how the storage tanks have been colonised by house martins. This facility is also visited several times a week by oil tankers so be on the look out for loaded craft manoeuvring above Fleet Bridge. The river by Fleet Lock was the site of a disastrous breach which occurred in March 1988, when the ground separating it from the adjacent St Aidens open-cast mine collapsed and the water poured in. Apparently the river below the breach flowed backwards for half a day, such was the volume of water consumed, and the workforce only just managed to rescue the large cranes. There are visitor and long-term moorings available in the marina above the new Lemonroyd Lock (combining the old Lemonroyd Lock with the now-vanished Kippax Lock). Rejoining the river at Lemonroyd Lock, the mining village of Allerton Bywater appears at the end of the newly constructed section of waterway. There is a welcome waterside pub here, but make sure you moor securely if you stop, since passing commercial craft cause a considerable wash. There is a waterways 'crossroads' at Castleford.

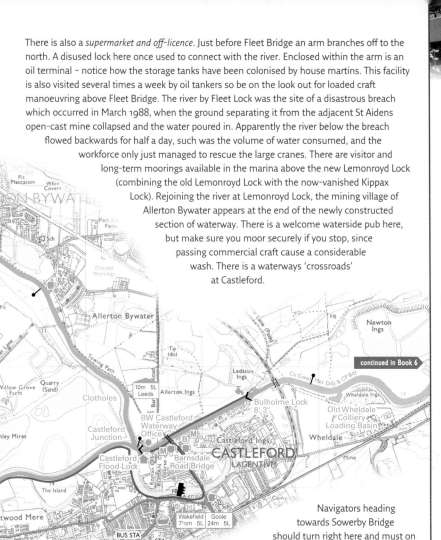

continued in Book 6

Navigators heading towards Sowerby Bridge should turn right here and must on no account go straight across – since that way leads to the huge Castleford Weir. To the left, through the Flood Lock, are a *sanitary station*, *showers* and good *moorings*, beyond which lies the route to Sheffield (*see* Book 6), Goole, Hull, York, the River Trent and ultimately the North Sea. The large commercial craft which trade to Fleet and Whitwood emerge from here, so boats travelling downstream on either the rivers Aire or Calder, though not entering the flood lock, must still observe the traffic signals to avoid collision with vessels leaving the lock. Entering the River Calder, navigators will notice that its course here has been straightened, as the oxbow lakes either side will testify. After ducking under a large road bridge and two railway bridges, a path which gives access to two fine pubs at Whitwood can be seen to the south. Your nose will also tell you there is a large sewage works here. Pressing on, the large, deep mechanised Woodnook Lock is reached. This replaced the earlier Fairies and Altofts locks (now disused) to the south. By comparing the sizes of the locks, an impression of the improvements carried out on the navigation during the last 100 years can be gained. Beyond the large motorway bridge is King's Road Lock (also mechanised) and paths from here lead to Altofts, although there is little reason to walk the ½ mile or so, except for supplies.

21

Temple Newsam House and Garden Temple Newsam Road, off Selby Road, Leeds LS15 0AE (0113 264 5535; www.leeds.gov.uk/templenewsam). Walk north from Swillington Bridge, fork left after the river – 2 miles. A superb Tudor/Jacobean house in 900 acres of parkland. Magnificent Georgian and Regency interiors. Walks in park and woods, magnificent displays of roses and rhododendrons in gardens. Regular events and activities. *House open: Nov–Mar Tue–Sun, and B Hol Mon, 10.30–16.00; Apr–Oct Tue–Sun 10.30–17.00.* Charge. *Park and gardens open all year.* Free.

Temple Newsam Farm A working rare breeds farm – home to 400 animals. Sheep, pigs, goats, chickens, ducks and largest Vaynol herd in the world. Three-hundred-year-old Great Barn and other traditional farm buildings housing a collection of old agricultural tools and machinery. *Open Tue–Sun 10.00–17.00 (16.00 winter).* Shop and café. Charge.

● **Mickletown**
W. Yorks. PO, tel, stores. Claimed by the locals to be the second largest village in England – it is suggested that Wroxham in Norfolk is the largest – Mickletown has clearly had its problems since the neighbouring colliery closed. The next-door village of Wood Row is close by, and the *pub, store and PO* there can be easily reached via a path from Caroline Bridge.

● **Allerton Bywater**
W. Yorks. PO, tel, stores. A mining village, but the pit is now closed. Coal was once loaded from wagons onto barges from a small staithe here.

● **Castleford**
W. Yorks. All services. Once the Roman settlement of *Lagentium*, now a busy industrial town which has grown up at this important waterways junction, it is also the birth place of the sculptor Henry Moore. The Waterway Office can be seen by the Flood Lock, and Allinsons mill is situated by the huge weir – here they produce their popular stoneground flour. **Castleford Museum** Carlton Street, Castleford WF10 1BE (01977 722085). In the library. Victorian Castleford theme exhibition. *Open daily during library opening hours.* Free.

● **Altofts**
W. Yorks. PO, tel, stores. Originally a mining village and now a suburb of Wakefield. There was once a pub by the river, but it is now a private house. There are still two pubs in the village.

Near Legard Flood Lock, Mirfield on the Calder & Hebble Navigation (see page 50)

Boat Inn Boat Lane, Allerton Bywater, Castleford WF102BX (01977 552216). An attractive riverside pub where once a ferry operated carrying miners and boat horses across the river, now replaced with a micro-brewery serving their own real ales and guest beers. Food is available *L and E, daily*. Riverside seating. Children's room and outdoor play area. Quiz *Thu and Sun*. Take care when mooring here, as passing commercial craft can create a sizeable wash.

Victoria Hotel Main Street, Allerton Bywater, Castleford WF10 2BZ (01977 516438). Friendly, modernised local dispensing real ale and good cheer. Children welcome. Garden. Quiz *Sun*.

Griffin Lock Lane, Castleford WF10 2BX (01977 557551). Real ale. Dogs welcome; children welcome. Outside seating. Quiz and bingo *Wed*; quiz and open box *Sun*. Try also **The Britt**, nearby on Lock Lane (WF10 2JU).

Garden House Wheldon Road, Whitwood, Castleford (01977 552934). On the south bank of the river. An ideal, comfortable, family pub with food available *L and E, daily*. The Goole packet boat used to leave from outside but now the friendly landlord is more concerned with serving real ale. Children welcome *until 21.00*. Outside seating. Large screen with Sky TV. Quiz *Thu*.

Bridge Inn Hotel Altofts Lane, Whitwood, Castleford WF10 5PZ (01977 550498; www.thebridgeinncastleford.co.uk). A most interesting pub, newly built but with old bricks and timbers. There is a lofty ceiling over the bar, with more intimate drinking and eating areas off to the sides. Good bar and restaurant meals – *L and E, daily* – friendly staff and a selection of real ale. Patio. Children welcome. B & B.

New Wheatsheaf Altofts Lane, Whitwood, Castleford WF10 5QB (01977 553052; www.wheatsheaf.com). Large, brightly decorated traditional pub, where someone clearly takes a great pride in their flower arrangements. Real ales, and a wide range of interesting and appetising food served *L and E* (not *Sun E* in restaurant) in both bar and restaurant – 3-course *Sun L* a speciality. Children welcome, patio. Quiz *Sun*. Regular events and entertainment.

WALKING & CYCLING

Currently there is no continuous towpath from Caroline Bridge to Castleford so walkers and cyclists wishing to follow the navigation are presented with two choices:

1 Leave the towpath ½ mile east of Shan Bridge and follow the Trans Pennine Trail signs onto Mickletown Road and thence to the junction of Savile Road and Church Road. Turn left along Savile Road and right along Pinfold Lane at the T junction. At the main road (Barnsdale Road) turn left and follow this road – along the pavement – round a sharp right-hand bend (ignore the left-hand turning here into Micklefield) and then south to Methley Bridge over the Wakefield Branch of the Aire & Calder Canal. Join the towpath here and follow it east into Castlefield. For those following this diversion in reverse (i.e. from Castleford) leave the navigation at Barnsdale Road Bridge and head south, over the river and turn right along Savile Road. Immediately past the roundabout look for a Public Footpath sign leading you back onto the river bank.

2 Follow the directions above to Methley Bridge where, by turning west along the towpath, it is possible to reach Wakefield and, with the assistance of the excellent Metro bus/rail system (0113 245 7676; www.wymetro.com) complete a circular walk/ride that might have commenced in Leeds. N.B. A section of the towpath Methley Bridge to Wakefield is only cyclable with care and at the cyclist's own risk!

3 A third option is to make use of the Trans Pennine Trail throughout its route in the Leeds area. Starting at Crown Point Bridge (*see page 16* near the city centre, it follows the canal to Mickletown (*see* 1 above) where, by following the excellent waymarking west along a minor road and a disused railway line, it heads to Wakefield making use of a further section of canal (the Aire & Calder Wakefield Branch) at Stanley Ferry. This is part of Euro-route E8 (ultimately running from the west coast of Ireland to Istanbul). For further information (free) and detailed guides (charge) contact the Trans Pennine Trail Officer on 01226 772574 or visit www.transpenninetrail.org.uk.

Wakefield

Birkwood Lock was for a long time the last mechanised lock when travelling upstream. At Stanley Ferry the canal is diverted over the new aqueduct, which stands alongside the original and was opened in 1981. The original aqueduct was thought to be at risk from the large craft which can now navigate here. There is a British Waterways repair yard and lock gate building workshop immediately before the aqueduct, and a marina with a pub beyond. This has been built in a defunct loading basin beside the splendid, stone wharf office. It was here that empty 'Tom Puddings' were hauled onto railway wagons and, after loading at the nearby colliery, re-launched en route for Goole. After Ramsden's Swing Bridge (*sanitary station, pump out and showers*) the navigation continues in a dead straight line, passing Broadreach Flood Lock and Heath Old Hall before turning west to join the Calder & Hebble at Fall Ing Lock. There are craft moored here by an old loading chute, a *picnic area* and convenient *pub*. Below Wakefield Flood Lock the river is navigable for a short distance towards the weir, although much cluttered by large craft undergoing refurbishment at the boatyard here. Leaving Wakefield you pass under a splendid curving brick railway viaduct known locally as 'the 99 arches'. A careful count will reveal only 95.

Stanley Ferry Aqueduct

It is a good idea to moor at Stanley Ferry Marina and walk to the road bridge for a full view of this fine structure – a trough suspended from a two-pin cast iron arch – built on the same principle as the Sydney Harbour Bridge, which it predates by 100 years. Nearly 7000 tons of Bramley Fall stone and 1000 tons of cast iron were used in its construction. The first boat to pass across it was the *James*, a schooner of 160 tons drawn by three grey horses, on 8 August 1839. The 700 men who worked on it were fed at the nearby public houses, one of which, The Ship, still stands. Designed by George Leather, the strength of the structure was severely tested when, soon after opening, the largest flood for 20 years caused the river below actually to flow into the trough. The towpath is carried on a separate steel girder structure designed to protect the aqueducts during such floods. The concrete aqueduct was built in 1981, and the original, by its side, is still in water.

NAVIGATIONAL NOTES

1 Take heed of the notices and flood indicator boards at the locks. Pleasure craft should only proceed if the water level is in the *green* or *amber* sectors. Amber indicates that the river is above normal levels and that boaters should proceed with caution to and THROUGH the next lock.
2 Most locks on the Calder & Hebble have a unique type of paddle gear, consisting of a small perforated wheel which is turned using a 'handspike'. These are obtainable from boatyards on the navigation, and from the BW office at Castleford. Or a piece of 3" x 2" hardwood, 3ft long (and planed down to size), will do just as well.
3 When coming downstream (from Sowerby Bridge direction) keep a sharp lookout for the entrance to Wakefield Flood Lock. There is a large weir on the river, a short distance beyond the boatyard, by the bridge.

49

THORNES

Thornes Portobello
Lock
8' 3"

WALKING & CYCLING

1 At Stanley Ferry the Trans Pennine Trail (*see* page 17) joins the towpath and it continues south east of Broadreach Lock over the river footbridge and under the railway arches. Once under the railway bridge, those wishing to follow the navigation into Wakefield – and beyond – should bear round to the right and back onto the river bank. In the wooded area, around Heath Old Hall, it may be necessary in the summer to make a slight detour along tracks to avoid the dense vegetation. A slightly longer detour at this point could bring you to the excellent Kings Arms, in the delightful village of Heath itself (*see* page 26).

2 At Wakefield Flood Lock cross over the navigation and head north along Bridge Street to cross the river. Bear left on to Thornes Lane and follow this road along the river bank. Stay on Thornes Lane when it meets Thornes Lane Wharfe and turns away from the river. Go under two railway bridges and turn left at the roundabout, past The Queen's Arms and under a third railway bridge. Turn left down Holmfield Lane (there is a *takeaway* on the corner) and then right past the industrial units along Green End Lane. Rejoin the navigation at Thornes Lock.

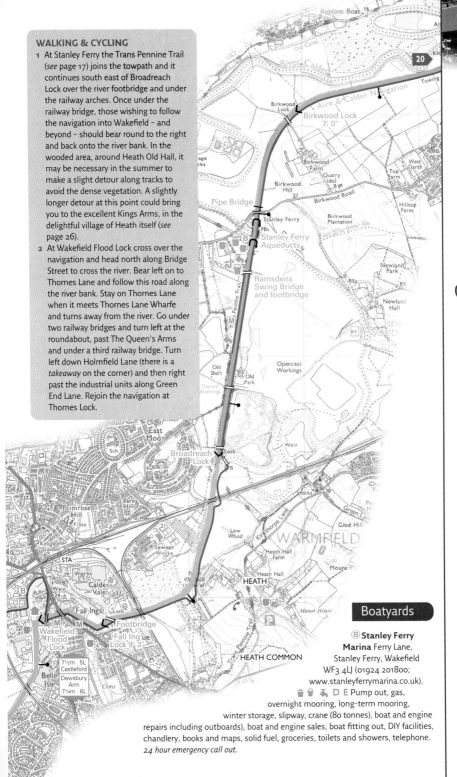

Boatyards

Ⓑ **Stanley Ferry Marina** Ferry Lane, Stanley Ferry, Wakefield WF3 4LJ (01924 201800; www.stanleyferrymarina.co.uk). 🚽 🚿 ⚓ D E Pump out, gas, overnight mooring, long-term mooring, winter storage, slipway, crane (80 tonnes), boat and engine repairs including outboards), boat and engine sales, boat fitting out, DIY facilities, chandlery, books and maps, solid fuel, groceries, toilets and showers, telephone. *24 hour emergency call out.*

Wakefield

W. Yorks. All services. The city centre is north of the navigation. The regional capital of West Yorkshire, it gained city status in 1888 when the cathedral was granted its charter. Mainly 15th-C Perpendicular in style, the cathedral's 247ft spire is a landmark for miles around. On a much smaller scale, but perhaps of equal interest, is the Chantry Chapel of St Mary, a rare 14th-C example of a bridge chapel, just a short walk north of Fall Ing, by the weir. Industrial pollution has meant that the entire front of the building has had to be replaced twice in the last two centuries: the original now graces the entrance to a boathouse at Kettlethorpe. The city itself is set on a hill, and still contains some quiet streets and dignified Georgian houses, notably those in St John's Square, with its delightful church and handsome council buildings. Wakefield's prosperity was founded on the textile and engineering industries, both of which have taken a battering in recent years. However, the city has been successful in attracting new industry, such as Coca Cola/Schweppes; and the vast and spectacular Ridings shopping complex has created many new jobs. **The Theatre Royal & Opera House** 12 Drury Lane, Wakefield WF1 2TE (01924 211311; www.wakefieldtheatres.co.uk) provides a lively and varied programme of entertainment. **Wakefield Art Gallery** Wentworth Terrace, Wakefield WF1 3QW (01924 305900; www.wakefield.gov.uk). Sculpture by local artists Barbara Hepworth and Henry Moore, plus contemporary paintings, prints and drawings. Also **Elizabethan Gallery** showing a wide range of temporary exhibitions. *Open Mon–Sat 10.30–16.30 and Sun 14.30–16.30.* Free. **Yorkshire Sculpture Park** at Bretton Hall, West Bretton WF4 4LG (01924 830302; www.ysp.co.uk). displays some important works by Barbara Hepworth and Henry Moore, both local artists. *Open daily 10.00–18.00 summer and 10.00–16.00 winter.* **Wakefield Museum** Wood Street, Wakefield WF1 2EW (01924 305351; www.wakefield.gov.uk). Local history and archaeology, excavations from Sandal Castle, and the Waterton collection of exotic birds and animals. The building, designed in 1820, was originally a music saloon. *Open Mon–Sat 10.30–16.30 and Sun 14.30–16.30.* Free. **Tourist Information Centre** Bull Ring, Wakefield WF1 1HB (0845 601 8353; www.wakefield.gov.uk). *Open Mon– Fri 08.30–17.00 (16.30 Fri) and Sat 09.00–12.00.* **Heath Village** 2 miles east of Wakefield. A beautifully preserved village with some 18th-C merchants' houses amongst other substantial buildings. Heath Hall is a fine Georgian house by John Carr (1753) with carved woodwork and moulded plaster ceilings. The gas-lit King's Arms pub is a gem (*see* below).

Pubs and Restaurants

◉ ✕ **Mill House and Forbisher Suite** Ferry Lane, Stanley Ferry, Wakefield WF3 4LT (01924 290596). A selection of real ales served in one of the old converted wharf-side buildings. Food *L* and *E*, *daily (all day Sun).* Children's room and extensive outdoor play area, patio and canalside seating. Children welcome *until 21.00.* Quiz *Tue and Fri,* live music *Wed,* adult and children's karaoke *Thu.*

◉ ✕ **Ship Inn** Ferry Lane, Stanley Ferry, Wakefield WF3 4LY (01924 372420). Close to the marina. Comfortable, family pub, pleasantly decorated. There must have been much merriment here on the day in August 1839 when the new aqueduct opened. Today real ales and an interesting bar and restaurant menu served *L and E daily* contribute more directly to the conviviality. Children welcome. Large garden and outdoor children's play area. Moorings.

◉ ✕ **King's Arms** Heath Village, near Wakefield WF1 5SL (01924 377527). Overlooking the common, originally built as houses in the 18th C and converted into a pub in 1841. A wide choice of real ale is served in an exceptional setting with a gas-lit, wood-panelled bar, a range of different rooms, stone-flagged floors, and full of antiques. Open fire, excellent bar and restaurant food *L and E* - beef in ale pie is a speciality. Children welcome. Two walled gardens and a lawn in front.

◉ **Fernandes Brewery Tap** 5 Avison Yard, Kirkgate, Wakefield WF1 1UA (01924 369547). Once a malt store and conditioning room for Beverley Brewery – and a malt kiln before that – this pub resurrects the original brewer's name and now dispenses both the present incumbent's own beers and that of guests. Food *L*; a dearth of electronic machines; brewery memorabilia and an open fire *in winter* makes this popular hostelry a real ale drinker's dream.

◉ **Henry Boon's** Westgate, Wakefield WF2 9SR (01924 378126). West of the cathedral, next to the prison. Fine traditional brewery tap for Clark's Brewery, also serving other real ales in an enthusiasts' pub, with live music *Sat.* Outside pavement seating.

✕ ◉ **Redoubt** 28 Horbury Road, Wakefield WF2 8TS (01924 377085). Little changed in 150 years, this heritage pub dispenses real ales *all day, every day.* Pub games, its own cricket and football teams and outside seating. A 'bring your own food' regime operates in lieu of a more local provision.

◉ **Wagon** 45 Westgate End, Wakefield WF2 9RQ (01924 372478). Near the railway station. A selection of real ales served in this popular, friendly local with outside seating and bar games. Small garden with play area. Quiz *Sun.*

◉ **Jolly Sailor** 46 Thornes Lane Wharfe, Wakefield WF1 5RL (01924 374172). Opposite Wakefield Flood Lock. Traditional pub with a friendly atmosphere serving real ales and inexpensive bar food *L (not Sun).* Children welcome. Garden. Pub games. Varied *Sat* night entertainment. Wakefield Folk Group play *once a month.*

BRIDGEWATER CANAL

MAXIMUM DIMENSIONS
Length: 70'
Beam: 14' 9"
Headroom: 8'
Draught: 2' 6"

LICENCES
Manchester Ship Canal Company, Land Planning,
Peel Dome, The Trafford Centre, Manchester
M17 8PL
Enquiries: 0161 629 8266;
www.bridgewatercanal.co.uk.

All craft using the canal must be licensed. They
must also be insured against third party risks which
should include the cost of salvage and removal of
wreck. Any boat holding a British Waterways canal
and river licence may cruise on the Bridgewater
Canal for seven consecutive days free of charge.

MILEAGE
PRESTON BROOK to:
Lymm: 10½ miles
Waters Meeting, junction with
Leigh Branch: 22 miles

CASTLEFIELD JUNCTION, start of
Rochdale Canal: 23½ miles
No locks

DUCIE STREET JUNCTION, start of
Ashton Canal: 25 miles (Rochdale Canal, 9 locks)
Preston Brook to Runcorn: 4¾ miles, no locks
Leigh Branch: 10¾ miles, no locks

The Bridgewater Canal received Royal Assent on 23 March 1759, four years after the Sankey
Brook, or St Helens, Canal and 18 years after the Newry Canal (once known as Black Pig's
Dyke), which linked Lough Neagh to the sea below Newry, in Northern Ireland, and was
probably the first 'modern' canal in the British Isles. The Bridgewater was built by Francis
Egerton, third Duke of Bridgewater, to enable coal from his mines at Worsley to be
transported to Manchester and sold cheaply. His agent was John Gilbert and his engineer
was James Brindley, who designed a lockless contour canal which crossed the River Irwell
on a stone aqueduct – a revolutionary concept and one that was ridiculed by many sceptics.
However, the line was open to Castlefield by the end of 1765.

While the canal was under construction, there began the excavation of a remarkable system
of underground canals to serve the Duke's mines, reached through two entrances at
Worsley Delph. Eventually 46 miles of underground canal were built, some on different
levels and linked by an ingenious inclined plane built along a fault in the sandstone. The
craft used in the mines were known as 'starvationers', double-ended tub boats which could
carry up to 12 tons of coal. This whole system remained in use until the late 19th C.

In 1762 the Duke received sanction to extend his canal to the Liverpool tideway at Runcorn
– this was later amended in order to connect with the new Trent & Mersey Canal at Preston
Brook. The route between Liverpool and Manchester was opened in 1776, although Brindley
did not live to see its completion. In 1795 the Duke, then 60 years old, received the Royal
Assent for the final part of the network, which linked Worsley to the Leeds & Liverpool Canal
at Leigh.

The coming of the railways did not initially affect the prosperity of the canal. In 1872 the
newly formed Bridgewater Navigation Company purchased the canal for £1,120,000, and
they in turn sold it to the Manchester Ship Canal Company in 1885. When the building of
the new Ship Canal meant that Brindley's original stone aqueduct over the River Irwell was
replaced, its successor, the Barton Swing Aqueduct, was no less outstanding than the
original, being a steel trough closed by gates at each end, pivoting on an island in the Ship
Canal.

The Bridgewater Canal is a tribute to its builders in that it continued to carry commercial
traffic until 1974 – indeed its wide gauge, lock-free course and frequent use of aqueducts
makes many later canals seem retrograde. It is now an oasis of tranquillity amidst the
burgeoning new industry of Manchester.

▌Preston Brook

Although the main line of the Bridgewater once locked down to the Mersey in Runcorn, this is now a dead end, with the locks being closed in 1966. It does, however, still make an interesting diversion – there is a *supermarket* and *PO* south of bridge 74.What is now the main canal route to Manchester bears to the right immediately after the big M56 motorway bridge, and its direct course to the south of the Mersey affords good views of the Manchester Ship Canal. The canal frontage at Moore is attractive, with moored boats, a *PO, shop and off-licence*, and a *telephone box* right by the canal.

Boatyards

Ⓑ **Claymoore Navigation** The Wharf, Preston Brook WA4 4BA (01928 717273; www.claymoore.co.uk). 🛈 ♨ 🅳 Pump out, gas, narrowboat and day-hire craft, overnight mooring, boat repairs, engine sales and repairs, toilets, books, maps and gifts, laundrette. *Emergency call out service.*

Ⓑ **Preston Brook Marina** Preston Brook WA7 3AF (01928 719081). 🛈 🛈 ♨ Gas, long-term mooring, slipway, boat sales, toilets, showers, solid fuel.
Ⓑ **Boat and Butty Company** Ockleston's Wharf, Ringway Road, Runcorn WA7 5QN (01928 500101; www. waterworthobats.co.uk). 🛈 🛈 ♨ Pump out, gas (next door), long-term mooring, winter storage, DIY facilities.

BOAT TRIPS
Tunnel Top II is a licensed floating restaurant based at Claymoor Navigation, the Wharf, Preston Brook WA4 4BA (01928 718181).

● **Preston Brook Tunnel**
1239yds long and forbidden to unpowered craft. *A notice indicates when you may enter – see* page 194.
● **Preston Brook**
Ches. PO, tel, stores. A village which grew to serve the canal, where goods were transshipped from wide beam craft of the north west to narrowboats of the Midlands. Unfortunately, little remains as evidence of this activity, and the M56 dominates.
Norton Priory Museum and Gardens Tudor Road, Manor Park, Runcorn WA7 1SX (01928 569895; www.nortonpriory.org). Access from mooring north east of bridge 75. Only the undercroft survives from the 11th C. A recorded commentary describes points of interest. Walled garden, pleasant woodland and sculpture gardens. Regular events and hands-on activities for children. Seasonal fruit and vegetables for sale. *Open Apr–Oct, Mon–Fri 12.00–17.00, Sat, Sun and public holidays 12.00–18.00; Nov–Mar, daily 12.00–16.00. Charge.*
● **Runcorn**
Ches. All services. The old town is to be found down by the docks, where the elegant curved 1092ft single span of the steel road bridge (built 1961), with the railway beside, leaps over the Ship Canal and the Mersey. The massive flight of 10 double locks which connected the Bridgewater

Canal to the Mersey was abandoned in 1966 and filled in, much to the dismay of industrial archaeologists and canal enthusiasts. Since 1964 Runcorn has been a 'new town', its rapid growth being carefully planned.
Tourist Information Centre 6 Church Street, Runcorn WA7 1LT (01928 576776, www.halton-borough.gov.uk). *Open Mon–Thu 08.45–17.15, Fri 08.45–16.30, Sat 10.00–12.30.*
● **Daresbury**
Ches. Tel, stores. Half-a-mile up the road from Keckwick Bridge, this was the birthplace of Charles Lutwidge Dodgson, better known as Lewis Carroll. The church of All Saints (WA4 4AE; www.daresburycofe.org.uk) has a pretty Lewis Carroll memorial window in the Daniell Chapel, where he is shown with characters from *Alice in Wonderland*: the Dormouse, the Mad Hatter and the Cheshire Cat. This window was designed by Geoffrey Webb, and was dedicated in 1934. The original church on this site dates from the 12thC, and was a daughter house of nearby Norton Priory (*see* above). The present tower dates from around 1550, with the rest of the church being rebuilt in the 1870s. The fine oak pulpit, dating from 1625, and the rood screen incorporated into the panelling behind the altar, are both worth a look. *The church is open daily.*

Pubs and Restaurants

🍺 **Ring O' Bells** Old Chester Road, Daresbury, Warrington WA4 4AJ (01925 740256). There has been an ale house here since 1641, although this building dates from 1841. The adjoining stables are older than the pub: to the other side the old Petty Sessions room has been incorporated. Pleasantly busy, with a relaxed atmosphere and open fires. Real ale, and good food, including fresh fish specials *12.00–22.00 (21.30 Sun)*. Children are welcome *until 21.00 when dining*. Outside seating. Quiz *Mon*.

🍺 **Red Lion** Runcorn Road, Moore, Warrington WA4 6UD (01925 740527). A friendly and traditional pub just a few minutes' walk west of bridge 7. Real ale, and meals, with an excellent choice *all day*. Children are welcome in the tap room. Quiz on *Tue*. Garden.

There are plenty of pubs in Runcorn, including:

🍺 **Grapes Inn** 82 Halton Road, Runcorn WA7 5SB (01928 575091). Between bridges 82 and 83. Families are welcome in this pub, which has a bowling green in the garden.

🍺 **Waterloo** 88 High Street, Runcorn WA7 1JH (01928 772276). Between bridges 88 and 89. A Victorian pub with a canal boat theme in the bar. Patio garden. Families welcome. Karaoke *Thu and Sat*. B & B.

WALKING & CYCLING

The towpath is in good condition throughout, but is only open to walkers. The towpath on the main line forms part of the Cheshire Ring Canal Walk, which makes a circuit with the Ashton, Peak Forest, Macclesfield and Trent & Mersey canals. Leaflets giving details of cycle routes in Runcorn can be downloaded from www2.halton.gov.uk. A Cyclists Map and Guide to Runcorn can be obtained from www.cycling. org.uk. The Trans Pennine Trail is a 350-mile national route which crosses Runcorn on its way from Liverpool to Warrington. Maps and an Official Accommodation and Visitor Guide are available from www.transpenninetrail. org.uk, www.sustrans.gov.uk or Barnsley Metropolitan Borough Council, Central Offices, Kendray Street, Barnsley, South Yorkshire, S70 2TN (01226 772574; www.barnsley.gov.uk).

Bridgewater Canal

Preston Brook

A short rural stretch is interrupted by the estate village of Higher Walton, which can be seen among trees, and this is followed by a secluded tree-lined length in a shallow cutting before the outskirts of Stockton Heath are approached. The building occupied by Thorn Marine was once a fodder store, stables and

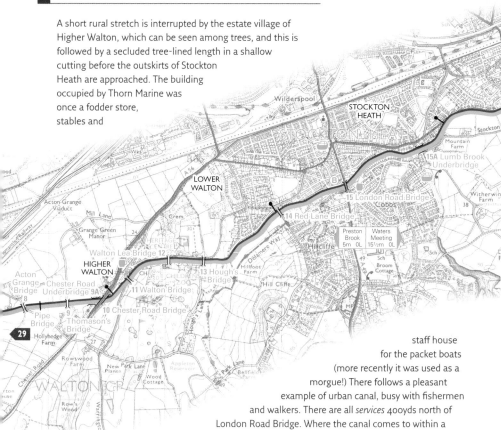

staff house for the packet boats (more recently it was used as a morgue!) There follows a pleasant example of urban canal, busy with fishermen and walkers. There are all *services* 400yds north of London Road Bridge. Where the canal comes to within a ¼ mile of the Manchester Ship Canal, the houses of Stockton Heath merge into those of Grappenhall crowded to the north, while to the south the old village survives, surrounded by open country. The canal makes a dog-leg turn past Thelwall and then proceeds under the M6 motorway south of the vast Thelwall Viaduct, which climbs laboriously over the Ship Canal.

Boatyards

Ⓑ **Thorn Marine** London Road, Stockton Heath, Warrington WA4 6LE (01925 265129; www.thornemarine.co.uk). 🛈 ♨ D Pump out, gas, day-boat and short breaks hire, engine sales,

boat and engine repairs, chandlery, toilets, showers, books, maps and gifts, solid fuels. Public telephone and shopping centre *nearby*.

● **Higher Walton**
Ches. PO, tel, stores. A pretty, late-Victorian estate village among trees.
Walton Hall Walton Lea road, Higher Walton, Warrington WA4 6SN (01925 601617; www.warrington.gov.uk/waltongardens/).

Twenty acres of parkland and gardens *open from dawn to dusk.* Facilities include children's zoo, outdoor games, heritage centre, play area, café and Ranger Service organising activities for the public and groups (telephone for details). Charge for facilities only.

WALKING & CYCLING

The Delamere Way parallels the canal near Red Lane Bridge. This is a 21-mile route following rights of way and quiet roads, from Frodsham to Warrington via Delamere Forest. A leaflet describing the entire route is published by the Mid Cheshire Footpath Society and is available from local shops, or details from www.mcfs.org.uk.

Stockton Heath

Ches. PO, tel, stores. Shops and services north of London Bridge. An outer suburb of Warrington, England's centre for vodka distilling and a useful place for supplies.

Stockton Quay Bridge 15. The terminus of the canal from 1771 to 1776, before the Duke of Bridgewater completed his route from Manchester to Runcorn, and consequently a major transshipment point with stables, yards, wharves, warehouses and a canal company office. Passenger packet boat services also ran from here from 1771 to the mid 1880s, one of the craft being the renowned *Duchess-Countess*. The historic

canal-side building here is under threat of demolition as we go to press.

Grappenhall

Ches. PO, tel, stores. A fine group of buildings on cobbled streets survive around the church of St Wilfred, where the village stocks remain. There are two excellent pubs, which makes a stop here very worthwhile.

Thelwall

Ches. PO, tel, stores. A short walk north from Thelwall Underbridge will bring you to 'The Penny Ferry' where, for a minimal charge, you can be carried across the Ship Canal (*see also* Pubs and Restaurants).

Pubs and Restaurants

🍺 ✕ **Walton Arms** 148 Old Chester Road, Higher Walton, Warrington WA4 6TG (01925 262659). North of bridge 11. Real ale in a comfortable 'Country Carvery'. Traditional food *all day, every day*. Children welcome if eating. Outside seating.

🍺 **London Bridge** 163 London Road, Appleton, Warrington WA4 5BG (01925 267904). By bridge 15. A homely and welcoming pub with a canalside terrace, offering real ale and food *all day*. Beer garden, and children are welcome *if dining*. Music quiz *Mon*, general knowledge quiz *Tue and Sun*.

🍺 ✕ **Rams Head** Church Lane, Grappenhall, Warrington WA4 3EP (01925 262814; www.ramshead-inn.co.uk). A comfortable old-fashioned pub on a cobbled street in a

conservation village, where *Sherlock Holmes* was filmed. À la carte meals are served in the restaurant *all day Mon–Sun*. Outside seating. Quiz night *Sun*. Curry night *Mon*. B & B.

🍺 **Parr Arms** Church Lane, Grappenhall, Warrington WA4 3EP (01925 267393). A comfortable and homely pub on the cobbled street, right beside the church, serving real ale. Good food *L and E*. Children welcome *until 20.30*. Outside seating.

🍺 **Penny Ferry Inn** 271 Thelwell Lane, Latchford, Warrington WA4 1NF (01925 638487). You can have a snack and a pint here while you wait for the ferry. Children are welcome, and there is a garden and a play park next door.

Lymm

There are fine views of the distant Pennines to the north before the canal makes a very pleasing passage through the heart of Lymm, where the streets come right down to the water's edge.

There are convenient *24 hour moorings* here. The canal then passes the village of Oughtrington (boater facilities including laundry, coal and gas) to the north before entering surroundings which are surprisingly rural. Rows of moored boats, some in an advanced state of decay, announce the presence of three useful boatyards and a fine pub, with a free ferry for towpath walkers (hit the clanger!) The fields then gently fall away into the valley of the River Bollin, which the Bridgewater crosses on a large embankment, with expansive views of the Manchester Ship Canal and Dunham Park. Dunham Underbridge is a new concrete and steel construction, built to replace the original stone trough which breached disastrously in August 1971 and resulted in a two-year closure and repairs amounting to £250,000 at the time. There are good moorings by Dunham Town Bridge.

● **Lymm**
Ches. PO, tel, stores, banks, fish & chips, laundrette. The 17th-C Lymm Cross stands just a few yards from the canal in the centre of this hilly and attractive little town. The dam at the back of the town was built to carry the turnpike road over a sharp ravine, thus creating a pleasant lake in the process.
● **Oughtrington**
Ches. PO, tel, stores. A good place for supplies.
● **Bollington**
Ches. A compact and attractive village, with a fine old pub and a converted mill.
Dunham Massey Hall NT Altrincham WA14 4SJ (0161 941 1025; www.nationaltrust.org.uk). Once the seat of the Earl of Stamford, this beautiful 18th-C house by John Norris stands in a wooded and well-stocked deer park, landscaped by George Booth, the Second Earl of Warrington, and now considered to be one of the north west's great plantsman's gardens. A sumptuous interior contains collections of Huguenot silver, paintings and walnut furniture. There is also an

18th-C orangery, an Elizabethan mount and a well-house. Concerts are staged in the gallery; exhibitions, fairs and services are held in the house and chapel; and there is a short programme of interesting conducted walks. Access is via Bollington, over the footbridge near the Swan with Two Nicks pub. *House open mid Mar–Oct, Sat–Wed 12.00–17.00 (Oct 12.00–16.00); garden open mid Mar–Oct, daily 11.00–17.30.* Admission charge. Restaurant and shop.
● **Dunham Town**
Gt Manchester. PO, tel, stores. A small, scattered, farming village with a pub.

WALKING & CYCLING
From Lymm Dam it is possible to access an excellent footpath network, details from www.warrington.gov.uk.

Boatyards

Ⓑ **Wharfage Boat Company** Agden Wharf, Lymm WA13 0SW (01925 754900). Pump out, ⚓ boat hire, gas, crane, boat sales, engine repairs, boat building, books, maps, gifts.
Ⓑ **Hesford Marine** Warrington Lane, Lymm WA13 0SW (01925 754639). ⚓ D Gas, long-term mooring, winter storage, slipway, crane (16 ton), dry dock, boat building, boat sales and repairs, engine repairs, chandlery, toilets, books, maps and gifts, solid fuel, DIY facilities.

Ⓑ **Lymm Marina Boat Sales** Warrington Lane, Lymm WA13 0SW (01925 752945 or 07798 752945; www.lmbs.co.uk). D Gas, day-boat hire, long-term mooring, winter storage, slipway, boat and engine sales, chandlery. *Closed Mon–Wed.*

Pubs and Restaurants

🍺 **Golden Fleece** 41 The Cross, Lymm WA13 0HR (01925 755538). By bridge 23. A picturesque canalside pub, serving real ale. Food is available *Mon–Sun 12.00–20.00.* Children welcome *until 20.00.* Garden with swings. DJ *once a month.*

🍺 **Bull's Head** 32 The Cross, Lymm WA13 0HU (01925 752831). By bridge 23. A cosy traditional village local serving real ale. Children are welcome *during the day.* Small courtyard.

🍺 **Spread Eagle** 47 Eagle Brow, Lymm WA13 0AG (01925 757467) Traditional local serving real ale and home-cooked food *all day.* Outside seating. Children welcome.

✕ 🍷 **Trattoria Baci** 18 The Cross, Lymm WA13 0HU (01925 756067). Smart Italian restaurant offering fresh authentic Italian pizza, as well as all other main Italian dishes. *Open every day from 12.00.*

🍺 ✕ **Barn Owl Inn** Agden Wharf, Warrington Lane, Lymm WA13 0SW (01925 752020). Between bridges 25 and 26. A friendly pub in a converted boatyard building, with fine views and serving a variety of real ales. Food *L and E, daily.* Children welcome, canalside garden. You can call for a ferry from the towpath side.

🍺 **Ye Olde No. 3** Lymm Road, Little Bollington, Altrincham WA14 4TA (01925 757222). Near Bollington Underbridge. An attractive former coaching inn with no less than three ghosts, which now has a selection of special nights, including live music. Bar meals *Mon–Fri L, Sat 12.00–21.30, Sun L and E.* Canalside garden. Children welcome for meals.

🍺 ✕ **Swan With Two Nicks** Park Lane, Little Bollington, Altrincham WA14 4TJ (0161 928 2914). By Bollington Underbridge (26A), and just a few minutes' walk into the village. A very fine, comfortable and cosy pub with a friendly atmosphere, serving real ale. Extensive menu for upmarket bar food and à la carte *Mon–Sat L and E, and Sun all day.* The name of the pub harks back to times when swans were taken as food: unmarked birds belonged to the monarch, who could dispense them at will. The nicks indicated ownership. It is all very similar to 'Swan Upping' on the River Thames, a ceremony which still continues today. Collections of key rings, bottles and bottle openers. Large garden. Children welcome.

🍺 **Axe and Cleaver Hotel** School Lane, Dunham Massey, Altrincham WA14 5RN (0161 928 3391). Village pub with log fires, candles and traditional decor, serving real ale and food *all day, every day.* Family room, garden with play area and bouncy castle. Regular club meetings take place here including Harley Davidson owners. Food theme nights *Sep–Dec.*

Sale

Beyond Seamons Moss Bridge, where *PO, stores, fish and chips* will be found to the south, buildings close in upon the canal, and the countryside rapidly disappears from view. Among the many industrial buildings, both old and new, stands the superb Victorian Linotype Factory, dated 1897, where metal printing type was manufactured. The Metrolink tramway closes in from the south east and escorts the canal all the way through Sale and on into Stretford. At Sale Bridge the area around the imposing Town Hall has been rebuilt, and a couple of pubs and a restaurant, along with The Robert Bolt Theatre and The Waterside Arts Centre, take full advantage of their canal frontage. There is another canalside pub before the waterway is crossed by the M60 motorway, which then crosses the River Mersey. A large expanse of graves opposite the Watch House Cruising Club heralds the entrance to Stretford.

Pubs and Restaurants

Bay Malton Hotel Seamons Road, Dunham Massey, Altrincham WA14 5RN (0161 928 0655). By Seamons Moss Bridge, number 29. A friendly community pub, offering real ale and food *L and E*. Children welcome *until 20.00*. The garden has a patio area, with a barbecue and outside heating.

The Waterside Waterside Plaza, Sale M33 7BS (0161 969 8966). By Sale Bridge. Smart modern bar, with dress code stating no sportswear or three-quarter length trousers. Bar meals are served *all day*. Patio seating overlooking the canal.

The Railway Inn Stamford Street, Altrincham WA14 1ES (0161 941 3383) By Sale Bridge. Traditional English pub dispensing real ale. Children welcome *until 21.00*. Outside seating. Quiz *Tue*.

✕ ♀ **Oca** Waterside Plaza, Sale M33 7BS (0161 962 6666) By Sale Bridge. Modern and stylish Italian restaurant serving traditional and gourmet pizzas alongside some great pasta dishes. *Open Mon–Sat 11.30–23.00, and Sun 12.00–22.30.*

King's Ransom Brittania Road, off Northenden Road, Sale M33 7BS (0161 969 6006). By Sale Bridge. In fine converted canalside brick buildings, which were at one time part of a coal yard. They extend under the railway, so the pub is larger than you might think. Real ale is served, and food is available *L and E*, including roast meat carvery *Sun L*. Children over ten years are welcome if eating. Live music *Thu and Sat*, quiz *Tue*. Fine selection of malt whiskies, and canalside seating on a floating pontoon.

Bridge Inn Dane Road, Sale M33 7QH (0161 969 7536). By bridge 36A. Comfortable canalside pub offering an ever-changing range of real ales, along with bar meals *all day*. Children welcome. Garden. Mooring. Live music *Sat*, quiz *Thu*.

STRETFORD

Boatyards

Ⓑ **Egerton Narrowboats**
Edge Lane Boatyard, Edge
Lane, Stretford M32 8HW
(0161 864 1066). 🛁 🛒 ⚓ D
Pump out, gas, long-term
mooring, winter storage,
crane, boat and engine
repairs, toilets.

● **Altrincham**
Gt Manchester. PO. A few black and white half-
timbered buildings remain in the market square of
what was once a small market town. Later in the
18th C it became a textile manufacturing centre, and
is now, inevitably, a dormitory town for Manchester.

● **Sale**
Gt Manchester. All services. A residential suburb of
Manchester, transformed from a farming community by
the building in 1849 of the Altrincham to Manchester
Railway – hence most of its buildings are Victorian or later.
St Martin's Church is, however, 18th-C and has a
hammerbeam roof. The clock tower of the town hall, built in
1914, is a prominent landmark. Look for the plaque in the wall
commemorating the work of James Prescott Joule, who was born
in Salford and calculated the mathematical relationship between
heat and electrical energy. The northern part of Sale merges without
boundary into Ashton upon Mersey, which is unremarkable except as
the birthplace of Stanley Houghton (1881–1913) who wrote *The Dear
Departed* in 1908 and *Hindle Wakes* in 1912. The area around Sale Bridge
has been imaginatively redeveloped.
Waterside Arts Centre & Robert Bolt Theatre Waterside Plaza, Sale
M33 7ZF (0161 912 5616). Music, drama and exhibitions. Robert Bolt
(1924–1995) was a dramatist and screenwriter, born in Sale.

ARTERIES OF INDUSTRY

A growing economy demands transport and power. The Romans recognised these needs
and built the Caer-dyke, a part of which still survives as the Fossdyke Navigation, to the
west of Lincoln. They realised a horse can pull only 2 tons on a good road, but up to 100
tons on a waterway.

Edward the Confessor ordered improvements on the Thames, Severn, Trent and
Yorkshire Ouse, and it was about this time that an artificial cut, a revolutionary idea at the
time, was made to improve navigation on the Itchen. The development of the 'flash' lock,
where a weir was used to build up a head of water which was then released to propel craft
over an obstruction, was eventually superseded by the 'pound' lock, still in use today.

But it was the Newry Canal, the Sankey Brook and the Bridgewater Canal, which was
built to serve the Duke's mines at Worsley and was still in commercial use until the 1970s,
which heralded the start of the Canal Age.

Waters Meeting

At Waters Meeting, marked with a fine vortex sculpture hidden amongst the bushes, the original main line of the canal is joined – to the north west is Barton, Leigh and the connection with the Leeds & Liverpool Canal; to the east is the centre of Manchester and the Rochdale Canal, which once again crosses the hills to Rochdale, having now been restored. The Bridgewater's route passes close to Manchester United football ground, where the new stand of this famous club towers above the canal, and the magnificent Salford Quays. Old Trafford cricket ground, the home of Lancashire Cricket Club and a Test Match venue, is a little further south. Near bridge 95 there is a fine mural, painted in 1993 by Walter Kershaw, depicting transport and industry. More empty docks are passed following the well-painted Throstle Nest Footbridge. The Manchester Ship Canal is now very close – indeed just across the towpath – with good views of the City Park buildings and the distant city centre. The new Metrolink towers above, before crossing high above Pomona Lock – the connection with the Ship Canal. Have a look on the towpath side for the circular overflow weir by bridge 97, and notice the disused basins beyond the towpath. These are followed by a railway bridge, more overgrown basins and the remains of the Hulme Lock Branch – the original junction with the Ship Canal. The excitingly restored Castlefield Junction is then reached. It is well worth stopping here to explore the basins under the railway bridge, and to visit the pubs and restaurants. Moor on the stretch below Grocers Warehouse (*laundrette* facilities are available at the YHA on the Staffordshire Arm). The first of the nine wide locks of the Rochdale Canal is right beside the restored Merchants' Warehouse. The gear is anti-vandal locked, so you will need to use the British Waterways key. The canal now passes between the backs of tall buildings and beneath elaborate railway arches, all of which have a certain faded grandeur. Tantalising glimpses of Victorian buildings invite exploration, but be wary of mooring away from Castlefield. You then pass the gay village, adjacent to Chorlton Street Lock, before finally the canal crawls under an 18-storey office block where you will find the top lock amidst concrete pillars. Ahead lies the Rochdale Canal (*see* page 172). Sharp right and left turns bring you to the start of the Ashton Canal, and the climb to Fairfield Junction (*see* page 162).

Boatyards

Ⓑ **Egerton Narrowboats** The Arches Boatyard, Potato Wharf, Castlefield M3 4NB (0161 864 1066; www.egertonnarrowboats.co.uk). 🛏 🛏 ⛽ D Pump out, gas, overnight mooring by arrangement – telephone in advance, long-term mooring.

NAVIGATIONAL NOTES

See Navigational Notes on page 168 if you intend to proceed up the Rochdale 9 – Locks 92-84.

BOAT TRIPS
City Centre Cruises Contact: 14 Falterley Road, Northern Moor, Manchester M23 9BR (0161 902 0222; www.citycentrecruises.co.uk). Based at Castlefield (opposite Castlefield Hotel M3 4JR), *L.S. Lowry* provides state-of-the-art restaurant and hospitality facilities on a wide-beamed boat. An unusual cruising venue for any occasion ranging from private functions to business meetings and corporate entertainment. Its spacious interior allows for a variety of settings and layouts for up to 50 diners. Licensed bar, and also available for private charter.

● **Manchester**
All services. One of Britain's finest Victorian cities, a monument to 19th-C commerce and the textile boom, its size increasing remorselessly with the building of the canals, and later railways. Unfortunately virtually no early buildings survived the city's rapid growth, although there is an incredible wealth of Victorian architecture surviving, in spite of redevelopment. The town hall and surrounding streets are a particularly rich area (north of Oxford Street Bridge). St Peter's Square, by the town hall, was the site of the 'Peterloo Massacre' in 1819, when a meeting demanding political reform was brutally dispersed by troops

37

carrying drawn sabres. Eleven people were killed and many more were injured. The Free Trade Hall, once the home of the Hallé Orchestra, is a little further along the road. Built in 1856, it was badly damaged in World War II, but was subsequently re-built to its original Palladian design. There is theatre, ballet and cinema, art galleries, and a wealth of interesting buildings, Victorian shopping arcades, many pubs with a choice of good beer and a variety of restaurants just a short walk from the canal. Sporting facilities are excellent, partly as a consequence of Manchester being the venue for the 2002 Commonwealth Games. The new developments at Salford Quays, on the Manchester Ship Canal, are quite breathtaking, and the building work continues elsewhere.

Imperial War Museum North The Quays, Trafford Wharf, Trafford Park, Manchester M17 1TZ (0161 836 4000; www.iwm.org.uk/north). Right beside the Ship Canal, in a stunning building by Daniel Libeskind, clad in shimmering aluminium representing a world shattered by war. Visitors enter through the 55-metres-high air shaft, giving fine views over the city. Exhibitions depict weapons, aircraft, the experience of war, science and war, interactive collections and a spectacular audio-visual display. *Open Mar–Oct, daily, 10.00– 18.00 and Nov–Feb, daily, 10.00–17.00. Free.*

Metrolink The new electric 'supertram'. G-Mex is a station close to the canal (G-Mex, Deansgate Railway Station, Manchester, M3 4LG), near to the second lock, if you fancy a ride. Information on 0161 205 2000; www.metrolink.co.uk.

Tourist Information Centre Town Hall Extension, Lloyd Street (off St Peter's Square), Manchester M60 2LA (0161 234 3157; www.manchester.gov.uk). To the north of Oxford Street Bridge. *Open 10.00–17.30 (Sun and B Hols 16.30).*

● **Manchester Ship Canal**
The Harbour Master, Manchester Ship Canal Company, Eastham Locks, Queen Elizabeth II Dock, Eastham (0151 327 1461; www.shipcanal.co.uk). The canal was opened in 1894 at a cost of £15½ million and carries ships up to 15,000 tons displacement. It is 36 miles long and connects the tidal Mersey at Eastham to Manchester. The Weaver Navigation, the Bridgewater Canal and the Shropshire Union Canal connect with it. All craft using the canal must be licensed. They must also be insured against third party risks which should include the cost of salvage and removal of wreck. There is a charge for the use of Pomona Lock, and advance notice is required – telephone 0161 629 8266. Any boat holding a British Waterways canal and river licence may cruise on the Bridgewater Canal for seven consecutive days free of charge.

Pubs and Restaurants

There are many fine pubs in Manchester. Those close to the canal include:

🍺 **Dukes '92** Castle Street, Castlefield, Manchester M3 4LZ (0161 839 8646; www.dukes92.com). Serving real ale, this very popular modern bar was once a stable for the nearby Merchant's Warehouse. Bar and restuarant meals, together with speciality cheese and paté *all day*. Canalside terrace and balcony overlooking the canal basin. Children welcome.

🍺♀✕ **Choice** Castle Quay, Castlefield, Manchester M15 4NT (0161 833 3400; www.choicebarandrestaurant.co.uk). Waterside. Bar and restaurant meals available *L and E*. Outdoor live acoustic stage. *Telephone or visit website for details.*

🍺♀✕ **Bar Ça** 8-9 Catalan Square, Castle Street, Castlefield M3 4LZ (0161 839 7099). Waterside bar. Meals and snacks are served *all day*. Children are welcome *until 21.00*. Outside seating.

🍺✕ **New Union Hotel** Princess Street, Manchester M1 6JB (0161 228 1492). Towpath side by Princess Street Lock. A comfortable pub in the gay village serving real ale, and sandwiches *L (not Sun)*. Entertainment throughout the *week*.

🍺 **Rembrandt Hotel** 33 Sackville Street, Manchester M1 3LZ (0161 236 1311). Towpath side between the Princess and Chorlton Street locks. A friendly hotel in the centre of the gay village, and serving real ale. Food is available *L and E (not Tue)*. Canalside seating. Children over 12 welcome upstairs. B & B.

🍺 **Churchills** 37 Chorlton Street, Manchester M1 3HN (0161 236 5529). Towpath side by Chorlton Street Lock. A traditional pub one side, with a café/bar on the other. Full disabled facilities. Meals are available *all day, every day*. Children welcome, plenty of outside seating. DJ and karaoke *nightly*. Mooring.

🍺 **Jolly Angler** Ducie Street, Ancoats, Manchester M1 2JW (0161 236 5307). Near the junction. A small, plain and friendly pub offering real ale and snacks *at all times* (or you can eat your own sandwiches!). Café nearby. Regular live music sessions. Children welcome. Moorings nearby, but don't leave your boat here overnight.

MANCHESTER SHIP CANAL

Harbour Master, Queen Elizabeth II Dock, Eastham, Wirral (0151 327 1461;
www.shipcanal.co.uk). The ship canal currently carries an increasing annual tonnage of
approximately 2,500 vessel movements per year. A great deal of it is hazardous, petro-
chemical traffic and therefore a no smoking régime is enforced. The canal company is
happy to allow pleasure boats use on the understanding that certain conditions are
adhered to. It is not a navigation for the novice boater and should be viewed as a daytime
transit corridor for the experienced boat owner (not hire boater) to access the River
Weaver, the River Mersey and the Shropshire Union Canal. In essence the company's
requirements are as follows:

1 The boat must carry £1 million third party insurance cover.
2 The boat is subject to an annual Certificate of Seaworthiness (not required for the
   passage from Pomona Lock *east* to Hunts Bank).
3 The appropriate fee is paid for each lock used, plus a fixed charge per passage.
4 The boater must contact the harbourmaster at least 48hrs in advance of passage to
   obtain copies of:
   a) Pleasure Craft Transit Notes;
   b) Port of Manchester Navigation By-laws.
   At this juncture boaters can discuss appropriate times of arrival and departure to
   coincide with scheduled shipping movements.
5 At all times the boater is required to act in a responsible manner and be aware that this
   is a *daytime* transit route only, with no lay-by facilities. Boaters should familiarise
   themselves with the geography of the canal before setting out.
6 VHF radio equipment is desirable (the Manchester Ship Canal Company call on channel
   14 in the canal; channel 7 in the River Mersey and operate on channels 14 and 20) and
   if not available a mobile phone should be considered essential. (Eastham VTS – 0151
   327 1242; Latchford Locks – 01925 635249).

The above synopsis is a brief note of the essential requirements and should be read in
conjunction with **The Transit Notes** and **Navigation Bylaws** referred to in 4 above. Also
available from the MSC at Peel Dome are notes for the transit of Pomona Lock and 'The
Upper Reach', for which a Certificate of Seaworthiness is NOT required.

Weston Marsh Lock Access to the River Weaver via Weston Marsh Lock is *only at
weekends Apr-Sep 10.00-18.00 and Oct 10.00-16.00. This includes B Hols.* All craft to arrive
30 mins before closing time to be guaranteed passage.Prior notice must be given to BW at
Northwich (01606 723800; enquiries.walesandbordercounties@britishwaterways.co.uk) *by
16.30 on the previous Thu.* VHF channel for the River Weaver is 74.

Ellesmere Port Bottom Lock Entry into the Manchester Ship Canal from the Shropshire
Union is restricted by a swing bridge over the first lock (adjacent to the Holiday Inn) which
is not under the control of BW. Boaters wishing to enter the canal must first contact
Ellesmere Port & Neston Borough Council (0151 356 6543) to make arrangements for the
bridge to be swung. Any difficulties in obtaining assistance should be referred to BW
(01606 723800; enquiries.walesandbordercounties@britishwaterways.co.uk).

Bridgewater and Rochdale Canals   Waters Meeting

Worsley

This is a surprisingly interesting section of waterway, well worth visiting for its own sake and a useful link with the Leeds & Liverpool Canal. What was the original line of the Bridgewater Canal leaves Waters Meeting through the vast Trafford Park Industrial Estate to cross the Manchester Ship Canal on the impressive Barton Swing Aqueduct, after passing an incongruous landscaped pagoda, and an even more incongruous 'lighthouse' at Parrin Lane Bridge. Curving through the suburbs of Salford and the leafy expanse of Broadoak Park, the navigation reaches the village of Worsley and what was the entrance to the underground mines which provided its *raison d'être*. It is well worth stopping to take a look around the Delph, to see at first hand what brought about the canals' construction, and a sturdy brick fountain built in 1905 to commemorate the Third Duke of Bridgewater in the park to the east of bridge 51. You will also notice that dissolved iron ore colours the canal bright ochre around here. After Worsley the M60 motorway and its attendant slip roads cross the canal as the Bridgewater then heads west through open country now only hinting at its industrial past, thanks to a vast clearing-up operation, still in progress. There is, however, more solid evidence of the area's mining connections at Astley, where it's worth stopping for a short while to visit the Colliery Museum. You will see the pit-head gear as you approach.

Boatyards

ⓑ **Worsley Dry Docks** The Boatyard, Worsley Road, Worsley M28 2WN (0161 793 6767). By bridge 51. Moorings, some chandlery and dry dock.
ⓑ **Bridgewater Marina** 14 Quayside Close, Boothstown, Worsley M28 1YB (0161 702 8622; www.bridgewatermarina.co.uk). By bridge 54.

🚽 🚿 🪝 D Pump out, gas, day-boat hire, overnight and long-term mooring, winter storage, boat sales and repairs, boat building, engine repairs, chandlery, toilets, showers, laundrette, solid fuel, DIY facilities. *Emergency call out.*

- **Salford**
  Gt Manchester.
  All services.
  Although now
  merged with
  Manchester,
  Salford was granted
  its charter in 1230,
  80 years before that
  of its now larger
  neighbour. It has a fine
  new university, built in
  1967, and a Roman
  Catholic cathedral dating
  from 1855. It is, however,
  most widely known as being
  the subject of many paintings
  by the artist L.S. Lowry
  (1887–1976). What is less widely
  known is that he gained his
  inspiration by walking the streets of
  Salford for many years as a rent
  collector, only painting in the evenings
  and at weekends – a fact to which he
  would never willingly admit. His work is
  exhibited at The Lowry Centre, Salford Quays
  (*see* page 37).
- **Salford Art Gallery and Museum** Peel Park, The
  Crescent, Salford M5 4WU (0161 736 2649,
  www.salford.gov.uk/salfordmuseum). In the centre of Salford
  University Campus. Stroll down a Victorian Street, admire the
  Landau Carriages and discover a Victorian heritage. Test your strength
  or listen to the Victorian Top 20. Experience the sights and sounds of
  Victorian Salford with original shop fronts and fascinating interiors. Victorian
  Gallery with paintings, pottery and fine art. Temporary exhibition programme, from
  hands-on activities to modern art. *Open all year, Mon–Fri 10.00–16.45, Sat and Sun
  13.00–17.00.* Free. Coffee shop.
- **Barton upon Irwell**
  Gt Manchester. Tel, stores, garage. In an interesting position overlooking the two canals. The richly
  decorated Catholic Church of the City of Mary Immaculate is by Pugin, 1867, and is considered to be one of
  his best works. Indeed the architect can be found featured in a painting on the south wall of the chancel.

- **Barton Aqueduct**

  One of the wonders of the waterways, it carries the Bridgewater Canal over the Manchester Ship Canal. Designed by Sir Edward Leader Williams, it was built in the early 1890s in a bold style comparable to contemporary railway engineering. Gates seal off the 235ft-long 1450-ton section that swings at right angles to the Ship Canal over a central island. It replaced Brindley's earlier aqueduct, built in 1761 and which carried the canal in a trough over 660ft long and 39ft above the Irwell, truly a wonder in its day. The aqueduct operates *summer, Mon–Thu 09.15–18.30, Fri–Sun 09.15–20.30; winter, daily 09.15–16.30. The aqueduct is usually closed for maintenance during the last two weeks of September –* telephone 0161 888 8266 for details.

- **Patricroft**

  Gt Manchester. All services. Here are the Bridgewater Mills, established in 1836 by Nasmyth, who invented the steam hammer.

- **Eccles**

  Gt Manchester. All services. The town peaked as a cotton and silk weaving centre between 1870-90, and little has happened since, although its name will always be remembered in connection with the famous cakes – round pastry filled with currants. The Church of St Mary has its origins in the 10th C, although the present sandstone building dates from the late 15th C.

- **Worsley**

  Gt Manchester. PO, tel, stores, garage. An attractive estate village dating from the 18th-19th C, and widely recognised as the place which triggered the 'canal age', in spite of the fact that the Bridgewater was not the first modern canal in the British Isles. Coal had been mined in Worsley since the 14th C, originally from the surface, and later by sinking shafts. It is thought that a drainage sough, common in underground workings, may have provided the germ of the idea for an underground canal network which could be used to bring the coal out. John Gilbert, the Duke of Bridgewater's agent, probably designed the system, which included an inclined plane on a 1 in 4 gradient 453ft long and 60ft wide. Work started at the same time on the building of the canal to Manchester,

and eventually 46 miles of tunnels were hewn out. A particular kind of simple double-ended tub boat was used underground, called a 'starvationer'. These carried up to 12 tons of coal. The old canal basin at Worsley Delph, with its entrance tunnels to the mines, is still intact, and information boards help to explain its workings. On the canal, look out for the Boathouse, built by Lord Ellesmere to house the royal barge, prepared for Queen Victoria's visit in 1851, and Duke's Wharf, an old oil store. Close by is Worsley Old Hall, the half-timbered Court House and The Old Reading Room, which was originally a nailers shop, shown on a plan of 1785 and painted on a Wedgwood dinner service presented to Queen Catherine II of Russia. The church, by George Gilbert Scott, 1846, has a spire decorated with crockets and gargoyles – inside there is a rich collection of monuments to the Dukes of Bridgewater.

- **Astley Green**

  Gt Manchester. Tel, stores. Canalside mining village dominated by a gaunt red-brick Victorian church.

  Astley Green Colliery Museum Higher Green Lane, Astley Green, Tyldesley M29 7JB (01942 828121; www.agcm.org.uk). To the north of the canal, perched on the edge of Chat Moss. The colliery was originally owned by the Pilkington Colliery Company, a branch of the Clifton and Kearsley Coal Company, which commenced the sinking of the first of two shafts in 1908. There are various pit relics to explore, plus a superb engine house containing a 3,300 HP twin tandem compound engine by Yates & Thom of Blackburn. This once wound the 8 ton lift which transported the miners to their work 873yds underground, at a maximum speed of 82ft per second (55mph!). Astley Green Colliery is situated in an area that was once full of collieries, but over the years they have all been closed, and demolished. There is now only one headgear and engine house left in Lancashire – this one, which ceased commercial activity in 1970. Being restored by the Red Rose Steam Society, it remains as a valuable reminder of life and work in this area in the recent past. *Open Sun, Tue and Thu 13.00-17.00. The site can also be visited at any other time by prior arrangement by school parties and groups.* No fixed charge, just give as you wish.

WALKING & CYCLING

Broadoak Park, to the north of Parrin Lane Bridge (50), contains some pleasant paths, suitable for a short walk. Bridgewater Park, Boothstown, has a few paths which can be enjoyed, while to the south of the canal is an area known as Chat Moss, a surprisingly remote area about 7,000 years old, and which was not reclaimed until the late 18th C. Close to the canal it consists mainly of reclaimed open-cast mine workings. A path from bridge 56 gives restricted access.

BIRD LIFE

Mallard ducks are widespread and familiar. The colourful male has a yellow bill and a green, shiny head and neck, separated from the chestnut breast by a white collar. Its plumage is otherwise grey-brown except for a black stern and white tail. The female has an orange bill and mottled brown plumage. In flight both sexes have blue and white speculum (patch on trailing edge of inner wing).

WILDLIFE

As water quality has improved, many different species of wildlife are being spotted in the Manchester Ship Canal (*see* page 38), including the *Grey Seal*. This large mammal is streamlined in water, but extremely cumbersome on land. It is frequently seen 'bottling', with its head and neck clear of the water. The coat colour is extremely variable, but usually some shade of blue-grey; the background colour of the male is generally darker than that of the female. Both sexes show an irregular and individually unique pattern of blotches and spots on their coats.

Pubs and Restaurants

🍺 **Dutton Arms** 56 Barton Road, Eccles M30 7AE (0161 786 7942). Old-fashioned beer drinker's pub. Outside seating and children are welcome. Live entertainment at *weekends*.

🍺 **Packet House** Liverpool Road, Eccles M30 8GF (0161 789 0047). By bridge 47. A corner pub serving real ale. Children welcome, garden with swings.

🍺 **Wellington** Worsely Road, Eccles M30 8PB (0161 789 1318). Between bridges 48 and 47. A local pub.

🍺 ✕ **Barge Inn** 1 Parrin Lane, Eccles M30 8AN (0161 788 8788). By bridge 50. A cosy real ale pub offering food *L and E, daily*. Children welcome *until 19.30*, and a large garden. Quiz on *Thu*, DJ *Fri*.

🍺 **Barton Arms** Barton Road, Worsley M28 2ED (0161 794 9373). Real ale is served in this traditional bar, along with food *available all day*. Quiz nights and other games are featured.

🍺 **Bridgewater Hotel** Barton Road, Worsley M28 2PD (0161 794 0589). By bridge 51. Large comfortable pub serving real ale and food *11.00–21.30, daily*. Children welcome if eating. Outside seating. DJ performs *Fri–Sun*. Nearby 🍴 🚻.

✕ 🍷 **Tung Fong** Worsley Road, Worsley M28 2NL (0161 794 5331). Smart Chinese restaurant, with interesting decor. *Open E daily.*

✕ 🍷 **Milan** Barton Road, Worsley M28 2PD (0161 794 5444; www.milanrestaurant.co.uk). Italian restaurant offering meals using seasonal and locally produced food. Theme nights throughout the year. *Open Mon–Fri 12.00–14.30 and 17.30–22.30; Sat 17.00–23.00; Sun 12.00–21.30*. Children welcome.

🍺 **Millers** 2 Quayside Close, Boothstown, Manchester M28 1YB (0161 702 6251). By bridge 54. In a lovely spot overlooking open country and the canal, on the corner of the Bridgewater Park Nature Reserve. Serving real ale, bar meals and snacks *all day, every day*. Children welcome, and there is a separate family dining area. Play area, canalside seating, mooring.

🍺 **Old Boathouse Inn** 164 Higher Green Lane, Astley, Tyldesley M29 7JB (01942 883300). By bridge 58. A comfortable canalside pub with a garden, serving real ale and food *L and E, daily*. Children welcome, mooring. Handy for the Colliery Museum. Karaoke *Sat*, various artistes *Fri*, and quiz *Wed*.

🍺 **Ross' Arms** 130 Higher Green Lane, Astley, Tyldesley M29 7JB (01942 874405). A 'food-led' pub which serves a range of real ales, plus meals *L and E, daily*. Children welcome *until 21.00*, large garden and conservatory. Fish & chips next door.

CHAT MOSS DESCRIBED

From hence [Warrington], on the road to Manchester, we passed the great bog or waste called Chatmos, the first of that kind that we see in England, from any of the south parts hither. It extends on the left-hand of the road for five or six miles east and west, and they told us it was, in some places, seven or eight miles from north to south. The nature of these mosses, for we found there are many of them in this country, is this, and you will take this for a description of all the rest. The surface, at a distance, looks black and dirty, and is indeed frightful to think of, for it will bear neither horse or man, unless in an exceedingly dry season, and then not so as to be passable, or that any one should travel over them. What nature meant by such a useless production, 'tis hard to imagine; but the land is entirely waste, except for the poor cottager's fuel, and the quantity used for that is very small.

Daniel Defoe, around 1720.

Leigh

After the excitement and interest of Barton, Worsley and Astley Green, the canal now passes through pleasant open country and reclaimed land towards the mill town of Leigh, where it transforms into the Leeds & Liverpool Canal, continuing the route to Wigan. Raised canal banks reveal past problems of subsidence in this area, caused by old mine workings. At Leigh the canal passes a sturdy warehouse by bridge 66 before it becomes the Leeds & Liverpool – the familiar stop plank cranes of the Bridgewater finish here, and signs announce you are back in British Waterways territory. Wigan is 7¼ miles away (*see* page 104).

● **Leigh**
Gt Manchester. All services. Once the archetypal mill town, most of the tall buildings and chimneys have now been demolished to be replaced with ubiquitous new developments. However, in the market place you can see the fine Edwardian baroque town hall, built 1904–7, facing the battlemented church of St Mary.

Pubs and Restaurants

● **Wheatsheaf Hotel** 298 Chapel Street, Leigh WN7 2AP (01942 709132). A sociable canalside pub on the corner of Warrington Road, serving real ale. There is a conservatory, and children are welcome. Live entertainment and karaoke *Sat and Sun*. B & B and shower facilities.
● **Moonraker Hotel** 77 King Street, Leigh WN7 4LJ (01942 740747). A friendly no frills pub with a garden. Children welcome *until 20.00*.
● **Bridge Inn** St Helen's Road, Leigh WN7 4HA

(01942 673573). Traditional pub serving real ale. Children welcome. Outside seating.
● **Waterside Inn** Twist Lane, Leigh WN7 4DB (01942 605005). This pub is contained within very handsome grade II listed canalside buildings, one a two-storey stone warehouse dated 1821, the other a brick warehouse dated 1894. A distinctive wooden tower adjoins. Real ale is served, and food is available *L and E*, *daily*. Children aged ten and over welcome if you are eating. Live music *Thu and Sun*, disco *Sat*.

WALKING & CYCLING

Pennington Flash is a 200ha country park, centred on a 70ha lake or 'flash', with a variety of well-maintained paths suitable for both walkers and cyclists. Over 230 bird species have been recorded in the park, and there is a wide variety of butterflies, dragonflies and damselflies. There is a small Information Centre.

NAVIGATIONAL NOTE

Plank Lane swing bridge is *open mid Mar-May 08.00-18.00; Jun-Aug 08.00-20.00; Sep-Mid Nov 08.00-18.00; mid Nov-mid Mar 08.00-16.30 Mon-Fri and 10.00-14.00 Sat-Sun. Closed for lunch daily 12.00-12.45.* The bridge is operated by a bridge keeper. Contact BW 01942 405700; enquiries.northwest@britishwaterways to confirm times.

Boatyards

Ⓑ **Lorenz Canal Services** Bedford Basin, Henry Street, Leigh WN7 2PG (01942 679690). Ⓓ Gas, overnight mooring *summer only*, long-term mooring, boat and engine repairs.

A VISIT TO THE MINES AT WORSLEY

'Arrived at Worsley, passing athwart the river Irwell, over which the canal runs, being raised on arches not less than fifty feet in height above that stream. Sent compliments to Mr Gilbert, the steward, asking the favour of seeing the duke's underground works, which was granted, and we stepped into the boat, passing into an archway partly of brick and partly cut through the stone, of about three and a half feet high; we received at entering six lighted candles. This archway, called a funnel, runs into the body of the mountain almost in a direct line three thousand feet, its medium depth beneath the surface about eighty feet; we were half an hour passing that distance. Here begins the first underground road to the pits, ascending to the wagon road, so called, about four feet above the water, being a highway for wagons, containing about a ton weight of the form of a mill-hopper, running on wheels, to convey the coals to the boats.

Arrived at the coal mine, which appearing about five feet through the roof, was supported by many posts, the area being about twenty feet square and the height scarce four. A hundred men are daily employed, and each turns out a ton a day; the miners' wages two shillings, and the laborers' about one shilling.'

Samuel Curwen, *Journal and Letters*, 7 June 1777.

CALDER & HEBBLE NAVIGATION

CALDER & HEBBLE NAVIGATION
Wakefield to Broad Cut
Length: 120'
Beam: 17' 6"
Headroom: 11' 10"
Draught: 6' 6"

Broad Cut to Sowerby Bridge
Length: 57' 6" (or 60' narrowboat)
Beam: 14' 2"
Headroom: 9' 4"
Draught: 3' 6"

HUDDERSFIELD BROAD CANAL
Length: 57' 6" (or 60' narrowboat)
Beam: 14' 2"
Headroom: 9' 6"
Draught: 2' 6"

MANAGER
0113 281 6800;
enquiries.yorkshire@britishwaterways.co.uk

MILEAGE
WAKEFIELD to
Cooper Bridge: 13 miles, 13 locks
Sowerby Bridge: 23½ miles, 27 locks including Fall Ing
Huddersfield Broad Canal: 3¾ miles, 9 locks

SAFETY NOTES
Where locks give access onto river sections of the navigation, river level gauge boards are located at each lock chamber indicating conditions as follows:

Green band – Normal river levels safe for navigation.

Amber band – River levels are above normal. If you wish to navigate the river section you are advised to proceed on to and through the next lock.

Red band – Flood conditions unsafe for navigation. Lock closed.

In an emergency telephone the manager's office or out of office hours telephone 0800 47 999 47. Mobile phone users telephone 01384 215785.

There is an excellent set of Navigational Notes available from British Waterways, downloadable from www.waterscape.com/boatersguides, which should be studied carefully before navigating this canal.

The construction of the Aire & Calder resulted in pressure to improve the Calder above Wakefield. After much opposition, the Calder & Hebble was built, with boats finally reaching Sowerby Bridge in the 1770s. The first survey had been made in 1740 and the Bill to implement it defeated by partisan landowners and millers. Sixteen years later John Smeaton produced a survey that was more acceptable and a Bill was finally passed in 1758. Construction was slow and conflict amongst the overseeing commissioners was rife. In 1765 Brindley was called upon to advise and Smeaton was dismissed. Three years later the position was reversed after serious flooding had damaged the recently completed navigation at Salterhebble. Further monies were raised to fund repairs and the waterway finally re-opened throughout in 1770.

From then on it was a case of continuous improvement and development with the addition of branch canals to profit from local pockets of trade. As always there were conflicts over water with mill owners, which curtailed some of the company's more ambitious plans to canalize large sections of the navigation but wherever possible the mills themselves were bought up. During the first half of 19th C, in line with developments on the Aire & Calder, further improvements were made (which included the cut at Horbury) but burgeoning railway competition severely blunted their impact. As a result the navigation was first leased to the Manchester & Leeds Railway and subsequently to the Aire & Calder. This second association led to a programme of lock enlargement under W.H. Bartholomew, which was of particular benefit to the section between Fall Ing Lock and Broad Cut Top Lock, above which the prevailing gauge remained consistent with the dimensions of the 57'x14' Yorkshire Keel. In 1885, on the expiry of the Aire & Calder's lease, the Calder and Hebble turned their attention to rebuilding their overbridges and establishing a carrying company: the Calder Carrying Co.

Beyond this there was little further investment, although the company continued to pay a dividend right through to Nationalization in 1948; often financed by the sale of assets. Never as successful as the Aire & Calder, it did, however, benefit from trade coming in from the Huddersfield Broad Canal and later, in 1811, from the Huddersfield Narrow. Commercial traffic ended in 1981, when the last coal barges unloaded at Thornhill Power Station. Becoming increasingly popular and yet still uncrowded, this waterway has much to offer, with great industrial interest and, in many places, considerable charm.

WALKING & CYCLING

The Calder & Hebble, as its name suggests, is largely a river navigation and it incorporates a series of lock cuts where weirs have been constructed to maintain a navigable depth. This approach, whilst excellent for boaters, can pose problems for those following the waterway along the towpath. These problems are twofold: erosion of the river bank during times of flood and the need to cross the river at either the head or tail of a lock cut in order to remain with the navigation. When boats relied upon horse power, before the invention of the internal combustion engine, both towpaths and horse bridges were maintained in a usable condition. Subsequently both have suffered from the ravages of time and the vagaries of flood – hence the need to come up with some 'creative alternatives' as detailed below.

1 At Thornes Flood Lock (*see* page 49) follow the river south west and under the motorway bridge. Strike off west across the mown sward through the clumps of trees at almost any point before reaching Broad Cut Low Lock and head west to meet the railway line where it intersects the north bank of the river. The bridge here incorporates an enclosed walkway accessible to walkers and cyclists and, in conjunction with a lane running south, returns you to Broad Cut beside the Navigation pub.
2 At Ledgard Bridge 17 (*see* page 50) cross over the navigation, go under the railway and over the river and turn right. At Chadwick Lane fork right and go through the industrial estate with Ledgard Boats on your right. Pass Navigation Garage on the left and as the road swings left, take the stone path on the right back towards the river, to the left of the PFS Factory Unit.
3 Due to severe bank erosion, only a small section of the towpath between Cooper Bridge and Brighouse (*see* page 52) remains, therefore walkers and cyclists should leave the navigation at Cooper Bridge, briefly heading south west along the A6107, before turning right at the garage along Lower Quarry Road. Cross the railway bridge and fork right down a track under the line signposted to Bradley Hall Farm. Just before the farm turn right and rejoin the waterway at bridge 11, below Kirklees Top Lock.

Brighouse (see pages 52–3)

Horbury Bridge

At Thornes Lock only one of the two chambers is now in use – you will need a Calder & Hebble handspike to operate this, and subsequent locks. Here the navigation enters a short cut and rejoins the River Calder at Thornes Flood Lock, before passing under the M1 motorway. Ahead is the tall spike of Elmley Moor television transmitter. The beautifully kept Broad Cut Low Lock marks the start of a 5-mile-long canal section with 8 locks. There was regular trade on this stretch until 1981, when West Country barges took coal from the British Oak Colliery to Thornhill Power Station. Remains of loading staithes can be seen opposite the Navigation Inn. There are good moorings at Horbury Bridge, and a *post office* and *farm shop* are close by. A short arm here used to connect with the river and this has now become an attractive long-term mooring with *showers* and the usual *facilities*. Beyond the bridge a tree-lined cutting leads to Figure of Three Locks. There are two locks on the navigation with another now disused which used to connect with the river. Is it this, or the fact that the river here makes the shape of a '3', which gives these locks their unusual name? Experts seem unable to agree. The towpath from Broad Cut to Dewsbury is good, having been improved in 1986–7. After Mill Bank look out for a milestone marked 'from FALL ING 7 miles' on the towpath side, by the next bridge. Thornhill Double Locks mark the junction with the Dewsbury Arm, which branches off to Savile Town Basin. Climbing Thornhill Double Locks (good *moorings* here) the navigation enters a deep, secluded cutting spanned by tall bridges.

NAVIGATIONAL NOTES

1   The Calder & Hebble joins the Aire & Calder Navigation (Wakefield branch) at Fall Ings Lock, outside Wakefield. Details of the last stretch, and information on Wakefield, *appear on* page 18 in the Aire & Calder section.
2   When ascending Broad Cut Low Lock both ground paddle and gate paddle outlets may be above the water level. Exercise caution when opening to avoid flooding your boat.
3   Take care when ascending locks, especially Kirklees Low Lock, to avoid trapping your tiller below the platform which extends over the locks, suspended from the lower gates.

Boatyards

ⓑ **Broadcut Marine** The Yard, Broadcut Road, Calder Grove, Wakefield WF4 3DS (01924 270070; www.broadcutmarine.co.uk). Marine engineering, boat repairs and restoration.
ⓑ **Calder Valley Marine** Savile Town Wharf, Mill Street East, Dewsbury WF12 9BD (01924 467976; www.cvmarine.co.uk). 🚿 🚽 🛒 D E Gas, pump out, overnight mooring, long-term mooring, slipway, winter storage, boat building, boat and engine repairs, boat sales, crane, books and maps, showers, laundry, toilets, telephone.

Pubs and Restaurants

Navigation Broad Cut Road, Calder Grove, Wakefield WF4 3DS (01924 274381). Broad Cut Top Lock, by the railway viaduct. A well-placed canalside pub serving real ales and inexpensive bar snacks and meals *all day, every day*. Children welcome; dogs outside only. Children's room and indoor ball pool. Massive garden and play area. Good moorings here; *PO and fish & chips* just a short distance to the south.

Bingley Arms 221 Bridge Road, Horbury, Wakefield WF4 5NL (01924 281331). A warm friendly establishment in another fine-looking pub serving real ales and food *L*. Children and dogs welcome. Garden with swings. Regular quiz and karaoke. Pub games and pool.

✕ **Ship Inn** 201 Bridge Road, Horbury, Wakefield WF4 5PR (01924 272795). Comfy local with a restaurant serving real ale. Excellent value food *L (not Mon)*. Children welcome if kept under strict control; dogs in bar only. Garden, children's play area and barbecue.

Leggers' Inn Savile Town Wharf, Mill Street East, Dewsbury WF12 9BD (01924 502846). A

tantalising array of real ales from their own 'Canal' range, brewed in the cellar below the pub and supplemented by an ever-changing selection of guest beers. Inexpensive bar snacks available from breakfast onwards. Children welcome *until 21.00*. Outside seating and pub games. *Open all day*.

✕ **Old Stables** Savile Town Wharf, Mill Street East, Dewsbury WF12 9BD (01924 488724). Good honest café fare – large portions, low prices and a wide selection including a range of salads. Takeaway or eat in. *Open Mon-Fri 08.00-14.00 and Sat 08.00-12.00*.

✕ **Agra** Warren Street, Savile Town, Dewsbury WF12 9LX (01924 467365). Turn left out of the basin, left again, over the bridge and bear left. Superb inexpensive Asian takeaway. Pizzas. Free delivery. *Open Mon-Thu and Sun to 23.30, Fri and Sat to 00.30. PO and grocers close by*.

Nelson Slaithwaite Road, Dewsbury WF12 9DW (01924 461685). Walk up the path west of Brewery Bridge. Real ales served in a pub atop the canal. Children welcome. Outside seating and games room. Quiz *Thu and Sun*.

● **Horbury Bridge**

W. Yorks. PO, tel, stores, takeaway, garage. A small town up a steep hill from the bridge. The hymn 'Onward Christian Soldiers' was written and first sung here by the Reverend S. Baring-Gould as a marching song for children.

National Coal Mining Museum for England Caphouse Colliery, New Road, Overton, Wakefield WF4 4RH (01924 848806; www.ncm.org.uk). On the A642, 2 miles south west of Horbury Bridge (bus service) and accessible by bus 263 from Huddersfield and Wakefield. Go 450ft underground to visit old- and new-style coalfaces. Audio-visual show, café, shop, picnic area. Wear warm clothes; not suitable for children under 5. *Open daily 10.00-17.00*. Charge.

● **Dewsbury**

W. Yorks. All services, station. The compact and attractive town centre is 1 mile away from Savile Town Basin.

Dewsbury Arm WF12 9BB Extending for 3/4 mile to Savile Town Basin.

49

Cooper Bridge

Before long the deep cutting gives way to an open industrial wasteland (for which there are large-scale redevelopment plans) around the site of Thornhill Power Station, where barges once used to unload coal. Between Thornhill Flood Lock and Greenwood Lock a short, wide, river section intervenes before the navigation enters another artificial channel to the south of Mirfield. Landscaping and pretty waterside gardens make this a pleasant spot. At Greenwood Flood Gates the river is briefly rejoined on a sweeping bend, before the navigation enters another artificial cut.

● **Thornhill**
W. Yorks. PO, tel, stores. This old stone-built mining village up on a hill above the canal offers fine views across the valley and an excellent pub.

● **Mirfield**
W. Yorks. All services. A useful place for supplies.

Kirklees Park *Mirfield.* In the grounds are the modest ruins of a priory founded in the 12th C for Cistercian nuns. Most of the stones were incorporated in the construction of Kirklees Hall during the late 16th C. It is believed that Robin Hood died whilst at the priory but before so doing he shot two arrows from the window to mark his burial place. One landed in the River Calder and floated away, the other landed in the grounds of the park. A tablet marks the spot thought to be his grave.

NAVIGATIONAL NOTES

1 When coming downstream, look out for the entrance to Ledgard Bridge Flood Lock. A large weir awaits those who miss it. This warning applies equally to boaters leaving Shepley Bridge Lock and approaching Greenwood Flood Gates.

2 There are landing stages below the locks which you can use, as well as ladders in virtually all the locks.

Boatyards

ⓑ **Mirfield Boatyard** 10 Station Road, Mirfield WF14 8NL (01924 492007). Below Shepley Bridge Flood Lock. D Gas, pump out, long-term mooring, winter storage, toilets and showers, laundrette, DIY facilities, solid fuel. *Closed Mon.*

ⓑ **Shepley Bridge Marina** Huddersfield Road, Mirfield WF14 9HR (01924 491872). 🚻 🚿 🛒 D E Pump out, gas, narrowboat hire, overnight mooring, long-term mooring, winter storage, slipway, boat sales, engine repairs, chandlery, books, maps and gifts, toilets, dry dock, wet dock, coffee shop.

The towpath is generally good on the canal sections, less so, or indeed non-existent, on the river sections (*see* note on page 47). At Battyeford there is a short canal section which rejoins the river opposite a large sewage works. A fine display of roses suggests they are not short of fertilizer! Cooper Bridge marks the junction of the Calder & Hebble with the Huddersfield Broad Canal (*see* page 64), which branches off to the south below the flood gates, overlooked by the tall chimney of Bottomley & Sons. Kirklees Park lies on a hillside to the north before the navigation passes under the M62 motorway.

Pubs and Restaurants

Perseverance Forge Lane, Thornhill Lees, Dewsbury WF12 9EJ (01924 463447). Spacious, airy pub serving real ale and home-cooked food *L and E, daily*. Children welcome as are dogs outside. Pool. Secure children's play area. Canalside garden. Moorings.

Swan Inn Huddersfield Road, Mirfield WF14 9HS (01924 492054). Above Shepley Bridge Lock. Smart real ale pub with a roadside patio. Bar food *L, Mon-Fri*. Karaoke *Thu-Sat*.

Savile Arms Church Lane, Thornhill, Dewsbury WF12 0JZ (01924 463738). North of Thornhill Lees. A genuine old village local that rather surprisingly shares consecrated ground with the nearby church, hence its other name – Church House. It dispenses an excellent range of real ales and totally eschews noisy machines. Pub games and outside seating. *Open Mon-Fri eves and Sat and Sun lunchtimes and eves*.

Bull's Head Huddersfield Road, Ravensthorpe, Dewsbury WF13 3LR (01924 503305; www.bullshead.org). 300yds from Greenwood Flood Lock. Bar meals *L and E* and a selection of real ales served in this pub set in 2 acres of parkland. Children welcome *until 20.00*. Regular events and entertainment.

Ship Inn Mirfield WF14 9HP (01924 493364). East of Shepley Bridge Lock. Large, smart and comfortable pub dispensing real ale. A carvery restaurant serves food *all day until 21.00, every day*. Children welcome. Garden, indoor and outdoor play area. Disco *Fri*.

Navigation Tavern Station Road, Mirfield WF14 8NL(01924 492476). Canalside near Shepley Bridge Flood Lock. Real ales and food *L and E*. Garden and limited moorings.

Railway 212 Huddersfield Road, Mirfield WF14 9PX (01924 480868). North of bridge 17. A selection of real ales together with two guests in a large pub serving food *L and E (until 21.30)*. Children over 12 allowed if eating. Outside seating. *Open all day Mon-Sat*. Pub games and disabled access. Quiz *Tue*.

Peartree Inn 259 Huddersfield Road, Mirfield WF14 9DL (01924 493079). Near Battyeford Lock. Riverside pub (complete with cellar-based ghost) serving real ales. Children's play area. Large beer garden overlooking the navigation. Live bands *Fri*, karaoke *Sat*, and jam night *Wed*. Moorings.

Bar Ra Me Café Unit 1, Fearnley Mill Drive, Calder Trading Estate, Leeds Road, Bradly HD5 0RX (01484 530818). Café and takeaway serving a selection of Thai and English food. *Open Mon-Fri 08.30-14.00 & 17.00-22.00; Sat 09.00-12.30 & 17.00-22.00*.

Brighouse

Leaving the river the navigation enters an artificial cut on its approach to Brighouse, completely enclosed by factories. There are good *moorings* between the two Brighouse Locks, and the passage through the town is pleasant, with gardens, seats and willow trees. At Brookfoot Lock there is evidence of a connection with the river giving some idea of how the navigation has evolved as canalised sections were progressively constructed.

Flooded gravel pits nearby are used for waterskiing. A milestone right by Park Nook Lock (*off-licence and grocers nearby*) reveals that you are now 18 miles from Fall Ing, with just a short distance to travel to Sowerby Bridge. Elland Basin, with its tastefully restored buildings and gardens, is worth more than a fleeting glance, however, and makes a good stopping place en route. There are several pubs close by. Have a look at the fine converted warehouse with its covered dock, before pressing on to the three superbly kept and picturesque Salterhebble Locks. The bottom lock here has an electrically-powered guillotine gate operated with a Watermate key. This was installed when the road was widened in the 1930s. The towpath passes separately through its own narrow tunnel. Immediately after this first lock the canal passes over a small aqueduct before climbing the top two. To the right is the Salterhebble Branch (where the old Salterhebble Basin has been restored providing visitor and long-term *moorings* and a range of boater *facilities*), to the left the route to Sowerby Bridge. The towpath improves above Brighouse.

BOAT TRIPS

M.V. Waylon featured as *Sally H* in the TV series *Stay Lucky*, and is available for both short and long trips for up to 12 passengers throughout the north eastern waterways. A converted working boat providing a flexible and participative, self-catering, cruising itinerary at very reasonable rates. An imaginative concept that introduces families and small parties to the waterways. For further details contact Mr Richardson at Brighouse Canal Basin, Brighouse HD6 1PS (01484 713424; www.melashton.co.uk)

Boatyards

Ⓑ **Sagar Marine** Victoria Works, Wharfe Street, Brighouse HD6 1PP (01484 714541; www.sagarmarine.com). Ⓓ Pump out, boat building, boat fitting out.

Ⓑ **Tayberg Steel Boats** Brookfoot Mills, Elland Road, Brighouse HD6 2QS (01484 400221). Boat building, welding, fabrication, boat repairs and alterations.

● **Brighouse**
W. Yorks. All services, station. A woollen textile producing village transformed into an important canal port with the building of the Calder & Hebble Navigation. In the 19th C silk and cotton were also spun here. Now there seems to be plenty of thriving new industry. The canal bisects the town, passing very close to the market place. A large Victorian church at the top of the hill is surrounded by trees and flowers.

Smith Art Gallery Halifax Road, Brighouse HD6 2AF (01484 719222; www.calderdale.gov.uk). Permanent display of 19th-C art works and touring exhibitions. *Open Mon–Sat, 10.00–12.30 and 13.00–18.00 (16.00 on Sat). Free.*

● **Elland**
W. Yorks. PO, tel, stores, bank. Elland has an enviable position on the steep south side of the Calder Valley, its narrow streets discourage through traffic, and its handsome church and terraces of stone houses give an air of tranquillity. The well-restored canal basin makes an excellent stopping point.

WALKING & CYCLING
At Anchor Pit Flood Lock follow the track around the outside of the river bend and join the straight road running north west through the industrial estate. Turn left at the T junction with Calder Street and right at its junction with Birds Royd Lane. At the junction with Huddersfield Road again turn right and rejoin the navigation at bridge 10.

Pubs and Restaurants

● **Prince of Wales** Betnal Street, Brighouse BD61JN (01484 400718). North of bridge 10. A handsome black and white half-timbered pub rebuilt in 1926 with timber from *HMS Donegal*, a wooden battleship launched in 1858. Real ales and meals are served. Children are welcome. Outside seating.

✗♀**Prego** Huddersfield Road, Brighouse HD6 1JZ (01484 715566). Beside bridge 10. Italian and continental cuisine served in a sophisticated contemporary setting. *Open daily L and E (not Sat L).* Children welcome.

● **Red Rooster** 123 Elland Road, Brookfoot, Brighouse HD6 2QR (01484 713737). North of Brookfoot Lock. Real ale enthusiasts' pub, with a real fire as well – always between seven and ten cask ales available. Also a selection of fruit wines and ciders. Outside seating. Children welcome *until 21.00. Mon* is cyclists and bikers evening; *Wed* quiz.

● **Colliers Arms** 66 Park Road, Elland HX5 9HZ (01422 372007). Between Elland and Park Nook locks. Traditional canalside pub offering real ale. Home-made food – cooked to order – is available *L daily.* Children welcome; dogs must be kept away

from eating areas. Award-winning canalside garden with quayside seating. Conservatory. Open fires in winter. Quiz, darts and dominoes *Thu.* Moorings.

● **Barge & Barrel** Elland Basin, Park Road, Elland HX5 9HP (01422 373623). An interesting choice of real ales from their own Barge & Barrel Brewery Co range together with guest beers in a comfortable Victorian-style pub. Inexpensive, home-cooked food *L.* Children welcome *until 20.30*; dogs in certain areas. Open fires in winter. Pub games and pool. Quiz *Wed* and *occasional* live music. Moorings.

● ✗ **The Watermill** Huddersfield Road, Salterhebble, Halifax HX3 0QT (01422 347700). Pub and hotel at the terminus of the Salterhebble Branch. Real ales served in this relaxed, family-orientated establishment. A range of food is available *all day, every day.* Outside seating and play area. Mooring. B & B.

● **Punch Bowl Inn** Huddersfield Road, Salterhebble, Halifax HX3 9LJ (01422 366937). By the Salterhebble Branch. Family-run pub serving real ale. Children and dogs welcome. Garden and play area. B & B.

Sowerby Bridge

The canal, now relatively narrow, clings to the side of a wooded hill, its clean water alive with small fish. A conspicuous building to the north is Wainhouse Tower, built in 1875 as a 253ft dyeworks chimney (but never used as such) and converted into a viewing tower. A superb example of stonemasonry, it is *open on Bank Holidays* (400 steps to the top). The buildings close in as the navigation approaches the basins at Sowerby Bridge, where the Rochdale Canal once again branches off to cross the Pennines. Now restored throughout its entire length, a third Pennine crossing has been made available offering the opportunity for two dramatic northern cruising rings. The towpath throughout this section is excellent.

Boatyards

Ⓑ **Shire Cruisers** The Wharf, Sowerby Bridge, Halifax HX6 2AG (01422 832712; www.shirecruisers.co.uk). Facilities either here or in the basin. 🛊 ⛽ 🔧 D Gas, pump out, narrowboat hire, overnight mooring, long-term mooring, winter storage, slipway, crane, boat sales & repairs, chandlery, books & maps, boat fitting out, engine sales and repairs, toilets, DIY facilities, gifts.

● **Halifax**
W. Yorks. All services. Well known as the home of the Halifax Building Society, founded in 1853, which now has ultra-modern offices in Portland Place; it is worth the journey north from the canal to visit this industrial town. The splendid **Piece Hall** Halifax HX1 1RE (01422 358087 - *open daily 08.00–18.00*), rebuilt in 1779, is the last remaining manufacturers' hall in the country. Here weavers traded their products, the continuation of an industry that dates back to 1275 in Halifax. Now restored, the hall houses arts and craft shops, a museum, art gallery, restaurant and the **Tourist Information Centre** (01422 368725). The parish church of St John the Baptist is Perpendicular in style, battlemented and with a mass of pinnacles, parapets and gargoyles.
Calderdale Industrial Museum Central Works Square Road, Halifax HX1 0QG (01422 358087) Next door to the Piece Hall. Steam engines, a Spinning Jenny, a Flying Shuttle loom and toffee wrapping machines, all working. Re-creation of 19th-C Halifax, coal mines and clay mines. *Open Tue–Sat 10.00–17.00, Sun 14.00–17.00.* Small charge.
Shibden Hall Folk Museum Shibden Hall, Godley Road, Halifax HX3 6XG (01422 352246). A 15th-C building with 17th-C furniture and extensive folk exhibits. *Open Mon–Sat 10.00–17.00, Sun 12.00–17.00 (16.00 Dec–Feb).* Charge.
Eureka Museum for Children Discovery Road, Halifax HX1 2NE (01422 330069; www.eureka.org.uk). Hands-on museum designed for children to touch, listen and smell. Three main exhibition areas: Me and my body, Living and working together, and Invent, create, communicate. *Open 10.00–17.00, daily except Christmas.* Charge.
Bankfield Museum Akroyd Park, Boothtown Road, Halifax HX3 6HG (01422 354823/352334; www.calderdale.gov.uk). Magnificent 19th-C mill owner's residence housing a fascinating range of costumes from around the world, displayed in exotic surroundings. *Open Tue–Sat 10.00–17.00, Sun 13.00–16.00. Closed Mon except B Hols (10.00–17.00).*
● **Sowerby Bridge**
W. Yorks. All services. Although this is an industrial town, the scale and grandeur of the surrounding landscape dominate the mill chimneys and factory roofs that are dotted about. This rare subservience to nature makes the town human and attractive. The 19th-C classical church is in a good position, overlooking the restored deep lock and tunnel.
● **Sowerby Bridge Basin**
PO, tel, stores. This great canal centre is a classic example of the functional tradition in industrial architecture, and has thankfully survived to be given a new life in restoration, while many other such examples have disappeared. The Rochdale Canal was built to accommodate vessels up to 72ft in length, so goods had to be transshipped here into the shorter Calder & Hebble craft before they could continue their journey; hence this important centre grew in stature.
● **Rochdale Canal**
One of three canal routes across the Pennines, its 92 wide locks over a distance of 33 miles virtually guaranteed its ultimate commercial failure. With the new tunnel and deep lock out of the basin open, it is once again possible to cruise across the Pennines to Manchester: hard work but the effort is amply rewarded.

Boatman and son statue at Sowerby Bridge Basin

Pubs and Restaurants

Navigation Inn 47 Holmes Road, Sowerby Bridge, Halifax HX6 3LF (01422 831636). By bridge 1. Friendly canalside pub dating back to 15th C complete with inglenook fireplace and Victorian cast iron range. Four rotating guest real ales, including the local Barge & Barrel Brewery Co's range, and an extensive bar menu. *Open all day* with food *available L and E, daily.* Children welcome *until* 21.00; dogs when food is not being served. Regular entertainment. Two gardens.

Moorings No 1 Warehouse, Canal Basin, Sowerby Bridge, Halifax HX6 2AG (01422 833940). A good choice of bar food is served together with real ale in this attractive conversion. Food *available L and E, daily.* Children welcome in dining area. Patio, family room.

Tenujin No 1 Warehouse, Canal Basin, Sowerby Bridge, Halifax HX6 2AG (01422 835500). Specialists in Mongolian barbecues. Children

welcome. *Open L and E, daily; early bird menu for families Sat 17.30-19.30.*

Java Restaurant Wharf Street, Sowerby Bridge, Halifax HX6 2AF (01422 831654). By the basin. A restaurant specialising in Indonesian food (*E only*). *Open 18.30-23.00 daily.*

William IV 80/82 Wharf Street, Sowerby Bridge, Halifax HX6 2AF (01422 833584). A good selection of real ales are served in this friendly pub close to the basin. Children welcome. Beer garden and pub games.

Rams Head Inn 26 Wakefield Road, Sowerby Bridge, Halifax HX6 2AZ (01422 835876). *Open evenings and all day Sat and B Hols.* The Ryburn Brewery's sole tied house, close to the plant, dispensing their full range of real ales. The pub is just as traditional as you'd expect: open fires, pub games and *weekend* sing-alongs. Food is also *available Mon-Sat L and E (until 21.00) and Sun 12.00-19.00.* Children welcome *until 20.00.* Garden.

HUDDERSFIELD NARROW CANAL

MAXIMUM DIMENSIONS

Length: 70'
Beam: 6' 10"
Headroom: 6' 2"
Draught: 3' 3"

MANAGER

Ashton-Under-Lyne to Diggle Portal, Standedge
Tunnel
01942 405700;
enquiries.northwest@britishwaterways.co.uk
Standedge Tunnel to Huddersfield
0113 281 6800;
enquiries.yorkshire@ britishwaterways.co.uk

MILEAGE

ASHTON-UNDER-LYNE
Junction with Peak Forest Canal to
Stalybridge: 2 miles
Mossley: 6 miles
Diggle: 8½ miles
Marsden: 12 miles
Linthaite: 16 miles
HUDDERSFIELD
Junction with Huddersfield Broad Canal: 19½ miles

British Waterways produces a set of navigational notes, available from the Waterway Unit offices listed above, or downloadable from www.waterscape.com/boatersguides, covering the safe use of the Huddersfield Canals.

To book a passage through Standedge Tunnel (*available Wed and Fri, mid Mar–end Oct*), contact 0113 281 6860 at least *three days* in advance of your intended passage. Boats may travel no further than Lock 32E or 24W without passage first being booked.

One of three transPennine canals, and by far the shortest route, this waterway was conceived in 1793, at the height of 'Canal Mania' (the bulk of canal construction was concentrated into the 1790s), and encouraged by the success of the Ashton and Huddersfield Broad canals. Benjamin Outram was retained as engineer and he reported in favour of a narrow canal (in the interest of cost saving) following the route of the present navigation. There was the inevitable conflict with local mill owners over water supply and a total reservoir capacity of 20,000 locks full of water was provided by way of appeasement.

As always optimism was in far greater supply than the capital raised from the initial share issue following the enabling Act passed on 4 April 1794. The estimated cost was some £183,000, of which nearly one-third was allocated to the construction of a 3-mile tunnel under the Pennines. As work progressed the canal was opened in sections to generate income; the first section opened in March 1797 between Huddersfield and Slaithwaite and two more, linking Slaithwaite to Marsden and Ashton to Greenfield, were completed late in the following year. It was not until 12 years later that the first boat passed through the completed Standedge Tunnel.

From the outset the waterway was dogged by shoddy workmanship and flood damage. In its 436ft rise to the eastern tunnel portal at Marsden, the canal follows the Colne Valley, whilst from the west end of the summit pound – 645ft above sea level – it follows the Tame Valley, dropping 334ft in 8½ miles to Ashton-under-Lyne. Damage extended along 16 miles of canal after flooding during the winter of 1799 and Robert Whitworth, called in to report during Outram's absence through illness, observed that the masonry and earthworks along the navigation 'were the worst executed of any he had seen'. Benjamin Outram resigned in 1801 and he was not replaced, although subsequently, five years later, Thomas Telford was asked to survey the work to date and advise on its completion. Two further Acts were passed to raise more capital before the navigation was officially opened on 4 April 1811 at a final cost of over £300,000. However, this was only after another disastrous flood occasioned after Swellands Reservoir (recommended by Telford as an addition to Outram's design) burst its banks and inundated large areas of the Colne Valley. Six people were drowned and many factories and mills severely damaged.

High tolls, in conjunction with an additional charge levied on boats using the tunnel, suppressed use of the waterway and although individual communities along the route expanded and thrived, within the climate of industrial prosperity brought by the canal, profits were disappointing. With the reduction of dues in the 1830s, trade was greatly stimulated, only to fall in the face of the inevitable railway competition which came with the completion of the Leeds and Manchester Railway in 1841. Three years later the Huddersfield and Manchester Railway Company was formed with the aim of building a line closely following the route of the navigation, which it acquired in 1845. The existing canal tunnel at Standedge was linked at intervals by cross adits to the infant railway tunnel during construction, thereby greatly reducing time and expense. Subsequent railway tunnels, built as traffic increased, also benefited immensely from the existence of the canal tunnel.

Much trade was surrendered to the railways over the years and by the time of its official abandonment in 1944, regular cargoes were limited to coal and iron ore. The last end-to-end voyage was made by Robert Aickman and fellow IWA members, in *Ailsa Craig*, during 1948.

WALKING & CYCLING

There is an interesting interpretation board beside the Roaches Lock pub (*see* page 61) detailing the industrial history of the area and setting out a short walk that takes in significant local features. The Oldham Way is a 40-mile trail, linking the newly opened Huddersfield Narrow and Rochdale canals, split up into seven more easily manageable sections. Visit the TIC for further details. The Medlock Valley Way leads walkers from the remote uplands of Saddleworth Moor above Oldham into the heart of Manchester linking meadows, rivers, moors, woodlands and canals along a trail of great diversity. Further information from local TICs. The Public Art Sculpture Trail links a number of pieces installed along the section of the canal running through Oldham. These images reflect life on the canal; they have been inspired by the geography of the area, by a local school and, in many cases, make use of recycled and reclaimed materials. Further details from local TICs and Brownhill Visitor Centre – *see* page 60. The Tameside Trail is a 40-mile circular walk that intersects with the canal at Division Bridge and broadly follows the Tameside boundary linking river valleys, country parks and other places of interest. Further details from Tameside Countryside Service (0161 330 9613; www.tameside.gov.uk/countryside). A section of the 268-mile-long Pennine Way runs through wild country along the eastern edge of Saddleworth Moor. *See* Leeds & Liverpool Canal, page 124 for further details.

To negotiate Standedge Tunnel, walkers and cyclists can make use of one of the several waymarked routes over the Pennines, commencing beside the Diggle Hotel. Walkers can also take a bus from Uppermill or a boat trip through the tunnel. Charge. See above for booking details.

The Colne Valley Circular Walk is 12 miles long and majors on the contrasts of impressive industrial buildings set against a backdrop of a striking river valley. Details from Huddersfield TIC (*see* page 66). The Kirklees Way beats the bounds of this eponymous district, totalling a demanding 72 miles. Again contrast abounds: landscape versus history, scenery versus industry. Details from Huddersfield TIC. The Marsden and Tunnel End Trail is a 'hands on' version of much that is depicted in The Old Goods Yard (*see* page 63 under Marsden Moor Estate) and as such is a fascinating insight into the area. There is a regular series of walks and events based on Marsden Moor Estate's 5,685 acres of unenclosed moorland. For a programme and copies of the trail detailed above, visit The Old Goods Yard or www.nationaltrust.org.uk/marsdenmoor, or telephone 01484 847016.

Apart from the range of walks detailed above, the presence of the transPennine railway line close to the waterway throughout makes planning expeditions along the canal straightforward. Trains run at frequent intervals, some stopping at all stations and some only at major stations. All trains carry bicycles free of charge although space is limited on First Transpennine Express services and it is advisable to book in advance during busy periods. Telephone 08457 48 49 50 for details.

To avoid the somewhat daunting trek over the top of Standedge Tunnel *see* note on page 63.

Stalybridge

The canal follows the River Tame east out of Portland Basin, crossing it just over 1 mile later to arrive at the first newly constructed lock in Stalybridge. In 1947 the section from here through the town was culverted and the enthusiasm for the recently exhumed navigation, ascending a series of locks amidst busy streets, is universal. Replacing a forgotten drain, there is now a vibrant waterway, a bustle of activity made colourful with boats: a scene reminiscent of a Dutch town, the canal its central focus, roads subservient. Good moorings are plentiful, well distributed between locks 4W and 8W. The Pennines beckon over the rooftops of Stalybridge, as the waterway continues on its steady climb towards Scout Tunnel, ducking directly between the legs of an unfortunately sited electricity pylon, more recently placed in its path. There are *showers and toilets* beside Grove Road bridge. The climb is unremitting, though largely through leafy glades with just the occasional glimpses of open hill views, punctuated with the dereliction of past industry – largely coal mining. Throughout its ascent, the waterway remains discrete, almost shunning the outside world, winding through woods and passing several attractively sited, waterside picnic areas. Whilst road crossings do briefly intrude, it is the transPennine railway that keeps constant company with the waterway: a not altogether unwelcome diversion bringing a source of well-ordered activity and flashes of colour on a dull day.

Pubs and Restaurants

🍺 **Station Buffet Bar** Platform 1, Stalybridge Railway Station, Rassbottom Street, Stalybridge SK15 1RF (0161 303 0007; www.buffetbar. freewebspace.com). The original station buffet, decorated with old railway photographs and memorabilia, and now dispensing an excellent range of real ales, cider and food *10.00– 20.00, daily*. Children and dogs welcome (dogs' water bowl provided). Outside platform seating and open fires *in winter*. No electronic machines – just the rattle of passing trains. *Open all day.*

🍺 **Q Inn** Market Street, Stalybridge SK15 2AL (0161 303 9157). In the *Guinness Book of Records* as the pub with the shortest name in the UK. Pool and darts. Regular live music. *Open all day.*

🍺 **Old Fleece Hotel** Market Street, Stalybridge SK15 2AL (0161 338 2827). Real ale and bar meals *available L and E*. Children welcome. B & B.

🍺 **White House** Water Street, Stalybridge SK15 2AG (0161 303 2288). Exposed brickwork, tiled floors and old cast iron radiators create the atmosphere in a pub serving food *L* together with real ale. Children welcome *12.00–15.00*. Pub games and beer garden. Quiz *Thu*, singer *Sun*. *Open all day.*

🍺 **Bridge Inn** Shepley Street, Stalybridge SK15 2AH (0161 304 0447). A traditional old pub with extensive wood panelling and a fine selection of wines and real ales. A reasonable standard of dress is required and only over-25s are admitted. *Open Mon-Fri 16.00-23.00, Sat and Sun all day from 12.00.* At rear of the pub is the entrance to **Harpers Bar**, open Fri-Sat 22.00-03.00 with regular live music.

🍺 ✕ **Mill Pond** Armentières Square, Stalybridge SK15 2BR (0161 338 4499). Beside lock 6W. A profusion of glass, a chandelier hanging through an opening in the balconied first floor and wooden floors set the tone in an establishment that maintains a casual/smart dress code and only admits over-21s. Real ale and food *served all day*. Pub and club activity in Armentières Square can make this a noisy area in which to moor.

🍺 **Bull's Head** Knowle Street, Stalybridge SK15 3AJ (0161 338 4182). Beside lock 7W. Traditional pub, beautifully furnished inside and dispensing real ale. Pub games. *Takeaways and laundrette* nearby.

Huddersfield Narrow Canal

Stalybridge

Saddleworth

The Pennines rear up ahead, although their full impact is softened by the fringe of woodland accompanying the navigation up the valley. To the west the imposingly situated building of Quickwood church, with its needle-like spire, oversees the bustle of road, rail and waterway activity below. Impressive mills, now sadly decaying, line the canal as it winds its tortuous path towards Uppermill, where it is greeted by what appears to be a castle keep, complete with portcullis. Closer inspection reveals a somewhat elaborate stone facing, topped with iron railings and employed to disguise a concrete box culvert, with further embellishment to hide a vertical gas main! By now the scale of the textile industry is subdued by the imposing bulk of Saddleworth Moor, while the sprawling conurbation of Manchester gives way to a straggle of attractive villages, constructed in the local gritstone and strewn randomly over the surrounding hillsides. Looking back towards the smoking chimneys below, there are wide open views now appearing over the high ground that had seemed to pose such a formidable obstacle when viewed from Stalybridge. Beyond the striking Wool Road Transhipment Warehouse *(all facilities including toilets)* the waterway, still climbing relentlessly, breaks out alongside the railway and together they both pick their way across heathered moorland towards their interlaced passage, deep beneath the Pennines.

● **Mossley**
Gt Manchester. Tel, stores, takeaway, station. A small agricultural hamlet of 1,200 souls in 1821, Mossley had grown into a prosperous cotton town by 1885 with a population of 15,000. There is a useful stores, *open 06.30-19.30*, near Roaches Lock; also an off-licence, takeaway, newsagent and Italian restaurant (01457 833495).
Mossley Industrial Heritage Centre Longlands Mill, Queen Street, Mossley OL5 9AH (01457 832813). Memories abound and are brought to life in an old cotton spinning mill now owned by Emmaus, a charitable organisation which provides work and a home for people who would otherwise be homeless. The Centre now seeks to answer questions about past times in a boom era of cotton and woollen manufacture. Shop and café. Heritage Centre *open Wed-Sat 14.00-16.00*; Emmaus shop *open Mon-Sat 09.00-17.00*. Café *open Mon-Sat 10.00-16.00*.

● **Greenfield**
Gt Manchester. Tel, stores, station. Another cotton community attempting to adjust to the demise of a past prosperity. The nearest station to Uppermill is here.

● **Uppermill**
Gt Manchester. PO, tel, stores, bank, chemist, butcher, garage. A traditional Pennine village and once the centre of the local cotton and cottage weaving industry, it has become a focus for the tourist trade that has long supplanted all such activity. Now the largest settlement in Saddleworth, it only gained its supremacy in the late 18th C with the coming of the canal and turnpike road, ousting nearby Dobcross.
Saddleworth Museum & Art Gallery High Street, Uppermill, Oldham OL3 6HS (01457 874093; www.saddleworthmuseum.co.uk). By Wade Lock. A family-friendly museum full of intriguing objects from the past telling the story of the people who have created Saddleworth's landscape and character. Gallery with changing exhibitions, many of local interest. Shop. *Open Easter-Oct, Mon-Sat 10.00-17.00, Sun 12.00-17.00; Nov-Mar, daily 13.00-16.00.* Charge.
Tourist Information Centre Saddleworth Museum & Art Gallery, High Street, Uppermill, Oldham OL3 6HS (01457 870336/874093; www.visitoldham.co.uk). *Open Mon-Sat 10.00-17.00, Sun 12.00-17.00.*

● **Dobcross**
Gt Manchester. PO, tel, stores. A delightful village, quintessentially Pennine, every building and winding narrow street a gem, the whole presided over by the charming Saddleworth Bank – now fulfilling a more homely role.
Brownhill Countryside Centre Wool Road, Dobcross, Oldham OL3 5PB (01457 872598). Wildlife and historical interpretation centre for the area with changing exhibitions and displays, a woodland 'crawly tunnel' for children, shop, refreshments, toilets and a picnic area. *Open Wed-Fri 11.00-16.00, Sat-Sun 10.30-17.00 (16.00 winter). Outdoor facilities open at all times.*

● **Diggle**
Gt Manchester. PO, tel, bakery, takeaway. Together with its neighbours Dobcross and Delph, Diggle lay at the heart of local hand-weaving until, in the late 18th C, the Industrial Revolution spawned mills as the centres of production, sited further down the valley for easier access.

Pubs and Restaurants

🛶 **Roaches Lock** Manchester Road, Mossley OL5 9BB. Canal-oriented pub serving real ales and food *L and E*. Children welcome. Bar games, canalside patio and an interesting selection of reading matter.

🛶 **Tollemache Arms** Manchester Road, Mossley OL5 9BG (01457 832354). This pub serves real ale and inexpensive bar meals *12.00–18.00*. Children welcome. Outside seating overlooking the canal. Regular *summer* barbecues. *Open all day.*

🛶 **King William IV** 134 Chew Valley Road, Greenfield Oldham OL3 7DD (01457 873933). East of the canal in the village centre. A cosy village local that welcomes families and serves a good selection of real ales. Traditional bar meals *available all day, every day.* Pub games and outside seating.

🛶 **Railway** 11 Shaw Hall, Bank Road, Greenfield, Oldham OL3 7JZ (01457 872307). West of the canal, opposite the station.

Photographs of old Saddleworth adorn the bar in a local that serves a variety of real ales. Pub games and open fires in *winter*. Live music *Thu and Fri and Sun afternoon*. B & B.

🛶 **Granby Arms** 28 High Street, Uppermill, Oldham OL3 6HR (01457 873028). Real ale and traditional pub food *served daily 12.00–18.00* in this traditional village local. Children welcome.

🛶 **Waggon** High Street, Uppermill, Oldham OL3 6HR (01457 872376). Cosy village local dispensing real ale and food *L daily*. Outside seating and children welcome. B & B.

🛶 **Navigation Inn** Wool Road, Dobcross, Oldham OL3 5NS (01457 872418). West of Wool Road Bridge. Serves real ale and food *L and E*. Children welcome. Outside seating and pub games. Brass bands play on *summer Sun afternoons*. Camping.

🛶 **Swan Inn** The Square, Dobcross, Oldham OL3 5AA (01457 873451). Also known locally as The Top House, this 18th-C hostelry serves real ale and home-cooked food *all day*. Children welcome until 19.00. Open fires in *winter*. Outside seating. Rhythm and blues *Sat*, folk *Thu*, quiz *Tue*.

🛶 ✕ **Hanging Gate** 217 Huddersfield Road, Diggle, Saddleworth OL3 5PQ (01457 871164). Just east of Bridge 66. Welcoming family pub serving freshly prepared, home-cooked food *L and E Mon-Fri and all day Sat-Sun*. Live entertainment *Sat*. B & B.

🛶 **Diggle Hotel** Station Houses, Diggle, Saddleworth OL3 5JZ (01457 872741; www.saddleworthlife.com/digglehotel). Close to the western tunnel portals (both canal and railway) this one time merchant's house went on to become a store, and then a pub, and now dispenses real ale and home-made food *L and E Mon-Fri and all day Sat and Sun*. Children welcome. Garden with superb Pennine views. B & B.

Marsden

It comes as almost something of a relief to leave the activity centred around the tunnel mouth and start the long steady descent into Huddersfield. Lock operation is no less arduous going downhill and there is a feeling akin to anti-climax as the waterway drops rapidly through a profusion of trees and almost into Sparth Reservoir. In places the hills lining the Colne Valley step back a little, leaving level grazing and fields for hay and silage making. The infant river is never far away and in places is separated only by a narrow band of trees. From time to time the landscape is punctuated by the gaunt remains of a splendid old mill as views open out briefly before the often tree-lined hills close in once again. Gas is available beside Shuttle Lock 24E. The railway shadows the canal into Slaithwaite where once again the harmony wrought by its focal position amidst shops and streets is most satisfactory.

Pubs and Restaurants

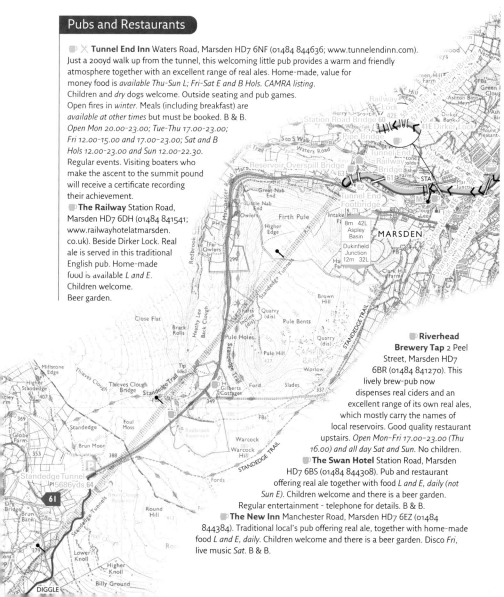

🍺✕ **Tunnel End Inn** Waters Road, Marsden HD7 6NF (01484 844636; www.tunnelendinn.com). Just a 200yd walk up from the tunnel, this welcoming little pub provides a warm and friendly atmosphere together with an excellent range of real ales. Home-made, value for money food is *available Thu–Sun L; Fri–Sat E and B Hols*. CAMRA listing. Children and *dry* dogs welcome. Outside seating and pub games. Open fires in *winter*. Meals (including breakfast) are *available at other times* but must be booked. B & B. *Open Mon 20.00–23.00; Tue–Thu 17.00–23.00; Fri 12.00–15.00 and 17.00–23.00; Sat and B Hols 12.00–23.00 and Sun 12.00–22.30.* Regular events. Visiting boaters who make the ascent to the summit pound will receive a certificate recording their achievement.

🍺 **The Railway** Station Road, Marsden HD7 6DH (01484 841541; www.railwayhotelatmarsden. co.uk). Beside Dirker Lock. Real ale is served in this traditional English pub. Home-made food is available *L and E*. Children welcome. Beer garden.

🍺 **Riverhead Brewery Tap** 2 Peel Street, Marsden HD7 6BR (01484 841270). This lively brew-pub now dispenses real ciders and an excellent range of its own real ales, which mostly carry the names of local reservoirs. Good quality restaurant upstairs. *Open Mon–Fri 17.00–23.00 (Thu 16.00) and all day Sat and Sun.* No children.

🍺 **The Swan Hotel** Station Road, Marsden HD7 6BS (01484 844308). Pub and restaurant offering real ale together with food *L and E, daily (not Sun E)*. Children welcome and there is a beer garden. Regular entertainment - telephone for details. B & B.

🍺 **The New Inn** Manchester Road, Marsden HD7 6EZ (01484 844384). Traditional local's pub offering real ale, together with home-made food *L and E, daily*. Children welcome and there is a beer garden. Disco *Fri*, live music *Sat*. B & B.

• **Marsden**
W. Yorks. PO, tel, stores, bank, chemist, garage, takeaway, station. Situated at an important transPennine crossing point, Marsden has always been a focus for the weaving industry and is associated with the Luddite riots. Enoch Taylor, pivotal figure in this industrial unrest, is buried beside the fine church and there is a set of stocks nearby. Its popularity as a location for TV soaps now make a different set of dramatic demands upon its environs. To the north of Colne Lock 38 there is a useful stores and off-licence (also snacks, sandwiches and hot drinks) *open daily 10.00–21.00.*

Marsden Information Point 20-26 Peel Street, Marsden HD7 6BW (01484 845595; www.kirklees.gov.uk). More than just a TIC – a fund of information and a community lifeline. *Open Tue 14.00–18.00, Wed–Sat 09.30–12.30 and 13.00–16.00.*

Marsden Mechanics Institute Peel Street, Marsden HD7 6BW (01484 844587; www.marsdenmechanics.co.uk). A striking stone building with a colourful wooden tower (the foundations of the main structure were considered inadequate to bear the weight of anything heavier) erected in 1861 to provide education for the betterment of the working man. Now the library and community hall. Also home to the evergreen Mikron Theatre Company (when not touring the waterways on their boat *Tysley*) who can be contacted on 01484 843701; www.mikron.org.uk.

Marsden Moor Estate The Old Goods Yard, Station Road, Marsden HD7 6DH (01484 847016; www.nationaltrust.org.uk/marsdenmoor). Over 5,000 acres of moorland in the hands of the NT and accessible through a series of walks and trails. The exhibition in the Old Goods Yard, beside the towpath at Marsden Railway Station, uses a series of excellent displays to provide a wealth of information about every aspect of the area, from natural phenomena through to the relatively recent industrial impact of weaving, water, canal and railway. Free.

Standedge Tunnels At first sight there appears to be an indecently large number of tunnels connecting Diggle with Marsden. The canal tunnel came first, completed in 1811, followed by the single bore of the Huddersfield and Manchester Railway dating from 1845. Two years later this railway company was taken over by the LNWR who built a second single – and parallel – track to cope with increasing demand. In 1894 the present double track tunnel was constructed to cope with the burgeoning traffic. In all instances the canal tunnel, now owned by the railway company and connected to its tunnels by cross-adits, proved invaluable for spoil removal during construction.

Standedge Interpretation Centre Waters Road, Marsden HD7 6NQ (01484 845624; www.standedge.co.uk). All the superlatives marshalled within the confines of one extremely long tunnel: highest, longest and deepest in Britain and largely hewn out of solid rock. The centre offers the opportunity to get to grips with all the facts, figures and dates. *Open Apr–Sep, Sat–Sun & B Hols 10.00–16.30 & daily during school summer holidays.* Free. Refreshments. Park at Marsden Railway Station and walk west along the towpath. A water taxi service operates *at weekends.* Disabled access and disabled parking at the centre itself.

BOAT TRIPS
Forty-five minute trips into Standedge Tunnel operate when the Interpretation Centre (*see* above) is open starting at *11.00*; last trip *15.15.*

Slaithwaite

The railway, as enthusiastic a companion to the navigation as ever, shadows the canal into Slaithwaite where once again the harmony wrought by its focal position amidst shops and streets is most satisfactory. It is a matter of intense speculation as to why it has taken so long to replace a secret subterranean trickle with this overtly delightful scene. East of the settlement the waterway settles into a broader valley bottom and the hills become a little more submissive. Attractive tree-lined glades alternate with views of a still bold landscape and everywhere there are the gaunt remains of mills: reminders of this area's supremacy as a textile producer and the canal's real purpose. The descent into Huddersfield is steady and not without contrast – pretty stone bridges vie with an imposing railway viaduct and many of the locks (although still in need of more use) appear in attractive settings.

● **Slaithwaite**
W. Yorks. PO, tel, stores, butcher, bank, chemist, garage, takeaway, station. Another settlement founded on the woollen and cotton industries with a fine Georgian church and the 16th-C Slaithwaite Hall. The juxtaposition of canal with the village streets is very pleasing.

● **Linthwaite**
W. Yorks. Tel. Although strung out and somewhat detached from the waterway, this village is not without charm and is home to several very striking (and very derelict) mills which tell of its former glory as a textile producer. Happily several of these structures are now undergoing renovation to fit them for their new rôle as appartments.

NAVIGATIONAL NOTES

See p67.

Pubs and Restaurants

✕ **Moonraker Floating Tearooms** Commercial Mills, Slaithwaite HD7 5HB (01484 846370). A boat-based tearoom, moored above Dartmouth Lock 23E, serving home-made meals, snacks, cakes, scones, sandwiches, salads, hot and cold drinks of all kinds and ices.*Open Apr–Sep, Tue–Sun 09.00–18.00 (Sun 10.00); Oct–Mar, Wed–Sun 09.00–16.00 (Sun 10.00). Also all B Hols except 25–26 Dec.*
▣ **The Shoulder of Mutton** Church Street, Slaithwaite HD7 5AS (01484 844661). Traditional pub serving real ale and food *available Tue–Fri 18.00–20.00; Sat–Sun 12.00–17.00.* Quiz Wed. Pool,

dominoes, darts and cards. *Open Mon–Fri 16.00–23.00; Sat 11.00–23.00 and Sun 12.00–22.30.*
▣ **The Commercial Hotel** Carr Lane, Slaithwaite HD7 5AN (01484 842920). Traditional English local's pub. Real ale and bar meals *L and E*. Children welcome. Beer garden.
✕ **The Captain's Table** 15 Carr Lane, Slaithwaite HD7 5AN (01484 841068). Fresh fish and chips with a difference. Eat in or take away.
✕ **The Full Muffin 39 Bridge Street** Bridge Street, Slaithwaite HD7 5JN (01484 844646). Selling hot and cold sandwiches to eat in or take out; a range of cakes and sticky buns; pies; hot and cold drinks and fresh bread.

HUDDERSFIELD BROAD CANAL

MAXIMUM DIMENSIONS

Length: 57' 6"
Beam: 14' 2"
Headroom: 9' 6"
Draught: 2' 6"

MANAGER

0113 281 6800;
enquiries.yorkshire@britishwaterways.co.uk

MILEAGE

ASPLEY BASIN, HUDDERSFIELD to:
Cooper Bridge: 3¾ miles
Locks: 9
British Waterways produces a set of navigational notes, available from the Waterway Unit office listed above, covering the safe use of the Huddersfield Canals.

To book a passage through Standedge Tunnel (*available Wed and Fri, mid Mar–end Oct*), contact 0113 281 6860 at least *three days* in advance of your intended passage. Boats may travel no further than Lock 32E or 24W without passage first being booked.

The Huddersfield Broad Canal was built to serve the rapidly expanding woollen industry of the 18th C. Known also as Sir John Ramsden's Canal, it was authorised in 1774 and completed in 1780. Costing £12,000, the waterway gave local textile manufacturers access to markets throughout Yorkshire as well as coal to feed the steam-driven mills. Despite the inevitable amalgamation with the competing railway company (the London and North Western Railway in 1847) the waterway remained a profitable concern until the late 1940s. It was conceived as a broad gauge canal to accommodate square-rigged, sailing keels or 'Yorkshire craft' – 58' 0" in length and 14' 0" beam. Due to the navigation's low bridges these had to be de-rigged at Cooper Bridge and bow hauled the remaining 3¾ miles. The Huddersfield Narrow Canal, completed some 30 years later, was built as a narrow gauge waterway unable to accept traffic from the Broad Canal; consequently warehousing and transshipment facilities were developed at Aspley Basin. The problem was partially overcome with the introduction of the West Riding narrowboat: a specially shortened craft able to negotiate locks on both systems. Immediately south west of Aspley Basin is a warehouse built prior to 1778 which is probably the oldest surviving example of such a building, demonstrating an early stage in the development of the large multi-storey warehouses of the 19th C. The crane beside it dates from the early 19th C.

The two factory tunnels are an ingenious solution to recent building on the old canal line and, in conjunction with the re-siting of the locks, represent the very best in Northern pragmatism! However, it is with some relief that you leave the stygian gloom of the second tunnel – the towpath employs an above-ground and altogether less elegant solution to the blockage – and, winding between university buildings, arrive at Apsley Basin. Beyond is the remarkable Turnbridge Loco Liftbridge dating from 1865; you will need a Watermate key to unlock it. The outskirts of Huddersfield present a mix of industry, a new waste incineration plant and by way

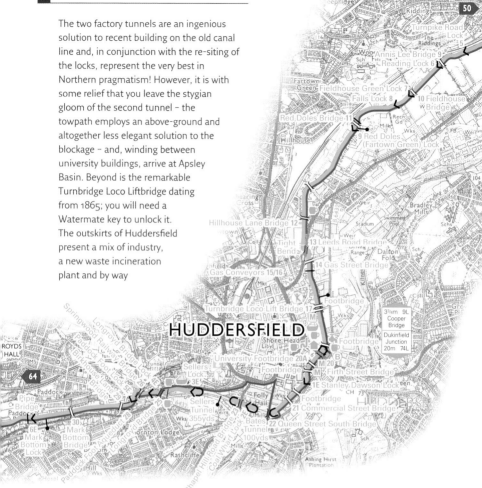

of relief, a vast expanse of green sports fields. The nine locks appear with a steady regularity and, passing through Cooper Bridge Lock, the canal finally enters a river section of the Calder & Hebble Navigation (*see page 50*). Before leaving this lock, boaters should be quite clear of the layout of the junction and of their intended passage.

Boatyards

Ⓑ **Aspley Wharf Marina** Aspley Basin, Huddersfield HD1 6SD (01484 514123; www. aspleywharfmarina.co.uk). 🛒 ♨ D Pump out, gas, overnight mooring, long-term mooring, slipway, chandlery, books and maps, boat sales, engine repairs (including outboards), boat repairs, telephone, toilets, showers, laundrette, gifts.

NAVIGATIONAL NOTES

1   When leaving or joining the Huddersfield Broad Canal at Cooper Bridge, take care to avoid the weir on the river just beyond the entrance to lock 1.

2   Holme Mill Services operate on a mobile basis offering water, pump out, etc and can be pre-booked by telephoning 01484 656139. *Available Mon-Fri 08.00-17.00 and Sat 08.00-13.00.* Charge.

3   Lock 24E has a guillotine-type tailgate. Read the operating instructions before use.

WALKING & CYCLING

Throughout both the Huddersfield Broad Canal and the adjoining Narrow Canal the towpath is in excellent condition making an attractive off-road trans-Pennine route for both walker and cyclist alike. To negotiate the section of canal in Huddersfield that tunnels under the floors of two separate factories, follow the copious blue and white signs along a succession of streets between Bridges 22 and 25. For those walkers daunted by the trek over the hills above Standedge Tunnel it is possible to travel with the electric tug hauling narrowboats through the tunnel itself, which operates on *Wed and Fri, mid-Mar-end Oct.* Contact 0113 281 6860 for further details. Charge. Note that cycles are not carried on the tug but a friendly boater might be persuaded to convey your machine in their front well deck.

● **Huddersfield**

W. Yorks. All services. Huddersfield is in the best tradition of Victorian industrial towns: all built to a grand scale of dark local stone, in a happy mixture of 19th-C styles. The most striking part of the town is around the railway station, built in 1847 with its powerful classical façade of Corinthian columns, considered one of the finest examples of railway architecture. The renowned Huddersfield Choral Society operates from the 19th-C town hall.

Art Gallery Princess Alexandra Walk, Huddersfield HD1 2SU (01484 221962). Above the library. Presents an international programme embracing all media together with changing displays from the permanent collection. *Open Mon-Fri 10.00-17.00, Sat 10.00-16.00.* Free.

Castle Hill and Victoria Tower off Lumb Lane, Almondbury, Huddersfield HD4 6TA (01484 223830). A striking local landmark occupied since the Stone Age and now topped by a Victorian tower. Splendid views and an exhibition tracing the hill's 4000 years of history. Bus no 304 from Huddersfield. *Open occasional days during Apr and May, and from end May-Sep, 12.30-16.30.*

Colne Valley Museum Cliffe Ash, Golcar, Huddersfield HD7 4PY (01484 659762; www.colnevalleymuseum.org.uk). The hand weaver's working life c.1850 depicted in a working exhibit in period settings. Also clog making by gas light and a range of changing craft exhibitions. Books, gifts and light refreshments available. *Open weekends and B Hols 14.00-17.00.* Small charge.

Regular buses – nos 301, 302 and 303 – from Huddersfield bus station; or walk up from Holme Mill Bridge on the Narrow Canal.

Holmfirth Nr Huddersfield. An essential visit for all *Last of the Summer Wine* devotees, easily accessible by bus from Huddersfield. Exhibition gallery contains photographs and memorabilia dating from the series beginning in 1972. *Sat* craft market and galleries.

Holmfirth Tourist Information Centre 49-51 Huddersfield Road, Holmfirth HD9 3JP (01484 222444; www.kirklees.gov.uk). *Open Mon-Fri 09.00-17.00, Sat 10.00-17.00, Sun 11.00-16.00.*

Kirklees Light Railway Park Mill Way, Clayton West, near Huddersfield HD8 9XJ (01484 865727; www.kirkleeslightrailway.com). Scenic ride on a narrow-gauge railway along a disused branch line. Children's playground and miniature fairground rides. Café. *Open daily Spring B Hol-Aug; weekends and most school holidays in winter.* Telephone for full details of event times. Charge. Bus no 484 from Huddersfield.

Tolson Museum Ravensknowle Park, Wakefield Road, Huddersfield HD5 8DJ (01484 223830). Fine Italianate mansion housing natural history, archaeology and local history exhibits. Workshops, events and children's activities. *Open Mon-Fri 11.00-17.00, Sat and Sun 12.00-17.00.* Free. There are buses from Huddersfield.

Tourist Information Centre 3-5 Albion Street, Huddersfield HD1 2NW (01484 223200; www.kirklees.gov.uk). *Open Mon-Sat 09.15-17.00.*

Pubs and Restaurants

Canalside Café Cooper Bridge, Huddersfield Immediately to the west of Cooper Bridge, in the middle of an industrial estate, above a dyeworks. Real down-to-earth café (in spite of its first floor location) serving an impressive selection of extremely inexpensive food from breakfasts (they come in all sizes) through sandwiches, hot drinks, soups and snacks, to a variety of full-blown meals. *Open Mon-Fri 07.00–14.00, Sat 07.00–12.00.*

Royal and Ancient Country Inn 19 Dalton Bank Road, Colne Bridge, Huddersfield HD5 0RE (01484 425461). East of bridge 2. A fine pub, tastefully furnished, achieving a balance between genuine olde worlde and traditional comfort. An intimate, cosy atmosphere in the separate restaurant area, together with interesting wall decorations and an intriguing array of curios to captivate the eye. An elaborate, varied and exciting range of food is available in both the bar and restaurant *L and E (not Mon E)* and a good selection of real ales is dispensed from a bar dominated by a dark burr-oak post, uncarved, but appearing to depict the head of a Hereford bull. Children welcome are well-behaved dogs in the bar only. Patio seating. Open fires *in winter*.

Spinners Arms Leeds Road, Huddersfield HD1 6NN (01484 421062). East of the canal, approaching Turnbridge. Inexpensive bar snacks *available all day, everyday*. Large pub geared up around entertainment which includes a stripper *Wed*, karaoke *Fri* and a live act *Sat*.

There are plenty of pubs and restaurants in Huddersfield. These are just a selection close to Aspley Basin:

County Hotel 4 Princess Street, Huddersfield HD12TT (01484 300494). As if to spite its narrow façade this pub is amazingly spacious inside and dispenses excellent real ale. Tucked away behind the Town Hall it serves traditional bar food *L, daily*. Outside seating. Pool.

Ship Inn Market Street, Huddersfield HD1 4SH (01484 311363). Large, one-roomed student pub with a poster-covered ceiling. Seven real ales always on tap. Live music *Thu* and quiz *Sun*.

Memsahib Eastern Eatery 37–39 Queensgate, Huddersfield HD1 2RD (01484 422002). Indian cuisine from a restaurant whose proprietor takes a real interest in serving authentic, regional dishes using fresh ingredients. Excellent value and *open E*. Children welcome. Takeaway service – within jogging distance of the basin.

Blob Shop Queensgate, Huddersfield HD1 2RD (01484 510974). Next to College Arms. Originally cottages, now with most of the first floor removed to give soaring ceilings. Real ales together with bar snacks *L, daily*. Children welcome if eating.

College Arms 33 Queensgate, Huddersfield HD1 2RD (01484 421 410). Close to the basin. Unusual, student pub – formerly the Dog & Gun. Children welcome *L only*. Pool.

New Wharf Wakefield Road, Huddersfield HD1 3AQ (01484 423009). South of Wakefield Road Bridge. A warm and friendly establishment serving an interesting selection of inexpensive bar food *until 21.00*. Beer garden. Children welcome.

Aspley Aspley Basin, St Andrews Road, Huddersfield HD1 6SB (01484 544250). Whitbread Brewers Fayre Chain. Real ales and food available in both bar and restaurant *all day, every day*. Children welcome. Canalside seating and moorings.

WILDLIFE

The *Freshwater Crayfish* was formerly common and widespread, but has become rather scarce and endangered today. Its numbers are threatened by pollution and the disturbance of favoured river and stream habitats, and by competition from the introduced North American species. It needs fast-flowing, well-oxygenated water and, during the daytime, hides under stones, in holes in the bank and in gaps in dry-stone walls. During the restoration of the canal in Huddersfield, British Waterways were able to create special habitat sites for the crayfish during construction of new tunnels built under factories that had been built over the canal. The crayfish has also successfully adopted the Rochdale Canal (*see* page 172).

LANCASTER CANAL

MAXIMUM DIMENSIONS	MANAGER
Preston to Tewitfield	01942 405700;
Length: 72'	enquiries.northwest@britishwaterways.co.uk
Beam: 14'	**MILEAGE**
Headroom: 8'	*PRESTON* to
Glasson Branch	Garstang: 16¼ miles
Length: 70'	Junction with Glasson Branch: 24 miles
Beam: 14'	Lancaster: 29¼ miles
Headroom: 8'	Carnforth: 37¼ miles
Ribble Link	*CANAL TERMINUS: 41¼*
Length: 62'	No locks
Beam: 10' 6'	
Headroom: 8'	Glasson Branch: 2¾ miles, 6 locks
Draft: 2'	Millennium Ribble Link: 4 miles, 9 locks

Construction on the Lancaster Canal began in 1792. The chosen route included several aqueducts, but only eight locks, at Tewitfield. By 1799 the canal between Tewitfield and Preston, including the aqueduct over the Lune, and the separate section between Clayton and Chorley, was opened. The route north was extended to Kendal in 1819, and the short, and very attractive, arm to Glasson Dock, falling through six locks, was opened in 1826, finally providing a direct link with the sea. In 1968 the canal north of Tewitfield was abandoned with the building of the M6 motorway (although eventual restoration now seems fairly certain), and the route in Preston was shortened by about a mile. What remains is remarkably rural, surprisingly quiet and worthy of exploration. The Ribble Link, opened in 2002, now provides a link to the national network.

NAVIGATIONAL NOTES

1. You will need a BW key to use the locks on the Glasson Branch.
2. Those who wish to use the Ribble Link MUST obtain the Millennium Ribble Link Skipper's Guide and booking form from 01942 405700; enquiries.northwest@ britishwaterways.co.uk, as this gives all ESSENTIAL navigational information. *Passages are booked up several months ahead, so planning well in advance is necessary. The passage is free. Opening times are dictated by tides in the Ribble estuary, but a journey can be made during daylight hours as directed by BW.* The staircase and sea lock are manned, and the link operates one way each day. There is no mooring on the Link. As the River Ribble is tidal, boats should carry, *as a minimum*: anchor, chain and warp, VHF radio or mobile phone, lifejackets for all on board, fire-fighting equipment, coastal flares. Your engine must be sufficiently powerful to cope with tidal conditions. Be sure to check that your boat insurance covers tidal waters.
3. If you need help or advice while on the River Ribble, contact Preston Riversway Control on VHF channel 16 (working on channel 14), or telephone 01772 726871.
4. If you wish to visit Preston Docks, contact Preston Riversway Control on 01772 726871.
5. Navigators entering the Rufford Branch of the Leeds & Liverpool from the sea should remember that they will need a BW key and a windlass to open the locks.

Preston

The canal in Preston, shortened many years ago by nearly a mile, now starts on an embankment just beyond Ashton Basin. From here it runs through urban areas until Haslam Park appears at bridge 12, where there is a BW sanitary station and showers. The Ribble Link leaves the main line just east of bridge 16 (*see* Navigational Notes on page 69) to link the Lancaster Canal with the rest of the network. A tall sculpture, *Gauging the Ripple*, overlooks the first new lock. Soon Preston is left behind and the canal reaches Salwick, where the moorings are administered by the Duchy of Lancaster. At Kellet's Bridge the navigation turns sharply east towards Catforth. At Swillbrook Bridge there is one of the few boatyards on this canal: the proprietor's house was formerly the old canal cottage.

Boatyards

Ⓑ **Arlen Hire Boats**
Ashton Basin, Tulkuth Brow, Preston PR2 2SD (01772 769183; www.arlen-hireboats.co.uk). 🚿 ♨
D Pump out, gas, narrowboat hire, overnight and long-term mooring, boat and engine repairs, solid fuel.
Ⓑ **Pendle Marine** The Boathouse, Canal Wharf, Preston PR4 0HE (01772 690232; www.pendlemarine.co.uk). D Gas, long-term mooring, winter storage, engine sales and repairs, boat sales, day-boat hire, chandlery, toilet. *Emergency call out.* Café.

● **Preston**

Lancs. All services. A large industrial town granted a Royal Charter by Henry II in 1179, with the right to hold a Guild Merchant. An outdoor market was also established and still thrives today. The teetotal movement was founded in Preston in 1834, and Joseph Livesey's Temperance Hotel (the world's first) used to stand at the corner of Church Street and North Road. There are many churches, such as St Walburge's (south east of the terminus), whose tall spires are a distinctive feature of the town. There is a good shopping precinct and a large modern bus station. Preston was awarded city status by the Queen in April 2002, in celebration of her Golden Jubilee.

Harris Museum & Art Gallery Market Square, Preston PR1 2PP (01772 258248; www.harrismuseum.org.uk). The largest gallery space in Lancashire, containing a specialised collection of the Devis family of painters and exhibits illustrating 18th-C and 19th-C art, including ceramics and costume. *Open Mon–Sat, 10.00– 17.00 and Sun 11.00–16.00; closed B Hols.* Free.

Tourist Information Centre Guild Hall, Lancaster Road, Preston PR1 1HT (01772 253731; www.visitpreston.com).

Pubs and Restaurants

🍺 **Last Orders Inn** Water Lane, Ashton-on-Ribble, Preston, PR2 2NL (01772 721567). A ¼-mile south of Ashton Basin. A good basic pub serving bar meals *12.00–19.00 daily.* Singers on *Sun.*

🍺 **Lime Kiln** Aqueduct Street, Ashton-on-Ribble, Preston PR1 7RF (01772 493247). Just east of Ashton Basin. This is a very friendly and extremely handy corner pub serving real ale and bar meals *L.* Children welcome.

🍺 **Fylde Tavern** 300 Fylde Road, Ashton-on-Ribble, Preston PR2 2NJ (01772 722514). South west of the terminus. Real ale is served, and children are welcome *until 19.00.* There is a garden, and a 60s, 70s and 80s disco *Fri,* live singer or groups *Sat.*

🍺 **Grand Junction** Watery Lane, Ashton-on-Ribble, Preston PR2 2NN (01772 726698). South west of the terminus. Traditional local's pub dispensing real ale and offering bar meals *L and E, daily.* Children welcome and there is outside seating.

🍺 **Lane Ends Hotel** Weston Road, Ashton-on-Ribble, Preston PR2 1HX (01772 671216). East of Blackpool Road Bridge. TVs and plasma screens. Real ale is served and children are welcome *until 19.30.* Meals *L and E.* Outside seating.

🍺 **Cotty Brook** Lea Road, Lea, Preston PR2 1RZ (01772 723484). A friendly pub serving real ale, and food *L and E Mon–Fri, and 12.00–17.00 Sat–Sun (no food Mon).* Children are welcome. Garden.

🍺 **Hand & Dagger** Treales Road, Salwick, Preston PR4 0SA (01772 690306). Canalside at bridge 26. Once the Clifton Arms. A welcoming country pub serving real ale and freshly prepared food *L and E and all day Sat–Sun.* Children welcome, and there is a play and barbecue area. Mooring. Live music.

PRESTON
Works

Bilsborrow

Passing the marina at Moons Bridge, the canal gently meanders along its remote route to eventually enter the village of Bilsborrow on a minor embankment: the A6 joins the canal here, as does the main railway line to Scotland, and the M6. Generally these rival transport routes keep their distance and the canal is for the most part delightfully quiet, still passing through peaceful green farmland, while the foothills of the Pennines begin to converge from the east. 'Owd Nell's' and 'Guys Thatched Hamlet' provide a single colourful intrusion. The River Brock is crossed on an aqueduct, with a good view to the west. There is a handy *garage and shop* at bridge 49, with limited temporary moorings giving direct access.

Boatyards

ⓑ **Moons Bridge Marina** Hollowforth Lane, Woodplumpton, Preston PR4 0BD (01772 690627; www.moonsbridgemarina.co.uk). ♿ D Gas, long-term mooring, winter storage, slipway, lifting trailer, boat and engine sales and repairs, chandlery, gifts, DIY facilities.

BIRD LIFE

The *Moorhen* is a widespread and familiar wetland bird: often wary, in urban areas they can become rather tame. The adult has brownish wings but otherwise mainly dark grey-black plumage. It has the distinctive yellow-tipped red bill and a frontal shield on its head, with white feathers on the sides of the undertail and a white line along the flanks. Juvenile birds have pale brown plumage. The moorhen's legs and long toes are yellowish. It swims with a jerky movement, with tail flicking. In flight the moorhen shows dangling legs.

Pubs and Restaurants

🍺 **White Horse Hotel** Garstang Road, Barton, Preston PR3 5AB (01995 640236). ¼ mile east of bridge 42. Small, comfortable pub serving home-made food *L* and *E*. Children are made very welcome.

🍺 ✕ **Owd Nell's** Canalside, St Michael's Road, Bilsborrow, Preston PR3 0RS (01995 640010; www.guysthatchedhamlet.co.uk). At bridge 44. A farmhouse-style thatched pub and restaurant complex, with all sorts of attractions. There are craft shops, a thatched terrace, a timber castle and games areas with cricket pavilion. Generous bar meals, with a children's menu *all day, every day*. When in season, local game features on the menu, as well as fresh fish dishes. Real ales, with a choice of well furnished bars in which to drink them. Children welcome. Hotel accommodation.

🍺 ✕ **Roebuck** Garstang Road, Bilsborrow, Preston PR3 0RN (01995 640234). A pub/restaurant/lodge serving real ale and meals *11.00–22.00 daily*. Children welcome, and there is a large garden.

🍺 **White Bull** Garstang Road, Bilsborrow, Preston R3 0RE (01995 640324; www.the-whitebull.co.uk). Canalside at bridge 44. Friendly village local with an open fire, dispensing real ales and food *L Mon–Sat, and E Fri, Sat*. Sunday carvery *12.00–18.00*. Children welcome, and there is a garden. Regular entertainment includes karaoke, singers or perhaps a quiz, and dominoes and darts.

FROM PRESTON TO KENDAL, BY WATERBUS

In an age when there is great personal freedom of movement, it is not always easy to imagine that canals, in their time, provided much the same opportunities as buses and trains today. As well as regular water bus services, special excursions were organised. Indeed as early as 1776 boats carried pleasure seekers from Beeston to the Chester Races, on what is now the Shropshire Union Canal.

Such services were scheduled on the Lancaster Canal until 1849. Initially a regular daily service operated between Kendal and Preston, the journey taking 14 hours, with refreshments being provided. In 1833, in order to compete with the stage coaches, an express service was introduced, cutting the journey time to 7 hours 15 minutes, and carrying an incredible 14,000 passengers in the first six months.

'For safety, economy and comfort no other mode of transport could be so eligible.'

Bilsborrow
*Lancs. PO, tel, stores,
garage, fish & chips.* A
village which straggles
along the A6. The church
of St Hilda, built 1926–7,
is set apart, up on a hill;
there are three pubs very
close to the canal.

73

Garstang

There is a flurry of canal interest around the Calder Aqueduct and Catterall Basin, and those who moor here and walk up the hills to the east of bridge 54 will also be rewarded with splendid views over Cockerham Sands and the Fylde. The canal then temporarily moves away from the hills and the remains of Greenhalgh Castle to cross the River Wyre on a fine stone aqueduct, 110ft long and 34ft high, attributed to John Rennie. There are steps down if you wish to have a better look at it. The attractive town of Garstang is soon reached; the area around Garstang Basin is a popular mooring for pleasure boats. There is a restaurant and museum in the restored wharf buildings here, with the town centre up to the north east. The canal then passes a new marina and continues to wind through countryside that is as green and pleasant as ever, but which is now overlooked by the steep slopes of the Pennines.

Boatyards

Ⓑ **Bridge House Marina** Crossing Lane, Nateby Preston PR3 0JJ (01995 603207; www.bridgehousemarina.co.uk). Between bridges 64 and 66. 🛏 🚿 ♿ D Gas, long-term mooring, winter storage, slipway, crane, chandlery, boat sales, boat and engine repairs, day hire, solid fuel, toilets, showers, telephone. DIY facilities. Also caravan park.

Pubs and Restaurants

Kenlis Arms Hotel Ray Lane, Barnacre, Preston PR3 1GD (01995 603307) East of bridge 54. A handsome red-brick pub serving home-cooked food *L Fri-Sun and E Mon-Sat*. Children are welcome, and there is a family garden with a play area. *Closed lunchtimes Mon-Wed*. Postbox outside.

Farmers Arms 8 Church Street, Garstang, Preston PR3 1PA (01995 6021950). Traditional local. Real ales and food *L and E, daily*. Children welcome and there is a beer garden. Quiz *Mon, Wed* and live music *Fri, Sat*.

Th'Owd Tithebarn The Wharf, Church Street, Garstang, Preston PR3 1PA (01995 604486). Canalside at bridge 62. A uniquely old-fashioned establishment where it is hard to discern where the bar ends and the museum, which the building contains, begins. They serve real ale and country fruit wines, and substantial bar and restaurant meals *L and E, daily*. Children welcome. Morris dancing *in the summer*. Canalside terrace.

Church Inn 33 Bonds Lane, Garstang, Preston PR3 1ZB (01995 602387). North of bridge 59. A cosy and traditional pub by the church, serving real ale, and food *L and E*. Children welcome.

Royal Oak Hotel Market Place, Garstang, Preston PR3 1ZA (01995 603318). A coaching inn, dating from the 1670s but with parts surviving from 1480. Real ale. Bar meals *L and E, daily*. Children, and dogs, welcome. B & B.

Eagle & Child High Street, Garstang, Preston PR3 1EA (01995 602139). Serves real ale and bar meals *L Mon-Sat*. Children welcome, and there is a small garden. Disco *Sun*.

Flag Parkside Lane, Nateby, Preston PR3 0JA (01995 602126). 200yds south of bridge 64. Real ale and bar meals *all day*. Indoor play area for children. Live music *Fri*, disco *Sat*.

Crown High Street, Garstang, Preston PR3 1FA (01995 602152). Serving real ale and meals *L (not Mon)*. Children welcome, and there is a play area and bowling green.

Kings Arms High Street, Garstang, Preston PR3 1EA (01995 602101). A sport-orientated pub serving real ale and home-made bar meals *L*. Children welcome, outside seating. DJ and large-screen football *Sun*.

Claughton Hall ¼ mile east of the canal. This hall was originally an Elizabethan mansion built next to the village church for the Croft family, but in 1932–5 the whole house, except for one wing, was dismantled and reassembled on top of the moor north of the village. It was quite a remarkable undertaking and still stands in defiant isolation.

Greenhalgh Castle Just north of the canal on a grassy knoll are the modest ruins of Greenhalgh Castle. It was built in 1490 by the Earl of Derby, who placed Richard III's crown on Henry Tudor's head after the victory at Bosworth Field. In the 17th C it was destroyed by the Roundheads during the Civil War, when the Royalists made a final stand there. Ask at the adjacent farm to visit the ruins.

Garstang
Lancs. PO, tel, stores, bank, garage. A friendly place, referred to as 'Cherstanc' in the Domesday Book, lying north east of the canal, which retains the atmosphere of a small market town. In the 18th C Garstang was a popular stopping point for coaches en route from London to Edinburgh, and the traditional market which still takes place every Thursday dates back to 1310, in the time of Edward II. Near the canal is the 18th-C church of St Thomas, surrounded by a tidy churchyard. Opposite the cobbled market place is an interesting town hall with diminutive bell-tower. Built 1755–64 to acknowledge the town's promotion by the king to borough status, it was rebuilt in 1939. The market cross, erected in 1754, is an elegant column topped by a ball. There was at one time a dozen ale houses in the town; a surprising number still remain!

Tourist Information Centre Discovery Centre, Council Offices, High Street, Garstang Preston PR3 1FU (01995 602125). *Open Apr-Oct, daily 10.30-16.30; Nov-Mar, daily 11.00-15.00.*

Potters Brook

Continuing northwards through quiet, modest and unspoilt pasture land, the canal passes countryside which is empty of villages but full of farms and houses which are dotted about the landscape. The absence of any locks certainly makes this an ideal waterway for restful cruising, while the wildlife and the generously proportioned stone-arched bridges always supply interest along the way. From Potters Brook Bridge (81) a lane across the A6 leads to a *telephone* and hotel beside what used to be Bay Horse Station. Just north of Potters Brook is the Ellel Grange estate with its remarkable spired church, ornamental canal bridge and the Grange itself, shrouded by tall trees; unfortunately the estate is private.

● **Ellel Grange** Bay Horse, Ellel, Lancaster LA2 0HN (01524 751651; www. ellelministries.org). On the banks of the canal. A very fine Italianate villa built for William Preston, a merchant, in 1857–9. It is a large mansion with two broad towers that compete in vain with the graceful spire of the charming little church of St Mary, built in 1873 at a cost of £7000, which stands in the grounds of the house. It was also built by William Preston. Purchased in 1986 by the Ellel Ministries, it was the first of their centres to be established and it still remains the international headquarters of the work. As well as holding Healing Retreats and Training Courses, Ellel Grange accommodates the Special Ministries Unit which provides longer-term help for those in need.

Pubs and Restaurants

▦ ✕ **Bay Horse** Bay Horse, Forton LA2 0HR (01524 791204; www.bayhorseinn.com). North east of bridge 81, across the A6. Real ale is served in this friendly and cosy country pub, which has an open fire *during the winter*. Restaurant and bar meals are available *L and E (not Sun E)*. *Closed Mon*. Children are welcome if you are eating, and there is a garden. B & B.

BIRD LIFE

The *Grey Heron* is a familiar large, long-legged wetland bird. The adult has a dagger-like, yellow bill and a black crest of feathers. The head, neck and underparts are otherwise whitish except for black streaks on the front of the neck and breast. The back and wings are blue-grey. In flight, the wings are broad and rounded with black flight feathers; the heron employs a slow, flapping wingbeat and holds its neck folded in a hunched 's' shape close to its body. The juvenile is similar to the adult but the markings are less distinct and the plumage more grubby in appearance. The heron is often seen standing motionless for hours on end on long, yellow legs, sometimes with its neck hunched up. It will occasionally actively stalk prey which comprise mainly amphibians and fish, especially eels. The call is a harsh and distinctive 'frank'. The heron nests in loose colonies mainly in trees but sometimes seen on coasts in winter.

The *Green Woodpecker*, despite its size and bright, colourful plumage, can be surprisingly difficult to see. It is usually rather wary and often prefers to hide behind tree trunks rather than show itself. Sometimes it is seen feeding on lawns or areas of short grass when the green back, greenish buff underparts and red and black facial markings can be seen. It uses its long tongue to collect ants. If disturbed the green woodpecker flies off revealing a bright yellow-green rump. The spiky tail gives support when climbing tree trunks. Its presence is often detected by a loud and distinctive yaffling call. The stout, dagger-like bill is used to excavate wood for insect larvae and to create nest holes. It favours open, deciduous woodland.

The Glasson Branch

Double Bridge marks the end of a rocky cutting and the junction with the Glasson Branch. Just around the corner on the main line is Galgate and a large boatyard and mooring site. The extremely attractive Glasson Branch leads off down to the west to connect the Lancaster Canal with the Lune estuary via Glasson Dock. The branch was finished in 1826, long after the main line of the canal was completed, and provided the canal with its only direct link with the sea. There are six wide locks whose bottom gates feature the same excellent type of sliding paddles seen on the Leeds & Liverpool Canal (*see* Navigational Note 2). Gates must be locked after use, and the locks left *empty*, even when going up. The arm falls through the Conder Valley, a pleasant, quiet stretch of countryside whose proximity to the sea is betrayed by the many seagulls cruising around. After the bottom lock, the canal runs in a straight line through saltings and marshland to Glasson Basin, where there is a large boatyard, mainly for seagoing yachts, and moorings.

The main line of the canal continues northwards through beautiful undulating green countryside, then passes through an unusually long wooded cutting, marked by Deep Cutting Bridge, and ends in the outskirts of Lancaster.

NAVIGATIONAL NOTES

1 The entrance lock from Glasson Dock up into Glasson Basin will take boats up to 87' 10" x 26' 3" with 11' 9" draught, and operates *2hrs* before high water. Anyone wishing to use the lock (for which *24hrs* notice is required) should telephone British Waterways Galgate office on 01524 751888. The basin links to a sea lock which is operated by the Lancaster Ports Commission: to use it telephone 01524 751724 giving at least *24 hrs notice during winter months. Summer opening* is arranged around the times of high water.

2 The locks on the Glasson Branch will take boats up to 67' 6" x 16' with 3' 10" draught. You will need a BW key to operate them. Gates must be locked after use, and the locks left *empty*, even when going up.

Pubs and Restaurants

Mill Inn Mill Lane, Conder Green LA2 0BD (01524 752852; www.thurnham-mill-hotel.co.uk). On the Glasson Branch. Hotel and inn offering real ale and food *L and E, daily*, in a sympathetically restored 17th-C grain mill, which was rebuilt in 1829. For over 100 years it was powered by canal water – an unusual innovation. Children welcome, garden and moorings close by.

Victoria Victoria Terrace, Glasson Dock, Lancaster LA2 0BT (01524 751423; www.victoriainnglassondock.co.uk). A fine family pub with an open fire and a nautical theme, taking its name from the *SS Victoria*. Real ale is served along with home-made bar meals *L and E (all day Sat and Sun)*. Children welcome, and there is a waterside garden. Regular entertainment.

Dalton Arms Ten Row, West Quay, Glasson Dock, Lancaster LA2 0BZ (01524 751213). Traditional family-run country pub. Real ale. Food *L and E*. Children welcome. Patio.

Green Dragon Main Road, Galgate, Lancaster LA2 0JH (01524 751062). Real ale in a village pub. Food *L and E (not Wed L)*. Children welcome. Outside seating. Live entertainment *Fri and Sat*, quiz *Sun*.

✕ **Lantern O'er the Lune Café** West Quay, Glasson Dock, Lancaster LA2 0BY (01524 752323). Overlooking the basin, this friendly café does main meals along with cakes, teas and coffee. *Open Tue-Fri 10.00-16.30, Sat 09.30-16.30, Sun 09.30-17.30.*

✕ **Lock Keepers Rest** Glasson Basin. This converted caravan has provided tea, coffee, cakes and burgers to visitors for many years.

Boatyards

Ⓑ **Galgate Marina** Main Road, Galgate, Lancaster LA2 0LG (01257 481054). Pump out, long-term mooring, slipway, crane, petrol, toilets, showers, chandlery, laundrette.

Ⓑ **Glasson Basin Yacht Co.** Glasson Dock, School Lane, Lancaster LA2 0AW (01524 751491; www.bwml.co.uk). Gas, long-term mooring, winter storage, travel hoist, slipway, boat sales and repairs, chandlery, books and maps, showers, toilets, laundrette, café.

WALKING & CYCLING

The Lune Millennium Cycleway, which also forms part of the Lancashire Cycleway, follows a former railway line and connects Glasson to Lancaster and Bull Beck picnic site to the north. The route of this footpath/cycleway runs through Lancaster before heading up-stream on the River Lune towards Caton.

Galgate

Lancs. PO, tel, stores, garage. An unassuming village on the A6, dominated by the main railway to Scotland. The back of the village up the hill is quiet; by the church of St John, built 1906-7, are the buildings of what is apparently the oldest surviving silk spinning mill in England, built in 1792. There is another, apparently older, built originally as a corn mill, close by. Some of the nearby cottages were built for the mill-workers.

Canalside Craft Centre Pear Tree Barn, Main Road, Galgate Lancaster LA2 0LQ (01524 752223). A craft shop next to the marina. Tea, coffee, snacks and full meals. *Open 10.00-17.00, closed Mon except B Hols.*

Glasson

Lancs. PO, tel, stores, garage. A fascinating tiny port built in 1787 to serve Lancaster. The huge basin is now only occupied by an assortment of pleasure boats using its excellent sheltered moorings. In the tidal dock, however, there are often coasters which discharge into lorries.

Lancaster

The canal now enters Lancaster, losing its rural identity as buildings close in. There are useful *stores* just west of bridge 98. At bridge 100 the towpath returns to the west side of the canal, where it stays for the rest of the journey northwards. The canal passes through the heart of Lancaster, passing well-restored mills, including Moor Lane with its conspicuous red-brick water tower and now the home of Reebok UK, and continues north, passing an old dry dock by bridge 103, to cross an aqueduct, built in 1961, over the A683. The imposing aqueduct which carries the canal over the River Lune quickly follows, affording fine views along the Lune valley. The canal then rejoins the side of the valley, turning west, then north again to head towards the sea at Hest Bank.

● **Lancaster**
Lancs. All services. Today Lancaster's quay, once a great shipping port handling more cargo than Liverpool, is a quiet backwater, with pleasant walks. There are some fine canalside buildings.
Lancaster Castle Castle Parade, Lancaster LA1 1JY (01524 64998; www. lancastercastle.com). On the site of Roman fortifications, this is a mainly 13th-C and 14th-C construction, except for the Norman keep, which is surmounted by a beacon tower. *Open daily 10.00–17.00.* Guided tours (Court sittings permitting) from *10.30–16.00.* Charge. Gift shop.
Cottage Museum 15 Castle Hill, Lancaster LA1 1YS (01524 388716). Opposite the castle, this is part of a 1739 house containing the artifacts of an artisan, c. 1820. *Open Easter–Sep 14.00–17.00.* Charge.
Lancaster Priory & Parish Church Castle Hill , Lancaster LA1 1YZ (01524 65338; www.priory.lancs.ac.uk). There has been a church on this site since AD 630. The present building is an attractive 15th-C church in late Perpendicular style, with an original Saxon western doorway. Church *open all year round 09.30–17.00.* Free. Guided tours *Jul–Sep.* Refectory *open Easter–Oct, 10.00–16.00.* Interesting book stall. Nearby are the excavated remains of a Roman bath house.
Lancaster City Museum Old Town Hall, Market Square, Lancaster LA1 1HT (01524 64637; www.lancashire.gov.uk). Lancashire's past, the King's Own Regiment Museum, portraits and landscapes, changing exhibitions, events and activities. *Open Mon–Sat 10.00–17.00.* Free.

Ashton Memorial Williamson Park, Quernmore Road, Lancaster LA1 1UX (01524 33318; www.williamsonpark. com). Dominated by the Ashton Memorial folly, which contains an exhibition gallery. Also tropical butterfly house and over 50 acres of parkland including landscaped gardens, children's playground and an ornamental lake. Shop and café. *Open Easter–Oct, daily 10.00–17.00; winter, daily 11.00–16.00.* Charge.
Maritime Museum Old Customs House, St George's Quay, Lancaster LA1 1RB (01524 382264; www.lancaster. gov.uk). Walk towards the river from bridge 99, turning left into Damside. Lifeboats, fine models and artefacts from Glasson Dock. *Open Easter–Oct, daily 11.00–17.00; winter 12.30–16.00.* Charge. Café. The riverside path to the west connects with Glasson Dock about 5 miles away.
Tourist Information Centre The Storey, Meeting House Lane, Lancaster LA1 1TH (01524 32878, www.citycoastcountryside.co.uk). *Open Mon–Sat 10.00–17.00.*
● **Lune Aqueduct**
This splendid edifice carries the navigation for some 600ft across the River Lune, which is 60ft below. Designed by John Rennie, it was built between 1794–7 by Alexander Stevens, a Scotsman who died before it was completed. The bottom of the channel is apparently 7 or 8ft deep, containing a layer of puddled clay about 3ft thick. There is said to be a plug which can be pulled to drain the structure onto the River Lune below. Its total cost was £48,320 18s 6d.
● **Hest Bank**
Lancs. PO, tel, stores, bank, Chinese takeaway. The seashore is only a couple of hundred yards from the navigation, and at low water miles of sandy beach are uncovered.

Pubs and Restaurants

▣ ✕ **Water Witch** Aldcliffe Lane, Lancaster LA1 1SU (01524 63828; www.thewaterwitch.co.uk). Canalside between bridges 98 and 99. Warm and friendly, with a stone floor and a good variety of fresh food, including an excellent cheeseboard, in the restaurant *L and E (all day Sun).* A wide selection of local real ales is available. Outside seating, mooring.
▣ ✕ **White Cross** Quarry Road, Lancaster LA1 4XQ (01524 384981). Canalside at bridge 100. Real ales, bar and restaurant meals *L and E, and all day Sat and Sun.* Children welcome. Canalside seating.
▣ ✕ **Farmers Arms Hotel** Penny Street, Lancaster LA1 1XT (01524 36368). A friendly family-run pub close to the canal, serving real ale and a wide range of bar and restaurant meals *L and E, daily.* Children welcome.

▣ **Golden Lion** Moor Lane, Lancaster LA1 1QD (01524 842198). North-west of Penny Street Bridge. Traditional English local's pub. Real ales.
✕ **Whale Tail Vegetarian Café** 78a Penny Street, Lancaster LA1 1XN (01524 845133; www.whaletailcafe.co.uk). Imaginative vegetarian and vegan meals, plus an organic snack menu. *Open daily for breakfast and L; also in E Thu–Sat.* Patio garden. Well-behaved children welcome.
▣ **Waggon & Horses** St George's Quay, Lancaster LA1 1RD (01524 846094). Worth a look in if you are visiting the Maritime Museum, this pub serves real ale, and food *L.* Waterside seats outside.
▣ ✕ **Hest Bank** 2 Hest Bank Lane, Lancaster LA2 6DN (01524 824339). Canalside at Bridge 118. *See* Pubs and Restaurants page 83.

Lancaster

WALKING & CYCLING

Themed walks and tours, local history walks, ghost and murder walks and treasure hunts are run in the Lancaster area by Catwalks (01524 792089;www.catwalks-lancaster.co.uk). There are guided tours of many of Lancaster's historic landmarks, plus Old Calendar Walks which leave from John O'Gaunt Gateway at Lancaster Castle at *19.00 on New Year's Eve, Valentine's Day, St George's Day, May Day, Midsummer Eve, Michaelmas Day, Hallowe'en and St Nicholas' Day*, telephone the Tourist Information centre on 01524 32878 for details. Some excellent walks and cycle rides in this area are suggested at www.losethesparetyre.co.uk/walkcycle, and www.greenwalks.net.

BOAT TRIPS

Daily waterbus service *June-mid Sept* between Lancaster and Carnforth. Ring 01524 389410 for details or visit: www.budgietransport.co.uk for timetable details.

81

Carnforth

The canal now passes Hest Bank and Bolton-le-Sands, with the sea never far away to the west and the A6 beside and below. As the waterway comes into Carnforth, it often affords grand views over Morecambe Bay before sneaking quite inconspicuously through the town, mostly in a cutting, passing a *sanitary station*, *pump out* and *showers*. It then dives under the motorway spur road and finds itself diverted along a new channel for several hundred yards before going under the main line of the M6: this diversion was presumably cheaper to build than a long, finely-angled skew motorway bridge over the navigation. Beyond the motorway lies peaceful green countryside backed, unmistakably, by the foothills of the Lake District. At Capernwray the canal crosses the River Keer on a minor aqueduct built by John Rennie in 1797; the nearby railway, which goes to Leeds, also crosses the Keer, on a very impressive viaduct.

BOAT TRIPS

Daily waterbus service *June-mid Sept* between Carnforth and Lancaster. Telephone 01524 389410 for details or visit: www.budgietransport.co.uk for timetable details.

Boatyards

Ⓑ **Nu-Way Acorn** Lundsfield, Carnforth LA5 9NB (01524 734457). Pump out, gas, overnight mooring, long-term mooring, winter storage, slipway, boat and engine sales and repairs, toilets, showers, DIY facilities.

● **Bolton-le-Sands**
*Lancs. PO, tel, stores,
fish & chips.* A pleasant
village of narrow streets,
with a pub at each end, and a
pie shop in the middle.

● **Carnforth**
Lancs. PO, tel, stores, garage, bank, station. Not
particularly attractive but useful for supplies, especially the
superb selection of pies at Madisons in Market Street, 01524 732021,
and of interest as an important railway junction. It is possible to catch trains not only
north–south but east over the beautiful green hills to Skipton and Leeds, west to Barrow and
right round the coast to Carlisle. Carnforth was the last town in the country to lose its regular British Rail
steam locomotive service in 1968: it is now a centre for steam-hauled railtours over the national railway
system. The Tearooms, as featured in the film *Brief Encounter*, have been restored.

Pubs and Restaurants

▣ ✕ **Hest Bank** 2 Hest Bank Lane, Lancaster LA2 6DN (01524 824339). Canalside at bridge 118. You can still see the window for the guiding light, which once showed the way across the sands. Now this old coaching inn, which dates from 1554, is justly popular and you can share the shelter it once offered to abbots and monks, soldiers and highwaymen, the Duke of Devonshire and Prince Frederick of Prussia. Real ale and fresh local food, and seafood *L and E, daily*. Children welcome (not in the public bar), and there is a fine canalside garden. Quiz *Wed*. Mooring.

▣ ✕ **Blue Anchor** Main Road, Bolton-le-Sands, Carnforth LA5 8DN (01524 823241; www.blueanchorhotel.co.uk). An 18th-C coach house serving real ale and bar and restaurant food *L and E (all day Sun)*. Children welcome. Garden with an aviary. Quiz *Wed*. B & B.

▣ **Packet Boat Hotel** Main Road, Bolton-le-Sands, Carnforth LA5 8DN (01524 822289). A friendly pub with 'something for everyone', serving real ale and food *L and E (all day Fri–Sun)*. Children welcome *until 20.30*. Outside seating. *Weekend* entertainment and quiz *Sun*. Live TV premiership football.

▣ **Royal Hotel** Main Road, Bolton-le-Sands, Carnforth LA5 8DQ (01524 732057). A choice of real ale, plus a good range of excellent food *L and E (all day Sun)*. A large and very comfortable pub. Dart board, pool table and sports TV. Children welcome, and there is a play area. Garden. B & B.

▣ ✕ **Canal Turn** Lancaster Road, Carnforth LA5 9EE (01524 734750; www.thecanalturn.co.uk). A very attractive canalside pub in cottages once known as 'Pig & Piano Row', and which housed workers from nearby iron and gas works. Meals are served *L and E, daily*, along with real ale. Children are welcome, and there is a waterside garden. Regular quiz nights and entertainment.

▣ **Shovel** North Road, Carnforth LA5 9NA (01524 733402). West of bridge 128. A friendly pub serving real ale. Children welcome, and there is a garden. Quiz nights.

▣ **Carnforth Hotel** Lancaster Road, Carnforth LA5 9LD (01524 732902). Real ale. Home-cooked meals available *L and E*. Beer garden. B & B.

▣ **Queens Hotel** 34 Market Street, Carnforth LA5 9JX (01524 732978; www.queenshotelcarnforth.co.uk). Real ales, meals and bar snacks available *all day*. Open fire, traditional pub games, pool table, regular quiz nights and entertainment at *weekends*. Children welcome. Beer garden. B & B.

▣ ✕ **Royal Station Hotel** Market Street, Carnforth LA5 9BT (01524 732033; www.mitchellshotels.co.uk). Bang in the centre of town, this handsome establishment played host to Trevor Howard, Celia Johnson and Stanley Holloway in the Noel Coward film 'Brief Encounter', which was filmed around Carnforth Station. Queen Victoria is also reputed to have stayed here. They offer real ale, plus bar and restaurant meals *L and E (all day Sun)*. Children welcome. The Sports Bar has a large-screen TV. B & B.

83

Borwick

Beyond Keer Aqueduct and the railway viaduct is the Capernwray Arm, a short branch to a worked-out quarry, and now offering some attractive sheltered moorings. The canal then winds around the hillside to end abruptly just beyond Borwick and right beside the M6, but fortunately with a decent pub just a stone's throw away. The abandoned Tewitfield locks begin across the road from the present terminus, and it is well worth taking the fenced path by the motorway and under the bridge to go and have a look, and to imagine how they will look when hopefully restored! It is possible to walk the 15 miles or so from Tewitfield to the original terminus at Kendal (and get a bus back). Boats can be left at the moorings here.

● **Borwick**
Lancs. Tel. A small, old and attractive village, spread around a green. Overlooking the canal is Borwick Hall, a large and sombre Elizabethan manor house, built around a high 15th-C tower and with extensive gardens.

● **Warton**
Lancs. PO, tel, stores. About 2 miles west of Borwick. Ancestors of George Washington lived in this village and their family crest, containing the famed Stars and Stripes, is to be seen on the 15th-C tower of the church of St Oswald.

Pubs and Restaurants

🍴 ✕ **Longlands Hotel** Tewitfield Locks, Tewitfield, Carnforth LA6 1JH (01524 781256; www.longlandshotel.co.uk). Just north east of the canal terminus. This popular country pub serves real ale and home-made bar and restaurant meals *L and E*, in a friendly atmosphere. Children are welcome, and there is outside seating by copious baskets of flowers. Regular entertainment. B & B.

LEEDS & LIVERPOOL CANAL

MAXIMUM DIMENSIONS

Liverpool to Wigan, and Leigh Branch
Length: 72' 0''
Beam: 14' 3''
Headroom: 8' 0''

Wigan to Leeds
Length: 60' 0''
Beam: 14' 3''
Headroom: 8' 0''

Rufford Branch
Length: 62' 0''
Beam: 14' 3''
Headroom: 8' 0''

MANAGER

Liverpool to winding hole upstream of Greenberfield Changeline Bridge 158:
01942 405700;
enquiries.northwest@britishwaterways.co.uk.

Winding hole upstream of Greenberfield Changeline Bridge 158 to Leeds: 0113 281 6800;
enquiries.yorkshire@ britishwaterways.co.uk.

MILEAGE

LIVERPOOL. Canal terminus to Burscough, junction with Rufford Branch: 24¹/₂ miles
Wigan, junction with Leigh Branch: 35 miles
Johnson's Hill Locks: 47¹/₄ miles
Blackburn, Top Lock: 56 miles
Burnley: 72¹/₂ miles
Skipton: 98 miles
Bingley Five Rise: 110³/₄ miles
Apperley Bridge: 118 miles
LEEDS, River Lock: 127³/₄ miles
Locks: 91
Leigh Branch: 7¹/₄ miles, 2 locks
Rufford Branch: 7¹/₄ miles, 8 locks

BW produce an excellent navigation guide for this canal (obtainable-free-from lock keepers and the Waterway Unit offices listed above, or downloadable from www.waterscape.com/boatersguides) to assist boaters in the safe operation of the many swing bridges and staircase locks.

With a length of 127¹/₄ miles excluding branches, the Leeds & Liverpool Canal is the longest single canal in Britain built by a single company. The canal has its beginnings in the River Douglas, a little river made navigable by 1740 from Wigan to Parbold, Tarleton and the Ribble estuary. Several ambitious trans-Pennine canal schemes had been mooted; one for a canal from Liverpool to Leeds, to connect with the head of the Aire & Calder Navigation. The Leeds & Liverpool Canal was authorised in 1770, and construction began at once, with John Longbotham as engineer. The first (lock-free) section from Bingley to Skipton was opened within three years; by 1777 two long sections were open from the Aire & Calder at Leeds to Gargrave (incorporating many new staircase locks) and from Wigan to Liverpool. The L & L bought out the River Douglas navigation at an early stage to gain control of its valuable water supply. It was replaced by a proper canal branch to Rufford and Tarleton, where it joined the (tidal) River Douglas. In 1790 work began again, with Robert Whitworth as the company's engineer; but after 1792 and the outbreak of war with France, investment in canals declined steadily. The whole of the main line from Leeds to Liverpool was finished by 1816 actually *sharing* the channel of the Lancaster Canal for 10 miles from Wigan Top Lock to Johnson's Hill Bottom Lock. The Lancaster used to branch off up what became the Walton Summit Branch. In 1820 a branch was opened to join the Bridgewater Canal at Leigh. A short branch (the Springs Branch) was also made to rock quarries at Skipton and an important 3-mile-long canal from Shipley to Bradford. The cut down into the Liverpool Docks was made in 1846. The prosperity of the company after 1820 was not, at first, greatly affected by the advent of railways. The scale of the navigation (the locks were built as broad locks 62ft by 14ft, allowing big payloads to be carried along the canal) contributed to the high dividends paid to shareholders for several years. Water supply was, however, a problem and in spite of the building of copious reservoirs, the canal had to be closed for months on end during dry summers, driving carriers' custom away to the railways. Use of the navigation for freight declined throughout the last century; the hard winter of 1962/63 finished off many traders. Today this canal offers boaters, walkers and cyclists an exhilarating link between two superb cities.

Springs Branch at Skipton (see page 136)

Liverpool

At the time of going to press it is expected that the Liverpool Canal Link will be completed in time for the start of the 2009 boating season. It runs from the bottom of the existing Stanley Locks and linking Stanley Dock to Canning Dock, via the old West Waterloo Dock; Princes Dock and an underground section near Pier Head, in front of the Royal Liver Building. Canning Dock in turn provides a link into the revitalised Albert Dock which will, for the first time in its history (it is hoped), play host to a regular influx of narrowboats.

Navigation now begins just north of Vauxhall bridge B. It runs north from the city centre for about 6 miles, parallel and close to Liverpool Docks, before turning east to Aintree, Wigan and the Pennines. Liverpool, while at one time not an attractive place from the canal, is slowly changing and although some factories still have their backs to the waterway, considerable effort has been made to improve the access to the towpath which is alive with walkers, fishermen and cyclists. The water, however, is surprisingly clear. Eldonian Village forms an attractive backdrop to the moorings in the terminus basin. There is a *PO* beside bridge 2A together with a very comprehensive range of *shops*.

NAVIGATIONAL NOTES

1 Just north of the terminus is the Stanley Dock Branch, until recently used only by intrepid navigators as a useful link into the tidal River Mersey. Today this compact flight of locks gives access to the newly completed Liverpool Canal Link, leading across the historic Pier Head, in front of the Royal Liver Building and ultimately into Albert Dock. There are four locks on this branch leading down into Stanley Dock and at the time of going to press arrangements for their use had still to be finalised. Contact BW North West Office (01942 405700); enquiries.northwest@britishwaterways.co.uk for the current situation.

2 Navigators wishing to enter the Mersey should contact the Mersey Docks and Harbour Company (0151 949 6000) – the lock is operated *24hrs a day*.

3 Those navigating the Leeds & Liverpool Canal will need, as well as a windlass, a British Waterways handcuff lock key and a Watermate key.

4 Mooring at unrecognised sites in the city centre is not recommended.

5 If you wish to navigate between Liverpool and Aintree and need assistance or details of safe mooring locations, contact BW North West Office (01942 405700); enquiries.northwest@britishwaterways.co.uk. Currently *48hrs* notice to BW is required before navigating this length but the whole dynamic of this stretch of waterway is likely to change, with the opening of the Liverpool Canal Link and the almost certain increase in the volume of boats that this will produce. Again contact BW for the up to date situation and their navigational requirements.

● Liverpool

Merseyside. All services. In the first century AD it was 'lifrugpool', a settlement next to a muddy creek; now it is one of Britain's largest ports. Famous worldwide as the place where the Beatles began their march to fame, and equally well known for the exploits of Liverpool Football Club. Club. There is much to be seen in this ancient port. The Anglican Cathedral, begun in 1904 and finished in 1978, is the largest in the world; the Roman Catholic Cathedral has stained glass by John Piper and Patrick Reyntiens. On the pierhead is a memorial to the engineers lost on the *Titanic*, which sank in 1912. The superb Albert Dock development and Liverpool Tate and The Walker Art Galleries,

Pubs and Restaurants

There are many to be found here.

together with a wide range of theatres and museums, are attracting an ever increasing number of tourists. As a city it has more Georgian buildings than Bath, a UNESCO World Heritage waterfront and has convincingly re-establishing itself upon a reputation as a cultural and leisure centre which was recognised with the award of City of Culture 2008.

Albert Dock The Colonnades, Albert Dock, Liverpool L3 4AF (0151 707 0729; www.albertdock.com). The largest grouping of Grade I listed buildings in England-opened in 1846 as warehousing for a range of precious cargo from around the world, these buildings have been transformed into an award-winning tourist destination including shops, cafés, restaurants, galleries and museums.

Beatles Story Britannia Pavillion, Albert Dock, Liverpool L3 4AD (0151 707 0729). The title says it all. *Open daily 10.00-18.00. Last admission 1 hr before closing. Closed 25 and 26 Dec.* Charge.

Bluecoat Arts Centre Bluecoat Chambers, School Lane, Liverpool L1 3BX (0151 709 5297;www.thebluecoat.org.uk). A striking 18th-C building housing a varied selection of visual and performing arts. Also educational programmes, artists' studios, shops and a café.

Bluecoat Display Centre College Lane, Liverpool L1 3BX (0151 709 4041; www.bluecoatdisplaycentre.com). Craft and design centre in an adjacent street. *Open Mon-Sat 10.00-17.30.*

Chinese Arch Berry Street, Liverpool. The largest outside China from where it was originally shipped, the arch stands 15m high and spans Nelson Street complete with its five roofs and 200 ornate dragons.

Citysightseeing from Canada Boulevard, Liverpool (01708 866000; www.city-sightseeing.com). Hop on and hop off open-top buses where a ticket lasts for 24hrs. *Open daily mid-Mar-Oct.* **Maghull Coaches** (0151 933 2324/922 4284; www.maghullcoaches.co.uk) operate a similar service *daily all the year round.*

National Conservation Centre Whitechapel, Liverpool (0151 478 4999; www.liverpoolmuseums.org.uk). Housed in an impressively restored, listed Victorian warehouse (the former Midland Railway Goods Offices) this interactive exhibition provides a rare insight into work that normally goes on behind the scenes. Surrounded by classical sculpture, the Café Eros makes a good place to meet and eat. Shop. *Open Mon-Sat 10.00-17.00 and Sun 12.00-17.00.* Free. Full disabled access.

Croxteth Hall & Country Park Croxteth Park, Liverpool L12 0HB (0151 228 5311; www.croxteth.co.uk).Once the ancestral home of the Molyneux family, the Earls of Sefton, the estate now offers the opportunity to visit the historic Hall, the 500- acre Country Park, the Walled Garden and the Home Farm. Only the Country Park is free. *Open Easter-Sep 10.30-17.00 and farm, café and shop open weekends Oct-Easter.*

Empire Theatre Lime Street, Liverpool L1 1JE (0870 606 3536; www.livenation.co.uk/livempire). Year-round programme of ballet, opera, musicals and large scale-theatre in a 2300-seat auditorium.

Everyman Theatre Hope Street, Liverpool L1 9BH (0151 709 0398; www.everymanplayhouse.com). A popular theatre with a diverse programme of in-house productions and touring shows.

Fact Wood Street, Liverpool L1 4DQ (0151 707 4450;

www.fact.co.uk). Exciting, purpose-built arts centre, completed in 2003, housing a range of galleries; three very varied cinemas; a café; restaurant, shop and bar. *Open Mon-Sat 11.00-23.00 and Sun 12.00-22.30. Galleries closed all day Mon and Tue-Wed at 18.00; Thu-Sat at 20.00; Sun and B Hols at 17.00.* Free

HM Customs & Excise Museum Albert Dock, Liverpool L3 4AQ (0151 478 4499; www.customsandexcisemuseum.org.uk). The museum tells the exciting story of smugglers and duty men, from the 1700s to the present day. Shop and café. *Open daily 10.00-17.00, last admission 16.00.* Free).

24 Hour Museum Guide Visit www.24hourmuseum.org.uk/cityheritage to plan your day out and gain a unique perspective on the heritage of English cities. Non-commercial and free to use.

● **Liverpool Canal Link** Liverpool (*see* Navigational Notes on page 88; www.britishwaterways.com/liverpool-canal-link). A new canal across Pier Head, running in front of The Three Graces and linking Stanley Dock to Albert Dock, via Princes Dock and Canning Dock.

Liverpool Cathedral St James Road, Liverpool L1 7AZ (0151 709 6271; www.liverpoolcathedral.org.uk). The largest Anglican cathedral in Britain, resplendent in red sandstone, built to the design of Sir Giles Gilbert Scott and begun in 1904. The 331ft tower extends the full width of the building and is home to the heaviest ringing peal of bells in the world-all 30 tons of them. Inside there are soaring gothic arches, a massive organ and together with worship there are regular recitals and concerts. Refectory and shop. *Open daily 08.00-18.00.* Free-donations. Charge for Tower and Embroidery Gallery.

Liverpool Heritage Walk Liverpool. Provides a structured approach to explore Liverpool's unique historical and architectural features. The Heritage Walk comprises 75 gunmetal markers set in footways and pedestrian areas throughout the city centre. Themed sub-trails within the heritage walk provide an opportunity to focus on three specific areas of the city's rich architectural legacy: 1) Maritime and Commerce; 2) Arts and Heritage and 3) Learning and Religion. Contact the TIC for further details.

Martin Mere Fish Lane, Burscough (01704 895181; www.wwt.org.uk). A major Wildlife & Wetlands Trust site approaching 600 acres that in winter hosts thousands of migratory wetland birds. There is plenty to do and see at all times of the year and it makes a worthwhile visit either from the city (Merseyrail train to Ormskirk and then a No 3 bus) or as you follow the canal east through Burscough. Café, shop and picnic area. Children's activities. *Open daily 09.30-17.30 (Nov-Feb 17.00).* Charge.

Mendips & 20 Forthlin Road Allerton, Liverpool L24 1YP (0151 708 8574; www.nationaltrust.org.uk). Where Sir Paul McCartney lived with his parents and John Lennon grew up with his aunt and uncle. Both homes have been sensitively restored and can be visited on a tour commencing either in the city centre or from Speke Hall. Booking essential-no direct access to either property. *Tours mid Mar-Oct*

10.30 and 11.20 from city centre; 14.15 and 15.55 from Speke Hall. Charge.

Mersey Ferries Pier Head, Georges Parade, Liverpool L3 1DP (0151 330 1444; www.merseyferries.co.uk). A 50-min heritage cruise with commentary and spectacular views. *Daily cruises weekdays 10.00– 15.00; weekends and B Hols 10.00–18.00.* Also special (and often themed) river cruises and summer trips along the Manchester Ship Canal to Salford Quays. Shop and café. Charge.

Merseyguide Liverpool (01928 566969; www.showmeliverpool.co.uk). Registered guides available for groups or anyone who wishes to unravel the rich tapestry of Liverpool's history and heritage.

Merseyside Maritime Museum Albert Dock, Liverpool L3 4AQ (0151 478 4499; www.liverpoolmuseums.org.uk/maritime/). The chance to discover Liverpool's maritime heritage from tales of the Titanic to the transatlantic slavery trade. Shop and Café. *Open daily 10.00–17.00.* Free.

MerseyTravel 24 Hatton Garden, Liverpool L3 2AN (0151 236 7676; www.merseytravel.gov.uk). Also National Rail Enquiries 08457 48 49 50 *(24hrs)* and Traveline Merseyside 0870 608 2 608 *open 08.00–20.00.* Merseytravel also produce two excellent leaflets entitled Rideabout and Getabout detailing five cycle rides and six leisure trails in the area that can be undertaken in conjunction with Merseyrail.

Metropolitan Cathedral Mount Pleasant, Liverpool L3 5TQ (0151 709 9222; www.liverpoolmetrocathedral.org.uk). Standing on the site once occupied by the Poor Law Institute, today's striking building, with its interior lantern tower of multi-coloured glass, has had a somewhat chequered career. Of the original design by Sir Edwin Lutyens, dating from 1933, only the Crypt was built and after the war inflation had raised the estimated cost of completion to £27m. Sir Frederick Gibberd produced a design that met the new brief, namely, that the cathedral should be completed within five years, incorporate the original crypt and cost no more than £1m. Building recommenced in 1962 and the finished cathedral-known locally as 'Paddy's wigwam'-was consecrated in May 1967. Café bar and gift shop. *Open daily 08.00–18.00.* Free-donations welcome.

Museum of Liverpool Albert Dock, Liverpool L3 4AX (0151 478 4080; www.liverpoolmuseums.org.uk/mol/). An opportunity to explore the richness of Liverpool's cultural diversity through a series of galleries which include the River Room, City Soldiers and City Lives. *Open daily 10.00–17.00. Closed 23–26 Dec and 1 Jan.* Shop and café. Free.

Prince's Road Synagogue Prince's Road, Liverpool L8 1TG (0151 709 3431; www.princesroad.org). Arguably Europe's finest example of Saracenic or Moorish revival style of synagogue in a Grade II listed building. Guided talks covering its architecture and history available.

Radio City Tower St John's Beacon, 1 Houghton Street, Liverpool L1 1RL (0151 709 3285; www.radiocity.co.uk). Stunning views over the city and the Mersey estuary from the top of the 440ft Radio City Tower. Tours *every weekend*-booking essential. Charge.

Rice Lane City Farm No 2 Lodge, Walton Park Cemetery, Walton, Liverpool L9 1AW (0151 530 1066; www.visitliverpool.com). 224 acres of countryside-11 of which are woodland. There is a variety of rare breeds of farm animals together with ponies, goats and poultry. Also guided walks and talks *which must be booked in advance.* Free-donations welcome.

Mr Hardman's Photographic Studio 59 Rodney Street, Liverpool L1 9EX (0151 709 6261; www.nationaltrust.org.uk). The complete studio, housed in an elegant Georgian terrace, where one of the city's best known portrait and landscape photographers lived and worked. *Open mid Mar-Oct Wed-Sun 11.00-16.15 and Nov weekends 10.00-15.15.* Charge for timed ticket and guided tour.

Royal Court Theatre 1 Roe Street, Liverpool L1 1HL (0151 709 4321; www.royalcourtliverpool.co.uk). An impressive, 1500-seat Grade II listed building presenting a major events programme including drama, opera, comedy and popular music gigs.

Royal Liverpool Philharmonic Hall Hope Street, Liverpool L1 9BP (0151 210 2895; www.liverpoolphil.com). Art Deco building opened in 1939 to replace the original which was destroyed by fire and now home to the Royal Liverpool Philharmonic Orchestra. The hall hosts around 60 orchestral concerts a year together with drama, film and other arts.

St George's Hall William Brown Street, Liverpool L1 1JJ (0151 707 2391; www.stgeorgeshall.eu). A stunning reflection of the City's prosperity in the 19th C, built in the neo-classical style to house the law courts and as a music venue. One of the first buildings to greet the visitor arriving at Liverpool Lime Street Station and currently undergoing a £23m refurbishment. Shop and café. Tours available *Mon-Sat 11.30-12.30 and 13.30-15.00.* Telephone 0151 233 2008 for details and bookings. Charge.

Sefton Park Palm House Sefton Park, Liverpool L17 1AP (0151 726 2415; www.palmhouse.org.uk). An octagonal, three-tiered, Grade II listed Victorian glasshouse housing Liverpool's botanical collection. Inside and outside the palm house are beds of formal bedding and statues. Regular events. *Open Apr-Oct 10.30-17.00 and Nov-Mar 10.30-16.00.*

Speke Hall The Walk, Liverpool L24 1XD (0844 800 4799; www.nationaltrust.org.uk). Black and white, half- timbered house dating back to 1490 complete with priest hole, fine Jacobean plasterwork, a Great Hall, Victorian kitchen and servants' hall. Restaurant and children's play area. Charge. Hall *open mid Mar-Oct Wed-Sun 13.00-17.00 and weekends Nov.* Gardens *open daily 11.00-17.30.* Charge.

Sudley House Mossley Hill Road, Liverpool L18 8BX (0151 724 3245; www.liverpoolmuseums.org.uk/sudley/). Take the train to either Airburth or Mossley Hill stations. Victorian interior decoration and craftsmanship together with fine examples of 18th- and 19th-C art – the art collection of a Victorian merchant in its original setting. *Open as per World Museum.* Free. Victorian tearooms *open Sat and B Hols 10.00–16.30, Sun 12.00–16.30.*

Tate Liverpool Albert Dock, Liverpool L3 4BB (0151 702 7400; www.tate.org.uk/liverpool). One of the largest galleries of contemporary and modern art outside London housed in part of the splendidly converted Grade I listed warehouses surrounding Albert Dock. Shop and café. *Open Tue–Sun and B Hol Mons 10.00–17.50. Closed 24–26 Dec.* Free to see collection; charge for touring exhibitions.

The Walker Art Gallery William Brown Street, Liverpool L3 8EL (0151 478 4199; www.liverpoolmuseums.org.uk/walker). One of Europe's foremost art galleries with outstanding collections from 1300 to the present day. *Open daily 10.00–17.00.* Shop and Café. Free.

University of Liverpool Art Gallery Abercromby Square, Liverpool L69 7WY (0151 794 2348; www.liv.ac.uk/artgall). Collection of modern and classical art with works by Epstein, Audubon and Freud. *Open Mon–Fri 12.00–16.00. Closed throughout Aug.* Free.

Western Approaches – Liverpool War Museum 1–3 Rumford Street, Liverpool L2 8SZ (0151 227 2008; www.liverpoolwarmuseum.co.uk). Re-creation of the underground centre that orchestrated the Battle of the Atlantic during World War II. Shop. *Open*

Mar–Nov, Mon–Thu and Sat 10.30–16.30. Last admission 15.30. Charge.

Williamson Tunnels Heritage Centre The Old Stableyard, Smithdown Lane, Liverpool L7 3EE (0151 709 6868; www.williamsontunnels.co.uk). A unique labyrinth of tunnels under Edge Hill created by 19th-C philanthropist Joseph Williamson–'The Mole of Edge Hill.' The Visitor Centre offers an insight into the life and underground world of one of Liverpool's most eccentric characters. Also 45-minute guided tours through a small section of the tunnel system. *Open Tue–Sun 10.00–18.00 (17.00 in winter).* Charge.

World Museum William Brown Street, Liverpool L3 4AQ (0151 478 4393; www.liverpoolmuseums. org.uk/wml). Thousands of exhibits, including an exploration of the Earth and cosmos, with themes ranging from the oceans to the stars–much very hands-on and interactive. A wide ranging and ever changing programme of events for all the family. Shop and Café. *Open daily 10.00–17.00.* Free.

Yellow Duckmarine Anchor Courtyard, Britannia Pavilion, Albert Dock, Liverpool L3 4AS (0151 708 7799; www.theyellowduckmarine.co.uk). A one hour sight seeing tour of the city's docks, waterfront and centre in a converted WW II DUKW complete with live commentary. 'Wa-ter way to see Liverpool ....' *Open daily 11.00–dusk.* Charge.

Tourist Information Centres The 08 Place, Whitechapel, Liverpool L1 6DZ (0906 680 6886/0151 709 5111; www. visitliverpool.com). *Open Mon–Sat 09.00–17.3 0 (Tue from 10.00) Sun and B Hol 10.30–16.30.* Anchor Courtyard, Albert Dock, Liverpool L3 4AF (0906 680 6886; www.visitliverpool.com). *Open daily 10.00–17.00.*

The Pier Head buildings from across the River Mersey

Litherland

North of Litherland the canal turns east to Aintree. Soon the first of many swing bridges is encountered; for the first few miles these bridges have to be locked to combat vandalism. All navigators should ensure that they have both a Watermate and a Handcuff key before reaching these bridges.

● **Bootle**
Merseyside. All services. Now a busy suburb of Liverpool, this settlement was described in early Victorian times as 'containing, with the township of Linacre, 808 inhabitants. The village comprises several good houses and is very much resorted to during summer for the benefit of sea-bathing.'

Pubs and Restaurants

Cooksons Bridge Gorsey Lane Ford, Liverpool L21 0EJ (0151 476 7327). Beside bridge 4A. Pleasant pub offering pool; karaoke *Wed and Sun* and live music *Sat.* Children welcome. There is a useful selection of *shops and a PO,* beyond the pub to the north of the canal

Maghull

Aintree marks the limit of Liverpool's outskirts and here is of course the Aintree Race Course. At the east end of the racecourse is another swing bridge; this carries a main road and traffic lights are installed, but boat crews operate the bridge themselves. The canal turns north again and emerges into open countryside, although Maghull soon interrupts this with a series of swing bridges. On the offside, between bridges 13 and 14, there is a *PO, a bank and a variety of restaurants and takeaways.*

● **Melling**
Merseyside. Tel. The village stands on an isolated hillock at a safe distance from the big city. The church is a landmark in the area; it was built in the 15th C with rock from an adjacent quarry.

● **Maghull**
Merseyside. All services. A small town astride the canal, convenient for supplies.

St Andrew's Church Damfield Lane, Maghull, Liverpool L31 6DD. Just north of bridge 12A. Though separated from the rest of the town by a dual carriageway, it is well worth a visit. It was built in the late 19th C, but its style is in imitation of that of the 13th C to accord with the tiny 700-year-old chapel, known as Old St Andrew's, which sits in its grounds. To the west of 11B Drapers Bridge, close to the railway station, there is a pub and a useful parade of shops including a late closing store.

Pubs and Restaurants

Old Roan Copy Lane, Bootle, Liverpool L30 8RD (0151 526 8422). Near Old Roan Bridge 7D. Real ales are served amidst multiple TV screens. Sensibly priced bar food served *L and E Mon-Fri and 12.00-19.00 Sat-Sun*. Children welcome. Outside seating. Disco *Fri and Sun*.

Horse & Jockey Waddicar Lane, Melling, Liverpool L31 1DU (0151 546 9406). Near bridge 9C. Bar food *available L daily*. Children's play area. *Mon* Karaoke, *Wed* Quiz and live music *Fri-Sun*.

✕ **Bootle Arms** Rock Lane, Melling, Liverpool L31 1EN (0151 526 2886). Continental, Asian and traditional food is served *all day* together with real ale in this family restaurant and pub. Children are welcome; dogs in the bar area only. Garden with children's play area.

Great Mogul Hotel 31 Station Road, Maghull, Liverpool L31 3DE (0151 531 9256). West of Bridge 11B, beside the station. Real ale is served along with

food, *Mon-Wed 12.00-19.45; Thu 12.00- 18.45; Fri-Sun 12.00-16.45*. Outside seating. Children welcome when eating. Quiz *Thu*, disco *once a month*.

Hare & Hounds 53 Liverpool Road, Maghull, Liverpool L31 2HP (0151 526 1447). Near bridge 14. Real ales and traditional bar meals are available *12.00-20.00 daily* in this roadside pub. Patio seating area. Children welcome. Quiz *Mon and Wed*.

Red House 31 Foxhouse Lane, Maghull, Liverpool L31 3EW (0151 526 1376). Genuine, traditional, suburban local dispensing real ales. Food is available *12.00- 20.00 Mon-Sat and 12.00-17.00 Sun*. Children welcome; patio seating area. Occasional live music.

Coach & Horses 164-166 Liverpool Road North, Maghull, Liverpool L31 2HP (0151 526 1093). On A567 east of the canal between bridges 15 and 16. Snacks and bar meals are available *L and E daily* together with real ales. Children outside only. Garden and children's play area.

NAVIGATIONAL NOTES

Those who do wish to continue should contact BW North West Office (01942 405700); enquiries.northwest@britishwaterways.co.uk) for assisted passage into Liverpool, giving at least *48hrs notice*. You can also seek advice on where and where not to moor.

97

16 Bell's Swing Bridge

11¾m 0L
Burscough
Terminus
12¾m 0L
Schs

15 Methodist Swing Bridge

14 Shaw's Swing Bridge

13 Red Lion Bridge

MAGHULL

12A Northway Bridge

Maghull Hall
12 Swing Bridge

Drapers Bridge 11B

11A

M58 Bridge

Weavers Lane

16 Bradshaw's Farm

MELLING

Wood Hall Farm

11 Melling Stone Bridge

MELLING

M58

7 M58

Brewery Lane

New House Farm

Wadacre

93

Brooklea

10 Holmes Swing Bridge

Waddicar

M57

Carr Cottage

Brooklands Farm

7 Copy Bridge

7A
Dunning's Bridge

Aintree Hall Farm

Ledson's Bridge 9C

M57 Bridge

7D Old Roan Bridge
7C

AINTREE

Bull Bridge

8 Blue Anchor Bridge

AINTREE VILLAGE CP

AINTREE RACE COURSE

Golf Driving Range

Weir

Aqueduct

9 Hancock's Swing Bridge

AINTREE RACE COURSE

Haskayne

The canal now enters continuous open countryside, which soon establishes itself as extremely flat and intensively cultivated lowlands: indeed it is more akin to Cambridgeshire or Lincolnshire than to the rest of Lancashire. However, it is pleasant enough and the canal forms one of its more important features – a view which is borne out by the large number of people usually to be seen walking and boating upon it, as well as the hundreds of anglers enjoying their sport in this well-stocked length of canal. As if in compensation for the unexciting landscape, the traveller is offered a truly astonishing number (and variety) of pubs on or near the canal, all the way from Lydiate to Wigan. The digging of the canal is reputed to have commenced in the low cutting between bridges 24 and 25, and this clearly provided an excellent source of stone for local bridges.

● **Haskayne**
Lancs. Stores, tel. There are just two pretty houses here: the old post office and a thatched cottage opposite. The remainder of the village sprawls away from the navigation but there is no sign of a church.

FERTILE RELIEF

This was once an area of low lying marshland, much of it below sea level and, consequently, thinly populated. The original course of the River Douglas ran close by, joining the sea near Southport. At some point its course was blocked – possibly by giant sand dunes thrown up by a great storm – and it found a new, northern mouth in the Ribble estuary, leaving behind the area known today as Martin Mere. This once extended to 15 square miles but in 1787 Thomas Eccleston of Scarisbrick Hall, with the help of John Gilbert, set about draining it for agricultural use (it was Gilbert who, as agent to the Duke of Bridgewater, enlisted James Brindley's help in constructing Britain's first major canal). Once drained the mere required vast quantities of manure to raise its fertility for crop production. 'Night soil' was shipped in along the canal from the large conurbations of Liverpool and Wigan and off-loaded at a series of small wharfs, some still visible today. Part of the mere remains undrained, a haven for migrating geese.

Pubs and Restaurants

🍺 **Scotch Piper** Southport Road, Lydiate, Liverpool L31 4HD (0151 526 0503). 500yds west of canal, access from bridge 19, left at A567 junction. An attractive old world, thatched pub dispensing real ales and good conversation in generous measure. No large (or small) screen TV, fruit machines or juke boxes. Dogs are most welcome but strictly no children. Garden.

🍺 **King's Arms** Delf Lane, Haskayne L39 7JJ (01704 840245). 100yds north of bridge 21A. A selection of real ales served in this traditional, old-fashioned village local. Snacks available *L*. Outside courtyard seating. Live music *Tue and Sat*, and quiz with bingo *Thu*.

🍺 **Ship** 6 Rosemary Lane, Haskayne, Ormskirk L39 7JP (01704 840572). Canalside, at Ship Bridge.

A well-known canal pub with a garden and waterside terrace serving real ale. Excellent fresh food served in a homely, dark-beamed bar tastefully decorated with horse brasses available – including seafood, steaks and pasta – *L and E Mon–Thu and all day Fri–Sun*. Children welcome. Reputed to be the first pub on the canal, which was started in the adjacent cutting. Quiz *Tue*, folk evening *Thu*, and live singer *Fri*.

🍺✕ **Saracen's Head** 100 Summerwood Lane, Halsall, Ormskirk L39 8RH (01704 840204). Canalside, at Halsall Warehouse Bridge. Real ales together with a wide range of food served *all day every day*. Children welcome *until 20.00*; garden with children's play area. Quiz *Wed* and live music *Sat*.

Burscough

On now past a massive caravan site on one side and attractive woods containing the private Scarisbrick Hall on the other; then out again into the open flatlands. An attractively produced information board, at the north end of bridge 27A, offers a fascinating insight into the history of the parish and the past habitation of the hall. The Southport-Manchester line converges from the north west; it runs near the canal all the way into Wigan, and has some wonderfully remote stations. A flurry of swing bridges brings the canal into Burscough; just beyond is the junction with the Rufford Branch.

● **Halsall**

Lancs. PO, tel, garage. ½ mile west of canal. There is a handsome tall 14th-15th-C church here (St Cuthbert's), with a fine spire. The choir vestry, erected in 1592, was formerly a grammar school. There is an interesting pair of pulpits/lecterns. One of them is generously illuminated by a solitary overhead window; the other, more sheltered, gives the occupant the unfortunate air of being behind bars . . .

● **Burscough**

Lancs. PO, tel, stores, takeaways, garage, bank, stations. Formerly a canal village and a staging post on the one-time Wigan-Liverpool 'packet boat' run, this place attaches more significance nowadays to the benefits of road and rail transport. It still boasts two stations (one is on the Preston-Liverpool line) and suffers from heavy through traffic. A very convenient place for taking on provisions.

Boatyards

ⓑ **Red Lion Caravan Centre** Scarisbrick Bridge, Southport Road, Ormskirk L40 8HQ (01704 840032; www.rlcaravans.co.uk). 🛠 D E Gas, solid fuel, narrowboat hire, large selection of spares and parts for caravans, many of which are 'boat compatible'.

ⓑ **Lathom Marina** The Workshop, Crabtree Lane, Burscough, Ormskirk L40 0RW (01704 894782). Winter storage, slipway, chandlery, boat and engine sales and repairs, salvage, canopy manufacture and repairs.

Pubs and Restaurants

✗ **Blue Elephant** Southport Road, Scarisbrick L40 8HQ (01704 840317). Near Scarisbrick Bridge 27A. Formerly the Red Lion, now turned into a good, reasonably priced Indian restaurant.

🍺 **Heatons Bridge Inn** Heatons Bridge Road, Scrisbrick L40 8JG (01704 840549). Friendly unspoilt canalside pub, at bridge 28. Real ales together with inexpensive, traditional pub food served *all day, every day*. Children welcome (not in bar area); dogs welcome outside restaurant space. Garden and moorings.

🍺 ✗ **Martin Inn** Mescar Lane, Burscough L40 0RT (01704 893894; www.themartininn.com). 200yds north of bridge 29. Restaurant and inn attracting a wide-ranging clientele and serving real ale and an à la carte menu *L and E*. Children and dogs welcome. Patio seating. B & B.

🍺 ✗ **Farmers Arms** 36 New Lane, Burscough L40 8JA (01704 896021). Canalside, by bridge 31. A bright, friendly pub of great character with an open fire, serving real ale. Full à la carte menu

together with a wide and interesting range of bar food *L and E daily*, served in nicely furnished surroundings. Children welcome. Large patio area; open fires in winter. Good moorings.

🍺 **Slipway** 48 Crab Tree Lane, Burscough L40 0RN (01704 897767). Attractive canalside setting (beside bridge 32) for this pub serving real ales and food *L and E Mon-Fri and all day Sat-Sun (no food Mon Jan-Feb)*. Children welcome; dogs welcome but not inside while food is being served. Large garden with children's play area and patio. *Monthly* singer. Good moorings.

🍺 **Royal Coaching House** Liverpool Road North, Burscough L40 4BY (01704 893231). Real ales in a pub two minutes' walk from the canal. Wide range of interesting snacks and bar food L *daily*. Children welcome as are dogs *until 19.00*. Cobbled courtyard with pond. Quiz *Mon*, karaoke *Wed* and live music *Sat*.

NAVIGATIONAL NOTES

You will need a Watermate key, and a windlass, to open bridge 32.

Parbold and Rufford

The Rufford Branch leaves the Leeds & Liverpool main line just east of Burscough, through an imposing arched bridge dated 1816. A canal settlement, now a conservation area, surrounds the top lock and the roomy dry dock here (also *showers* and the usual *facilities*). The locks come thick and fast to begin with, as the canal falls through the fertile and gently sloping farmland towards the distant Ribble estuary and a connection with the Lancaster Canal. The country is generally quiet, flat and unspectacular. At times the busy A59 intrudes noisily. East of the junction with the Rufford Branch, the canal meanders through the flat countryside to the village of Parbold with its ancient sail-less windmill. Here the canal crosses the River Douglas and then joins the Douglas Valley, a pretty, narrow wooded valley which the canal shares with the railway. Appley Lock is reached: there are two locks alongside, now semi-derelict and therefore only the lock on the main line is in operation. The shallower locks were once used as a navigable sidepond for boats passing in opposite directions. **As with all subsequent locks, the gates should be closed and the paddles lowered and padlocked after use to combat vandalism and wastage of water.**

NAVIGATIONAL NOTES

You will need a Watermate key to open bridges 33 and 36 and a windlass and Watermate key to operate Lock 1 and Bridge 1 on the Rufford Branch.

White Bridge
Marina
103
Marina 7 Rufford Lock
Holly Farm
Holland Meadow
6 Marsh Meadow Swing Bridge
Marsh Moss Bridge
Causeway Farm
Marsh Moss
Sluice Lane
Canal Bridge
White Dial Farm
Springwell Farm
Prescott's Farm
Autocross Circuit
Low Mead
FB
NTL
Anchor Farm
5 Prescott Bridge
Wham Bridge
Saulthouse Farm
Chicken Lock 6
4 Baldwins Bridge
Lathom's Farm
3 German's Bridge
5 German's Lock
cough idge
Warper's Moss
Meadow Lane
Hoscar Moss
New Sutch House Farm
Old Sutch House
4 Moss Lock
Sutch Lane
Bleak Hall Farm
Bleak Lane
2A
6¾m 8L Tarleton
99
3 Runnel Brow Lock
Sandy Farm
HOSCAR
2 Runnel Brow Bridge
Lathom Locks
Henry's Farm
STA
Stocks Farm
Tawdside
Works
1 Junction Bridge
Hoscar Moss Road
Frog Lane
33 Glovers Swing Bridge
Carr Lane Farm
Towing Path
Moss Bridge
Deans La
37E
Giant's Hall
STA
Terminus 24½m 0L
Wigan 10½m 6L
Ring-o'-Bells Bridge 34
Briars Hall Farm
Ring o'Bells
Moss Bridge 35
Hollowford Lane
Sewage Works
Rigby's Farm
37A
Back Lane
37B
Parbold Bridge 37D
Pa Sta
Leeds
22
Taylor's Farm
Lowry Hill
18
Duttons Farm
36 Spencer's Swing Bridge
Aqueduct 35A
Course Lane
Newburgh
Sch
PO
Bound Farm
37C
Roborross Lane
Round Thorn
Nursery
Lawrensons
Cross (restored)
FB
Doug Farm

Parbold

Lancs. PO, tel, stores, butcher, chemist, takeaway, garage, library, station. Parbold is prettiest near the canal bridge, where the brick tower of the old windmill is complemented by an equally attractive pub. Unfortunately the rest of the village is being engulfed by acres of new housing. Local landmarks are the tall spires of Parbold's two churches, and Ashurst's Beacon high on a hill to the south. The latter was built in 1798 by Sir William Ashurst in anticipation of an invasion by the French. The beacon was intended as a local warning sign.

Douglas Navigation

The little River Douglas, or Asland, was made navigable in the first half of the 17th C, well before the great spate of canal construction. It provided the Wigan coalfield with a useful outlet to the tidal River Ribble, from which the cargoes could be shipped over to Preston or along the coast. When the Leeds & Liverpool Canal was built, the old river navigation became superfluous. The new company constructed their own branch to the Ribble estuary (the Rufford Branch). Between Parbold and Gathurst it is possible to find many traces of the old navigation, including several locks.

Pubs and Restaurants

Ship Inn Wheat Lane, Lathom L40 4BX (01704 893117). Near second lock down, on Rufford Branch. An old canal pub formerly known as the 'Blood Tub' – black puddings were once made here, and a bucket of pig's blood could be exchanged for a pint of beer. Busy, welcoming, comfortable with excellent bar food *L and E, daily (all day Sun).* Children welcome *until 21.00;* dogs *after 14.30.* Garden. Quiz *Mon.* Moorings.

Ring O'Bells Ring O'Bells Lane, Lathom L40 5TE (01704 893157). Canalside at bridge 34. Tastefully modernised country pub serving an interesting variety of bar meals *all day, every day* along with real ales. Canalside tables, indoor and outdoor children's play areas.

Railway Tavern Hoscar Station, Hoscar Moss Road, Lathom L40 4BQ (01704 892369). North east of bridge 35. Small country pub serving real ale and excellent food *L and E* daily. Children's menu and there is a beer garden.

✗ **Yours is the Earth** 2 Mill Lane, Parbold WN8 7NW (01257 262999). Canalside, bridge 37. Gift shop and traditional chintzy tearoom serving coffee, lunch and tea. Tasty ice creams. All food home-made including soups and cakes. *Open Mon and Wed–Fri 10.00–17.00; Sat 10.30– 17.00 and Sun 10.30– 16.30.*

Windmill Mill Lane, Parbold WN8 7NW (01257 462935). Beside bridge 37. Old village local dispensing real ale, and an imaginative selection of traditional, home-cooked food *L and E (not Mon E).* Children welcome *until 20.00;* dogs on a lead only. A huge collection of brassware decorates the pub, and there is outside seating.

✗ **Stocks Tavern** 16 Alder Lane, Parbold WN8 7NN (01257 462220). South of bridge 37. Fine traditional country pub, dating from 1810 and serving excellent meals *L and E Mon–Fri and all day Sat and Sun,* together with a selection of real ale. Children welcome; small outside seating area and quiz *Sun.*

✗ **Wayfarer Restaurant** 1–3 Alder Lane, Parbold WN8 7NL (01257 464600). South of bridge 37. Dating back to before 1668 this cosy pub-cum-restaurant serves real ale and food *L and E Mon–Sat and all day Sun.* The à la carte restaurant is *open daily 18.00–21.30* and good fresh local produce is used wherever possible. Children welcome; patio area with pond and Koi carp. Log fires *in winter.*

Water's Edge Mill Lane, Appley Bridge WN6 9DA (01257 253755). East of bridge 42. Family pub, *open all day,* serving real ale together with inexpensive home-cooked food *all day, every day.* Children welcome *until 21.00.* Moorings and outside seating.

BOAT TRIPS

Restaurant boat *Romance* is based at the Water's Edge pub (*see* above). Cruising along the Douglas Valley, offering lunches, afternoon teas, evening cruises, *Sun* roast dinner cruises and private parties. Contact the pub for more information.

◣ Tarleton

A line of trees and the spire of Rufford church are followed by the beautiful Rufford Old Hall, on the west bank. Then the waterway leads back out into open, flat and fairly featureless countryside, with the River Douglas never far away but initially out of sight. Beside Spark Bridge 8A there are *facilities including a pump out, showers and a toilet.* At Sollom there used to be a lock, but now it is no more. This is where the canal turns into the old course of the River Douglas, and it twists and turns as though to prove it. The 'new' course of the Douglas (which was once navigable from the sea right up to Wigan) comes alongside the canal at the busy road bridge near Bank Hall, a house hidden by trees. From here it is only a short distance to the final swing bridge and Tarleton Lock, where the canal connects with the tidal River Douglas – which in turn flows into the River Ribble near Preston forming the newly opened Ribble Link with the Lancaster Canal.

NAVIGATIONAL NOTES

1 Navigators entering the Rufford Branch canal from the sea should remember that they will need a padlock key – as well as a windlass – to open the locks up the branch. Both available from James Mayor's boatyard.

2 Those who wish to use the Ribble Link (www.ribblelink.co.uk) MUST obtain the Skipper's Guide and booking form from BW North West Office (01942 405700); enquiries.northwest@britishwaterways.co.uk, as this gives all ESSENTIAL navigational information. A booking form can also be obtained by email from: enquiries.northwest@britishwaterways.co.uk. *A minimum of five days' notice is required–during busy periods book as early as possible. Opening times are dictated by tides in the Ribble estuary, but a journey can be made Easter–Oct during daylight hours, Nov–Easter on request.* The staircase and sea lock are manned, and the link will operate one way each day. There is no mooring on the Link. As the River Ribble is tidal, boats should carry, *as a minimum*: anchor, chain and warp, VHF radio or mobile phone, lifejackets for all on board, fire fighting equipment, coastal flares. Your engine must be sufficiently powerful to cope with tidal conditions, and be sure to check that your boat insurance covers tidal waters.

3 If you need help or advice while on the River Ribble, call Preston Riversway Control on VHF channel 16 (working on channel 14), or telephone 01772 726871.

4 If you wish to visit Preston Docks, contact Preston Riversway Control on 01772 726871.

● **Rufford**
Lancs. PO, tel, stores, garage, station. Main road village noted for its Hall. The church is a small Italianate Victorian building containing many monuments to the Heskeths who owned Rufford Hall for several centuries; obviously a prolific family, judging by one large sculpture depicting a brood of 11 children, dated c.1458. The family now resides in Northamptonshire.
Rufford Old Hall NT 200 Liverpool Road, Rufford L40 1SG (01704 821254; www.nationaltrust.org.uk). On the west bank of the canal. A medieval timber-framed mansion with Jacobean extensions given to the National Trust in 1936. The interior is magnificently decorated and furnished in period style, especially the great hall with its hammerbeam roof and 15th-

C intricately carved movable screen – one of the few still intact in England. The Hall also houses a folk museum and an exhibition. Gardens and tearoom. *House open daily mid Mar–Oct 13.00– 17.00 (except Thu and Fri). Gardens as per house 11.00–17.30.* Charge.
Note: although the Hall is beside the waterway, it is not possible to enter the grounds directly from the canal. Navigators should therefore tie up near bridge 8, walk up to the village and turn left at the main road. The entrance is a few hundred yards along the wall on the left.
● **Tarleton**
Lancs. PO, tel, stores, garage, bank. A large village luckily avoided by the A59 road. There are some useful shops, and a good takeaway pizzeria opposite the Cock & Bottle.

Pubs and Restaurants

✕ **Rufford Arms** 380 Liverpool Road, Rufford L40 1SQ (01704 822040; www.ruffordarms.com). Immediately west of bridge 8A. Restaurant with a bar open to diners serving reasonably priced food ranging from bar snacks to full à la carte meals in the restaurant. Children welcome; dogs by arrangement. *Open L and E and all day Sat and Sun.* B & B.

✕ **Bay Leaf** Liverpool Road, Tarleton PR4 6HQ (01772 811858). Well-presented Indian restaurant. Good food served by friendly staff.

🍺 ✕ **Cock & Bottle** Church Road, Tarleton PR4 6UP (01772 812258). West of bridge 12. Village-centre pub dispensing real ale. Bar snacks and meals served *12.00–21.00, daily.* Children welcome. Garden seating.

✕ **Boathouse Brasserie** Diamond Jubilee Road, Rufford L40 1TD (01704 823697; www.stmarysmarina.co.uk). Part of St Mary's Marina complex. Informal dining. Meals prepared with locally grown ingredients wherever possible. Home baking and their own 'Feisty Cow' locally-made ice cream.

Boatyards

Ⓑ **St Mary's Marina** Diamond Jubilee Road, Rufford L40 1TD (01704 823697; www.stmarysmarina.co.uk). 🚿 🛢 ♿ **D** Pump out, slipway, hard standing, repairs and servicing, long- and short-term mooring, boat sales, toilets and showers, laundrette, chandlery, library service and visiting post office.

Ⓑ **James Mayor** The Boatyard, Tarleton PR4 6HD (01772 812250; www.tarletonboatyard.com). ♿ **D E** Overnight mooring, long-term mooring, winter storage, chandlery, slipway up to 65 feet, 3-ton crane, boat transportation, boat and engine sales, engine repairs, showers, toilets.

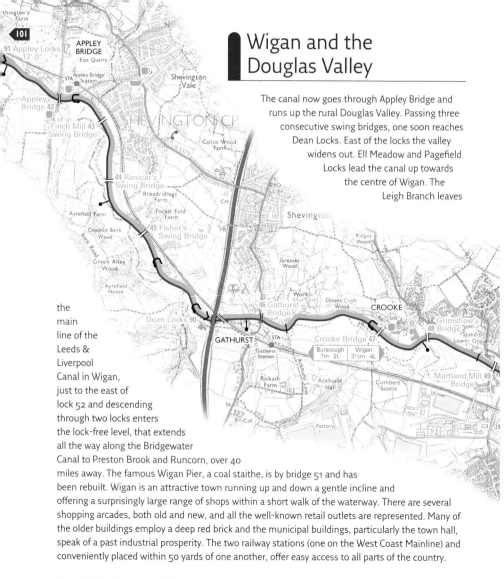

Wigan and the Douglas Valley

The canal now goes through Appley Bridge and runs up the rural Douglas Valley. Passing three consecutive swing bridges, one soon reaches Dean Locks. East of the locks the valley widens out. Ell Meadow and Pagefield Locks lead the canal up towards the centre of Wigan. The Leigh Branch leaves the main line of the Leeds & Liverpool Canal in Wigan, just to the east of lock 52 and descending through two locks enters the lock-free level, that extends all the way along the Bridgewater Canal to Preston Brook and Runcorn, over 40 miles away. The famous Wigan Pier, a coal staithe, is by bridge 51 and has been rebuilt. Wigan is an attractive town running up and down a gentle incline and offering a surprisingly large range of shops within a short walk of the waterway. There are several shopping arcades, both old and new, and all the well-known retail outlets are represented. Many of the older buildings employ a deep red brick and the municipal buildings, particularly the town hall, speak of a past industrial prosperity. The two railway stations (one on the West Coast Mainline) and conveniently placed within 50 yards of one another, offer easy access to all parts of the country.

Pubs and Restaurants

✕ **Baby Elephant** 162 Gathurst Lane, Gathurst, Shevington WN6 8HZ (01257 251155; www.babyelephant.co.uk). Formerly the Navigation Inn, now a restaurant serving contemporary Indian cuisine.

✕ **Crooke Hall Inn** Crooke, Standish Lower Ground, Wigan WN6 8LR (01942 247524). Near bridge 47. Cosy village pub, with friendly atmosphere, in the pretty Douglas Valley serving a selection of real ales. Inexpensive bar snacks and meals available *L and E (except Tue)*. Children welcome in dining room only. Canalside garden, moorings.

Moon Under Water 5-7a Market Place, Wigan WN1 1PE (01942 323437). Real ale dispensed in a busy, town centre, ex-building society premises. Food *available all day, every day*. Children's room.

Swan & Railway Wallgate, Wigan WN1 1BA (01942 495032). Friendly town pub serving real ales and food *L Mon-Fri*. Beer garden. B & B.

Orwell Wigan Pier, Wigan WN3 4EU (01942 323034; www.wiganpier.co.uk). Large converted cotton warehouse on Wigan Pier; a CAMRA pub of the year so there is always an excellent range of real ales available. Food served *L Mon-Sat* and there is a *Sun* carvery *13.00-15.00*. Children welcome. Canalside seating in summer.

Appley Bridge
Lancs. PO, tel, stores, station. Canalside hamlet.

Wigan
Gt Manchester. All services. A large, heavily industrialised town whose skyline is now a mixture of industrial chimneys and towering concrete blocks of offices and flats. There is a covered market hall in the traditional mould, and an Olympic-size swimming pool.
All Saints Church 192 Atherton Road, Hindley, Wigan WN2 3XA (www.wiganparishchurch.org). A very large and impressive parish church surrounded by beautiful rose gardens. There are several fine stained-glass windows, including a charming William Morris example depicting St Christopher.
History Shop Library Street, Wigan WN1 1NU (01942 828128; www.wlct.org). Heritage Service project offering a display depicting the impact of coal on the area, exhibitions, fine art collection, genealogical research centre, shop and meeting room. *Open Mon 10.00– 19.00, Tue-Fri 10.00–17.00 and Sat 10.00–13.00.*

Trencherfield Mill The Mill, now being converted to offices and apartments, still retains the engine shed - home to probably the largest working steam-powered mill engine in Europe, installed when the mill was built in 1907. At the time of writing this is steamed on *Sun mornings*, heralded by a loud blast on the steam whistle. The engine is in a beautifully restored condition; its operators are very knowledgeable and there is an audio-visual presentation linked to some clever lighting that shows off the engine to its best. There is also a range of working cotton spinning machinery which is used to demonstrate the processes that were carried out at this mill. This is a marvellous opportunity to get to grips with what made this area such a hub of the industrial revolution: a revolution whose successful was, to a large extent, dependant upon the presence of the Leeds and Liverpool Canal.
Tourist Information Centre 62 Wallgate, Wigan WN1 1BA (01942 825677; www.wigan.gov.uk). *Open daily 10.00–17.00.*

NAVIGATIONAL NOTES

1 You will need a Watermate key to open Bridge 43; however Bridges 43-45 are usually left open.
2 The locks (nos 85–1) between Wigan and Leeds are 6oft long and cannot accommodate a full-length narrowboat.
3 You will require a British Waterways handcuff key.
4 BW have a dry dock for hire in Wigan. Contact BW North West Office (01942 405700); enquiries. northwest@britishwaterways.co.uk

Boatyards

ⓑ Boatyard west of Bottom Lock 87 (offside) in Wigan operated by Derry Bent 07801 477457 – telephone for details.

105

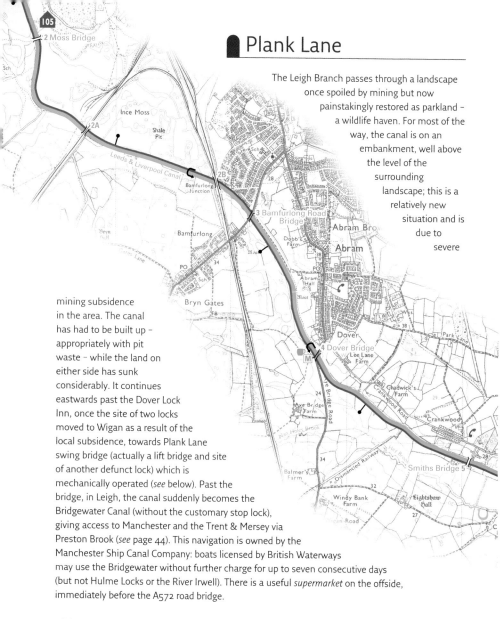

Plank Lane

The Leigh Branch passes through a landscape once spoiled by mining but now painstakingly restored as parkland – a wildlife haven. For most of the way, the canal is on an embankment, well above the level of the surrounding landscape; this is a relatively new situation and is due to severe mining subsidence in the area. The canal has had to be built up – appropriately with pit waste – while the land on either side has sunk considerably. It continues eastwards past the Dover Lock Inn, once the site of two locks moved to Wigan as a result of the local subsidence, towards Plank Lane swing bridge (actually a lift bridge and site of another defunct lock) which is mechanically operated (*see below*). Past the bridge, in Leigh, the canal suddenly becomes the Bridgewater Canal (without the customary stop lock), giving access to Manchester and the Trent & Mersey via Preston Brook (*see page 44*). This navigation is owned by the Manchester Ship Canal Company: boats licensed by British Waterways may use the Bridgewater without further charge for up to seven consecutive days (but not Hulme Locks or the River Irwell). There is a useful *supermarket* on the offside, immediately before the A572 road bridge.

Leigh

Gt Manchester. All services. Once the archetypal mill town, most of the tall buildings and chimneys have now been demolished. In the market place you can see the fine Edwardian baroque town hall, built 1904-7, facing the battlemented church of St Mary. This church was originally built in 1516 but was extensively rebuilt in the late 19th C and is the burial place of Thomas Tyldesley, killed at the battle of Wigan Lane.

Pennington Flash Country Park off St Helen's Road, Leigh WN7 3PA (01942 605253; www.wlct.org). 1100-acre park centred on the flash or lake. Walks, birdwatching, sailing, fishing, golf, picnic areas and information centre. *Open daily 08.30-dusk.*

Three Sisters Recreation Area Three Sisters Road, Bryn, Ashton-in-Makerfield WN4 8DD (01942 720453; www.wlct.org). Site of the Wigan Alps: three colliery spoil tips now landscaped to provide

Pubs and Restaurants

■ **Dover Lock Inn** Warrington Road, Abram WN2 5XX (01942 866300). Canalside at Dover Bridge on the Leigh Branch. Real ales are served together with bar meals and snacks *L and E daily during boating season (no food Mon–Thu L out of season)*. Children welcome *until 21.00*; no dogs. Large south-facing beer garden.

■ **Nevison** Plank Lane, Leigh WN7 4QE (01942 671394). 400yds from the swing bridge. An original old-fashioned pub with lots of brass and a piano, serving a good selection of real ales and home-cooked food with real chips *daily 12.00–19.30. No food Mon except by prior arrangement*. Children welcome outside bar areas; no dogs. Large enclosed garden with children's play area. Gas lighting in bar area

and real fires in winter. Quiz *Wed. Note: Winter afternoon drinkers take note of bridge operating times and moor appropriately!*

■ **Eagle & Hawk** Chapel Street, Leigh WN7 2PQ (01924 606600). Lively establishment dispensing real ales, good company and bar food *all day, every day*. Children welcome *until 19.00*. Pool and darts. Quiz *Thu*, disco/ karaoke *Sat* – also other regular entertainment. Outside seating area.

■ **Red Brick Inn** Twist Lane, Leigh WN7 4DP (01942 671698). A warm, comfortable boater-friendly pub offering real ales. Food available available *Tue–Sun L and E until 20.00*. Children welcome away from the bar. Outside seating. Disco *Fri*, karaoke *Sat*. B & B.

an international karting circuit (01942 270230), racing circuit, boating lake, picnic area and visitor centre. Telephone for details or visit their website.
Turnpike Gallery Civic Square, Leigh WN7 1EB (01942 404469; www.wlct.org). Home to major touring arts exhibitions. *Open Mon–Fri 10.00–18.00, Sat 09.30–15.30.*

NAVIGATIONAL NOTES

Plank Lane swing bridge is *open mid Mar–May: 08.00–18.00; Jun–Aug 08.00–20.00; Sep–Mid Nov 08.00–18.00 and mid Nov–mid Mar 08.00–16.30 Mon–Fri and 10.00–14.00 Sat–Sun. Closed for lunch daily 12.00– 12.45.* The bridge is operated by a bridge keeper. Contact BW North West Office (01942 405700); enquiries.northwest @britishwaterways.co.uk to confirm times.

Wigan Locks

Leaving the junction with the Leigh Branch, the main line reaches the Wigan flight of 21 locks. The Kirkless Hall at the top lock offers an embellished certificate to all boaters who complete the ascent, and the nearby boater facilities provide both toilets and showers. Here is a T-junction as the canal meets what used to be the southern end of the Lancaster Canal. Turning left, the traveller is soon aware of the great height climbed as the navigation winds along a hill.

● **New Springs**

Gt Manchester. A suburb of Wigan. Once an industrial hub with collieries and ironworks lining the canal as it struggled up the 21 locks to the summit. The acres of partially landscaped waste ground today belie the past activity of Rose Bridge Colliery (near bridge 54) and Ince Hall Coal and Cannel Company higher up (cannel is a dull coal that burns with a smoky, luminous flame). Hardest of all to imagine is the massive operation of Wigan Coal and Iron Co. who, at the turn of the century, employed 10,000 people at their works beside the top nine locks of the flight. Then one of the largest ironworks in the country, it mined 2 million tons of coal to produce 125,000 tons of iron annually. The skyline here was dominated by 10 blast furnaces, 675 coking ovens and a 339ft high chimney. It must have been an impressive sight on the night skyline, viewed from the streets of Wigan.

Haigh Hall Copperas Lane, Haigh, Wigan WN2 1PE (01942 832895; www.wlct.org). On east bank of the canal. The pre-Tudor mansion was rebuilt by its owner, the 23rd Earl of Crawford, between 1830 and 1849. The reconstruction was designed and directed by the Earl, and all the stone, timber and iron used on the job came from the estate. The Hall is now owned by Wigan Corporation, who allow the citizens to use it for private wedding receptions, etc. There is little to see in the house and it is not normally open to the public. The park and grounds around the hall are *open daily all year, except 25–26 Dec and 1 Jan* and contain much that caters for the family: there are children's amusements, gardens and woodlands, a nature trail and selection of waymarked walks, miniature railway, a model village, crazy golf course, shop and cafeteria. Entry to the park is free but there is a charge for the amusements which are *open May–Sep.* Audio trail for the blind and partially sighted using a braille map and tape player.

Stables Centre Haigh Country Park, Copperas Lane, Haigh, Wigan WN2 1PE (01942 832895). Daily art and craft workshops for groups and individuals. Hands-on creativity painting, batik, stencilling, clay, canal art for adults and children. *Available Mon–Fri 10.30–12.00 and 13.30–15.00. Weekends by arrangement.* Charge.

Pubs and Restaurants

🍺 **Commercial Inn** 21 Heath Road, New Springs, Wigan WN4 9DY (01942 726955). Canalside, at bridge 57. A small, sturdy working man's pub offering bar snacks on request *Mon–Sat.* Children welcome. Outside seating.

🍺 **Kirkless Hall** New Springs, Wigan WN2 1JW (01942 242821; www.geocities.com/kirklesshall). Canalside, near Wigan Top Lock. Distinctive black and white building housing spacious and comfortable bars. A wide range of excellent food is offered *L and E daily* from both table d'hôte and à la carte menus. Children welcome. Canalside patio. Karaoke *Sat.*

🍺 **Colliers Arms** 192 Wigan Road, Wigan WN2 1DU (01942 831171). Above bridge 59A. Real ale dispensed in a charming 17th-C listed hostelry overlooking the canal. Children welcome *until 21.00.* Patio seating.

🍺 **Crawford Arms** Red Rock Lane, Haigh, Wigan WN1 2UW (01257 421313). Inexpensive bar food *daily until 20.00.* Temporary jail to a 17th-C murderer, this pub now dispenses real ale rather than justice. Children welcome. Outside seating. Quiz *Thu. 48hr* mooring outside.

NAVIGATIONAL NOTES

1 The locks between Wigan and Leeds (nos 85–1) are 60ft long and, therefore, cannot accommodate a full-length narrowboat.

2 The Wigan Flight is not quite the daunting prospect it once was. It is *open throughout the year (Nov-Mar 08.30-16.30).* BW lock keepers are available to assist boaters *daily 08.30-16.00 (15.30 Fri).* It is possible to stop on the flight, between locks 77 and 78 where, to the east of bridge 54, there are *stores, takeaways and a PO.*

3 You will require a British Waterways handcuff key.

Adlington

The canal continues to run as a 9-mile lock-free pound – known as the Lancaster Pool – along the side of the valley from which the industries surrounding Wigan can be viewed in the distance. It enjoys a pleasant and quiet isolation in this lightly wooded area. Already the navigation is well over 300ft above the sea, and the bleak hills up to the east give a hint of the Pennines that are soon to be crossed. The conspicuous tower east of Adlington stands on a hill that is over 1500ft high. Wandering northwards, beyond the village, the waterway remains hemmed in for much of the way by woodland and is undisturbed by the railway and main roads that for a while follow it closely. Soon the greenery gives way to views of Chorley's rows of rooftops across the valley. The canal crosses this valley, but shuns the town. There is a *slipway* just to the north of Cowling Bridge 75A, on the towpath side.

Pubs and Restaurants

Bridge 11 Park Road, Adlington PR7 4HZ (01257 480507). East of bridge 69. Traditional local serving real ale. Pub games and outside seating. Moorings.

Waggon & Horses Market Street, Adlington PR7 4HE (01257 485343). East of bridge 68. Good value, home-cooked food available *all day, every day (except Sat and Mon, L)*, served until 20.00 (19.30 Sat). Dating from 1818, this busy pub dispenses real ale and offers live entertainment *Sat* and a Quiz *Tue*. Children welcome. Outside seating.

White Bear Market Street, Adlington PR7 4HE (01257 482357). West of bridge 69. An old roadside pub serving real ales and inexpensive bar food available *L and E (not Mon E) and all day Sun*. Tea and coffee *always available*. Garden with children's play area. B & B. *Open all day*.

Cardwell Arms Chorley Road, Adlington PR6 9LH (01257 480319). East of bridge 71. Real ales in a boisterous (*at weekends*) pub. Garden and outside play area. Food available *weekends all day until 19.00. Sun* disco and jackpot.

Mariners Coffee Shop Park Road, Adlington PR7 4HZ (01257 481054). East of bridge 69, beside the marina. Friendly establishment serving breakfasts, lunches, snacks (all home-made and predominantly low fat), coffee and tea. *Open 08.30–16.00.*

White Horse Chorley Road, Adlington PR6 9LJ (01257 481766). East of bridge 71, top of Rawlinson Lane. Smart, welcoming pub serving real ale. Reasonably priced food *L daily, Fri E and all day Sat and Sun (no food after 17.00 Sun)*. Children welcome. Patio, pool and pub games. Quiz *Tue*.

Hop Pocket Carr Lane, Chorley PR7 3JQ (01257 275597; www.hoppocket.co.uk). West of bridge 75. Real ale in a modern estate pub offering live artists on *Sat and Sun*. Food available *L daily*. Children welcome. Garden and outside seating area.

Boatyards

Ⓑ **White Bear Marina** Park Road, Adlington PR7 4HZ (01257 481054; www.bwml.co.uk). 🚿 🚽 🔧 D E Pump out, slipway, gas, overnight mooring, long-term mooring, winter storage, boat fitting out, boat and engine repairs, crane, DIY facilities, wet dock, laundrette, showers, toilets, solid fuel, chandlery, books, gifts and maps, café, telephone.

Ⓑ **L & L Cruisers** Rawlinson Lane, Heath Charnock PR7 4DE (01257 480825). 🔧 D Pump out, gas, narrowboat hire, day-hire craft, overnight mooring, slipway, chandlery, books and maps, boat building, engine sales and repairs, gift shop, ice cream, toilets.

Ⓑ **PB Mechanical Services/Ellerbeck Narrowboats** Rawlinson Lane, Heath Charnock PR7 4DE (01257 480825; www.pbmechanical.co.uk). D Pump out, gas, boat hire, slipway, boat sales, engine sales and repairs, DIY facilities, chandlery, solid fuels.

- **Adlington**
  *Gt Manchester. PO, tel, stores,
  garage, station.* A small
  industrialised town very useful
  for pubs and supplies – the local
  licensed store east of bridge 69 is
  open late most evenings and there
  is a park nearby.
- **Chorley**
  Lancs. All services. On the west bank of
  the canal, a busy town based on the
  manufacture of textiles and spare parts
  for commercial and public service
  vehicles. (Leyland, where the vehicles
  are built, is just a few miles away to the
  north west.) Chorley has avoided too
  much industrial grimness by maintaining
  its market town traditions and by
  extensive new housing development.
  Today there are two major markets: the
  Flat-Iron Market, dating from 1498, *held on
  Tue* and the Covered Market *held on Tue,
  Thu, Fri and Sat.* A collectors' market is
  also *held on Mon.* Sir Henry Tate, the
  founder of the Tate Gallery in London,
  was born in Chorley in 1819 and began
  his career here as a grocer's assistant.
  St Laurence's Church Church Brow,
  Chorley (01257 231360;
  stlaurencechorley.googlepages.com).
  Surrounded by trees in the centre of the
  town, parts of the church date back to the
  14th C. The bones that are enshrined in a
  recess in the chancel are believed to have
  belonged to St Laurence and to have been
  brought back from Normandy.
  Astley Hall Astley Park, Chorley PR7 1NP
  (01257 515555). At the north west end of
  the town just over a mile from Botany
  Bridge (78A). Set in 105 acres of wooded
  parkland beside an ornamental lake, the
  appearance of this Elizabethan mansion is
  very striking, for in the 17th C the existing
  timber framing was replaced by a new
  façade that is lacking in symmetry. The
  interior – more home than museum piece –
  is very fine, with splendid restoration
  ceilings, furnishings, tapestries and
  pottery. *Open Apr–Oct, Sat and Sun,
  12.00–17.00.* Charge.
  Tourist Information Contact
  Chorley Council on 01257 515151;
  www.chorley.gov.uk.

Withnell Fold

The canal sidesteps Chorley to the east, passing instead some large and resplendent outlying textile mills. There is a *slipway* just to the north of the M61 bridge, on the off-side. Now the boater enters a most delightful stretch of waterway. The junction with the old Walton Summit Branch features a canal cottage and the bottom lock in the Johnson's Hill flight. A short but energetic spell of windlass-wielding is required here, for the seven locks are very close together. It is rewarding work, for the steep countryside yields good views, and the locks are tidily maintained and painted. Near the middle lock is an old toll house and a *telephone*, while at the top lock there is a pub, a boatyard and, together with the usual facilities, showers, toilets and a self-operated pump out. The canal now changes course to north east and flows along a beautifully secluded and often wooded valley at a height of over 350ft above sea level. Even the old paper mills at Withnell Fold, which once brought a glimpse of industry, have been converted into small, discreet, industrial units. There is an excellent nature reserve developed in the old filter beds and sludge lagoons opposite which, derelict for many years, gradually infilled with silt and reedswamp to provide natural plant and animal habitats.

Pubs and Restaurants

Malt 'n' Hops Friday Street, Chorley PR6 0AH (01257 260967). Near the railway station. Guest real ales that change on a daily basis are dispensed in the congenial surroundings of this displaced antique dealer! Bar snacks are served *all day*. Children and dogs welcome. Quiz *Wed. Open all day*.

Malt House Farm Moss Lane, Whittle-Le-Woods, Chorley PR6 8AB (01257 232889). A listed farm house converted to an upmarket pub and restaurant. Open fires and exposed beams. Real ales are available together with an extensive range of home-cooked food served *daily 12.00–22.00*. Well-behaved children welcome *until 21.00*. Large garden and decking overlooking the canal. Gym and outdoor swimming pool for patrons' use. Jazz *monthly*. B & B.

Red Lion 196 Blackburn Road, Wheelton, Chorley PR6 8EU (01254 830378; www.redlionwheelton.com). A changing selection of real ales served in a popular village pub which is *open all day*. Meals (including steak & ale pie and kangaroo steaks) available *L Fri–Sun only*. However parties of four or more can pre-book meals *at other times*. Children and dogs welcome. Darts and pool. Regular events.

Lock and Quay Botany Bay, Chorley PR6 9AE (01257 460470). Modernised pub and restaurant serving meals *all day, every day*, with children's menu and outside seating.

Red Cat Blackburn Road, Whittle-Le-Woods, Chorley PR6 8LL (01257 263966). Inexpensive modern English, Mediterranean, and Italian menu served *L Fri, Sat, Sun, and E Mon–Sat* in pleasant surroundings in this listed building. Children's menu and play area. Patio. Quiz *Sun*.

Top Lock Copthurst Lane, Heapey, Chorley PR6 8LS (01257 263376). Real ales served in a canalside hostelry at the top of the Johnson's Hill flight of seven locks. Well placed to slake the toiling boaters' thirst, this pub serves traditional English food (*all day, every day*) and Indian food (*Fri–Tue from 14.00*) at very reasonable prices. Children welcome. Regular live music. Outside seating and moorings (below the lock please).

Dressers Arms Briers Brow, Wheelton, Chorley PR6 8HD (01254 830041). 3/4 mile east of bridge 82. A superb pub with a fine choice of value for money, home-made food at the bar *L and E Mon–Fri and all day Sat and Sun*. An excellent selection of regular and guest real ales together with their own Dressers Special, are dispensed in the unpretentious, traditional bar: the amalgamation of the original tiny beer house and neighbouring cottages. Children welcome. Quiz *Tue*. Garden seating.

Wan's Cantonese Restaurant Briers Brow, Wheelton, Chorley PR6 8HD (01254 830171). Above the Dressers Arms. A well thought of establishment offering all the Oriental favourites. *Open 18.00–23.00 Mon– Sat and 13.00–20.00 Sun*. Children welcome.

Golden Lion Blackburn Road, Higher Wheelton, Chorley PR6 8HP (01254 830855). A pleasant walk up the footpath south of bridge 86. Real ales in a small, welcoming main road pub. Extensive bar menu *served all day, every day*. Children welcome. Patio seating. Jukebox and free pool *Wed after 19.00*. Quiz *Thu*.

Boatyards

Botany Bay Boatyard 7 Botany Bay, Chorley PR6 9AE (07967 380464/07770 576288; www.botanybayboatyard.co.uk).Next to Bridge 78A. Short-term mooing, cranage, maintenance and servicing, storage, fitting out, DIY facilities, boat transport, engine repairs.

Classic Narrowboats Wheelton Boatyard, Kenyon Lane, Wheelton, Chorley PR6 8EX (01257 831444; www.classicnarrowboats.co.uk). Gas, boat servicing and repairs, boat building, DIY facilities, boat blacking and painting, chandlery, solid fuels, boat sales.

BOAT TRIPS
Royal Sovereign is a 60-seat charter and trip boat operated from Botany Bay, Chorley (north of bridge 78A) by Boatel Cruises, 7 Botany Bay, nr Chorley PR6 9AE (01257 273269; www.boatelpartycruises.com) for further details.

● **Wheelton**
Lancs. PO, tel, stores, laundrette, garage. The village is best accessed by walking east from bridge 82. Fish & chip shop *closed Sun, Mon and Thu.*

● **Walton Summit Branch**
The short branch used to be part of the Lancaster Canal, originally projected to run south from Preston to the Bridgewater Canal. The Lancaster Canal Company, after arranging with the Leeds & Liverpool Company to share a common course between Johnson's Hill Locks and Wigan Top Lock, was daunted by the prospect of constructing an expensive aqueduct over the River Ribble in Preston. A 'temporary' tramroad was built to connect the two lengths of canal between Preston and Walton Summit. The tramway, which opened in 1803, featured a short tunnel and a light trestle bridge over the Ribble. The tramroad was never replaced by a canal; indeed the whole line was closed by 1880. However in 2002, more than 200 years after the truncated Lancaster Canal was completed, the navigation has finally been connected into the rest of the waterways system with the opening of the Ribble Link, using the tidal rivers Douglas and Ribble. Most of the canal branch has been severed by the building of a motorway, although plenty of it still remains in an unnavigable state.

Botany Bay Village Botany Bay, Chorley PR6 9AF (01257 261220; www.botanybay.co.uk). Canalside near bridge 78A. Themed shopping centre in a converted mill together with restaurants and children's play area.

● **Withnell Fold**
Lancs. A remarkable, small estate village, built to house workers at the canalside paper mills which are now demolished. Grouped around three sides of a spacious square, the terraced cottages present an intimately united front which is almost unnerving to the casual visitor – especially as on the fourth side of the square is an old set of wooden stocks.

Blackburn

Passing under the new M65 extension the canal curls round a steep and thickly wooded valley, crossing it on a high embankment before entering the outskirts of Blackburn. Close to bridge 95 the delightfully named suburb of Cherry Tree provides an excellent range of *shops and takeaways*. There is also a useful *shop* at bridge 94. It seems to take a long time to get through this large town, as there is a flight of six locks here, raising the canal's level to a height of over 400ft above sea level. The lock keeper maintains a tidy flight – indeed most of the passage through the town is now pleasant – there is little rubbish or graffiti, and the views are excellent. There are *showers and toilets* beside Bridge 100 and a good towpath exists throughout the city.

Pubs and Restaurants

Boatyard Inn Bolton Road, Riley Green PR5 0SP (01254 209841). Bridge 91A. Real ale and English and Continental dishes *12.00–21.30 daily*. Children welcome. Terraces, games room, karaoke *Fri*. Overnight mooring for customers.

Royal Oak Blackburn Old Road, Riley Green PR5 0SL (01254 201445). North of bridge 91A. An oak-beamed pub dating from 1620 which serves real ale. Meals and snacks *L and E daily*. Three open fires, no electronic games. Children welcome. Outside seating. *Open all day Sun.* B & B.

Navigation Inn 2 Canal Street, Mill Hill, Blackburn BB2 4DL (01254 53230). Canalside, at bridge 96A. Real ale and butties *L* are available in this waterside pub. Children welcome. Darts and dominoes. Moorings. *Open all day.*

Sam's Water's Edge Bar Albion Mill Site, Albion Street, Blackburn BB2 4LX (01254 680950). Canalside at bridge 96B. Real ale and bar food *L and until 17.00 on Sun*. Children welcome when eating. Patio. Disco *Fri*, karaoke *Thu and Sat*, quiz *Sun*. Pool.

Moorings 106a Bolton Road, Blackburn BB2 3PZ (01254 664472). By bridge 99. Bar meals available *L and E Mon–Thu and 12.00–18.00 Fri–Sun*. Canalside patio and children's play area.

Blakeys Café Bar King George's Hall, Northgate, Blackburn BB2 1AA (01254 503238). Café serving coffee *09.00–16.00* and meals and snacks *09.00–15.30*. Beer Garden.

Malt 1 Barton Street, Blackburn BB2 1LJ (01254 699453). Busy, town-centre pub with a late licence dispensing Boddingtons, Flowers, Marston's and guest real ales. Food available *L, daily*. Children welcome. Large-screen TV. Outside seating.

Postal Order 15-19 Darwen Street, Blackburn BB2 2BH (01254 776400). West of bridge 102A. A good selection of real ales and no prizes for guessing the original use of this building now under the Wetherspoon banner. Food available *all day, every day*. Children welcome if eating.

NAVIGATIONAL NOTES

1. Gates giving access to the towpath in Blackburn are locked at night and those providing access to a secure mooring in the town can be opened with a BW Handcuff Key. For suitable moorings consult the lock keeper.
2. There is the usual range of services, together with showers and toilets, immediately above bridge 99.
3. Locks 57–52 require a Handcuff Key.

- **Blackburn**

Lancs. All services. Few of the Pennine towns which sprang up with the Industrial Revolution can be described as beautiful. In an attempt to rectify this, Blackburn has taken drastic steps in recent years to construct a new town centre. Nevertheless the most impressive features of the town are still the old cotton mills.

Blackburn Cathedral Cathedral Close, Blackburn BB1 5AA (01254 51491; www.blackburncathedral.com). Dating from 1820-6, the parish church was raised to cathedral status in 1926. Extensive renovations have been made inside. Very striking 13ft sculpture of 'Christ the Worker' in aluminium and black iron by John Hayward. Large churchyard.

King George's Hall Northgate, Blackburn BB2 1AA (01254 582579; www.kinggeorgeshall.com). Entertainment complex promoting a wide-ranging programme of music and theatre. Charge.

Museum & Art Gallery Museum Street, Blackburn BB1 7AJ (01254 667130; www.blackburn.gov.uk). Exhibits include natural history, pottery, early manuscripts and a large collection of English, Greek and Roman coins. In the art gallery are over 1200 beautiful Japanese prints, as well as English watercolours of the 18th C–20th C. Also incorporated is the Lewis Textile Museum: a series of period rooms demonstrating the development of the textile industry from the 18th C by means of full-size working models, including Hargreaves' Spinning Jenny. *Open Tue–Sat 10.00–16.45; closed B Hols.* Free.

Waves Waterfun Centre Nab Street, Blackburn BB2 1LN (01254 51111; www.blackburn.gov.uk). The town's own tropical paradise. Cafeteria. Full disabled access. Technical tours by arrangement. Charge.

Witton Country Park Preston Old Road, Blackburn BB2 2TP (01254 55423; www.blackburn.gov.uk). Nearly 500 acres of magnificent parkland, including the beautiful landmark, Billinge Hill. Tree and nature trails; wayfaring course; picnic sites and children's play area. Park *always open*. The **Visitor Centre** is *open Apr–Sep, Mon–Sat 12.00–16.45, Sun and B Hols 11.00– 16.45; Oct–Mar, Thu, Fri and Sat 12.00–16.30, Sun 11.00– 16.30.* Free. Restored stables and coach house, displays of carriages. The centre has a natural history room and a live British small mammal collection. Free.

Tourist Information Centre Visitor Centre, Church Street, Blackburn BB1 5AL (01254 688040 ; www.blackburn.gov.uk).Tourist and travel information, gift shop selling arts, crafts and books, café, gallery and exhibitions, garden. *Open Mon–Fri 10.00–17.00 and Sat 10.00–16.00.*

Hoghton Tower Hoghton, Nr Blackburn PR5 0SH (01254 852986; www.hoghtontower.co.uk). Past the Royal Oak at bridge 91A. So enjoyable was a joint of beef devoured during a visit, that James I knighted the remains 'Sir Loin'. More recently this 16th-C fortified hilltop mansion is visited for its dungeons, doll's houses, picturesque gardens, as well as for the magnificent banqueting hall. *Open Jul, Aug and Sep, Mon–Thu 11.00–16.00; Easter–Oct, B Hols and Sun 13.00–17.00.* Charge.

Rishton

Of particular interest to those on the canal are the fine canopied wharves of the Depot at Eanam Wharf, now converted for business use and also incorporating a pub. The canal leaves Blackburn and embarks upon a course of twists and turns that emphasise the hilliness of the countryside. The scenery varies all the time between heavy industrial development (and its effects) and – just around a corner – green fields, farms and distant views of wild moorlands. The Calder Valley motorway (M65) follows the line of the canal to Burnley. Of interest is the fine wharf building with a large central arch at Simpson's Bridge, now in a serious state of dereliction. Beyond Church, the first of four swing bridges appears (nos. 113, 114 and 115 require a handcuff key and a windlass): they are the only ones between Wigan and Gargrave.

● **Rishton**
Lancs. PO, tel, stores, chemist, takeaways, garage, bank, station. A small grey town that grew up around the cotton mills in the 19th C by courtesy of the Petre family of the Dunkenhalgh Estate, who used to be lords of the manor and are still local landowners. For more about the industrial archaeology of the Rishton area visit www.rishton.net.

● **Church**
Lancs. PO, tel, stores, garage, station. An industrial community which was originally based on calico printing, established on the canal bank by the family of the famous statesman Sir Robert Peel. The row of terraced houses is characteristic of so many of the towns in this industrial area. The parish church of St James is right on the banks of the canal; only the tower and font remain from the original 15th C building. There are two delightful windows designed by Edward Burne Jones. To arrange a visit telephone 01254 725450. The canal is close by and there are excellent moorings at this, the central point of the Leeds and Liverpool Canal, which is depicted by a sculpture. **Dunkenhalgh Hall** Clayton-le-Moors. Standing in 16 acres of gardens and woodland, it is a beautiful Elizabethan mansion, extensively altered in the 19th C. Its name is said to be derived from a Scottish raider named Duncan, who chose to settle htere. The hall is now used as a hotel.

Boatyards

Ⓑ **Altham Marine** Canal Wharf, Moorfield Close, Moorfield Industrial Estate, Altham BB5 5TX (01254 383900; www.althammarine.co.uk). Marine engineering, on-site and mobile services. Also mooring, cranage, storage, boat sales and chandlery

Pubs and Restaurants

✕ ♉ **The Depot**, Eanam Wharf, Blackburn BB1 5BY (01254 678776). Modern eatery offering meals *L*, *daily*. Childen welcome but no dogs. Outside seating.

🍺 **Rishton Arms** Station Road, Rishton BB1 4HF (0125488639б). Worth the walk for the friendly welcome in this comfortable local beside the railway station. A traditional pub with two rooms serving a range of ales (including a mild) from local brewer Thwaites. Pool and darts. Children welcome. Beer garden. *Open all day Sat and Sun and evenings Mon-Fri*.

✕ ♉ **Rialto Café** 2-4 Hermitage Street, Rishton BB1 4NL (01254 829697). Cheerful Italian café beside Bridge 108A, also operating a take-away service. Italian and North African menu. Children welcome; mooring close by. *Open Tue-Sun 17.00-23.00 (23.00 Fri and Sat)*.

🍺 **Thorn Inn** St James Road, Church, Rishton BB5 4JP (01254 399115). East of bridge 112, behind the church. Cosy, welcoming old pub dispensing real ale. Inexpensive bar meals and snacks *available L (except Sat)*. Traditional *Sun* roast and children's menu. Beer garden.

🍺 **Albion** 243 Whalley Road, Clayton-le-Moors BB5 5HD (01254 238585). Beside bridge 114A. An excellent selection of real ales from the Rossendale Brewer together with real cider served in a pub astride the halfway point of the canal. Bar food is available *Fri-Sun E during the season*. Children and dogs welcome. Moorings outside. Garden seating. *Open all day Wed-Sun and evenings Mon and Tue*. Shops and takeaways nearby.

Hapton

The navigation continues to wind eastwards along the side of what turns out to be the Calder Valley with the M65 motorway to the south. High ground rises on each side of the valley, and in the distance the summit of Pendle Hill (1831ft high) can be clearly seen when it is not obscured by cloud. This is an attractive length of canal, unspoilt by industry and greatly enhanced by the ever-changing views from the side of the hill along which the canal is cut, although the motorway is uncomfortably close throughout. Soon the distant mass of dwellings is recognisable as the suburbs of Burnley and the canal ducks through Gannow Tunnel (559yds long) to swing sharply over the M65. At Rose Grove there are *moorings* together with *showers* and *toilets* with full disabled access.

Pubs and Restaurants

🍺 **Railway** Manchester Road, Hapton, Burnley BB12 7LF (01282 773719). Along the road from the Bridge House. Traditional local's drinking pub. Pool and darts. Karaoke *Fri and Sat.*

🍺 **Gannow Wharf** Gannow Lane, Burnley BB12 6QH (01282 421908). Canalside at bridge 127A. Real ale and bar food *L and E.* Quiz *Wed;* music *Fri and Sat.*

🍺 **Dugdale Arms** Dugdale Road, Burnley BB12 6DW (01282 423909). Approach from western end of Gannow Tunnel. Thwaites beers served in a large, modern suburban pub. Children allowed and good disabled access. Bar snacks available *Fri–Sun.* Music quiz *Sun.* Outside seating and pub games. *Opens at 16.00 Mon–Thu.*

🍺 **Coal Clough** 41 Coal Clough Lane, Burnley BB11 4PG (01282 423226; www.coalcloughpub.co.uk). East of motorway slip road, above Gannow Tunnel. An end of terrace traditional northern pub full of friendly folk and good honest real ale. No children or dogs. Karaoke *Sun.* The only Burnley hostelry to dispense Bass Museum beer (Massey's Original). Pub games. *Open all day.*

Shipley (see page 134)

Boatyards

Ⓑ **Hapton Boatyard** Simpson Street, Hapton BB12 7LJ (01282 773178). ⚓ D E Gas, overnight mooring, long-term mooring, winter storage, crane, boat sales, engine repairs, boat building, DIY facilities, hull blacking, paint shop, welding, chandlery.

Ⓑ **Knott's Bridge Moorings** Hapton Boatyard, Simpson Street, Hapton BB12 7LJ (01282 774868). D Gas, overnight mooring, long-term mooring, DIY facilities.

WALKING & CYCLING

To rejoin the canal beyond Gannow Tunnel leave the towpath and follow the subway under the motorway. Bear round to the right under the A67 and take the path leading uphill to the right of the Derby Hotel. Cross the road and go up the steps and then follow the straight path leading steadily downhill to the eastern tunnel portal. The town of Accrington lies a little to the south of the waterway but is the centre for the Hyndburn District which covers Rishton, Church and Clayton-le-Moors. There is a beautifully produced range of walking and cycling guides to this area which can be obtained (for the most part free) from Accrington Information Centre at the Town Hall (01254 872595; www.hyndburnbc.gov.uk).

● **Hapton**
Lancs. PO, tel, stores, takeaways, laundrette, station.
A small and unmistakably northern village,
with regular streets of
terraced houses.

Burnley

This is an industrial stretch where the canal was once a main artery for the town and its industries. The area around bridge 130, known as the Weavers' Triangle, has been recognised to be of great interest – fine warehouses, tall chimneys and loading bays flank the canal here. At Burnley Wharf there is a museum in the old toll house and wharf master's house. The huge Burnley Embankment carries the navigation across part of the town – called 'the straight mile' it is 3/4 mile long, but no less dramatic for that; 6oft high, it incorporates an aqueduct over a main road. The whole area of the embankment has been tidied up and the towpath opened up offering excellent access to a wealth of pedestrianised shopping, together with good moorings. The town is within easy reach and the attractive Thompson Park (good play area and boating lake) can be found north of the aqueduct after bridge 130H. There is a BW slipway (01942 405700) immediately south of 130E Finsley Gate Bridge. Now the canal negotiates a landscape which alternates between open country, towns and semi-towns, with the massive distant bulk of Pendle Hill in the background. Cobbled streets of terraced houses run down to the canal and old wharves, some disused and overgrown, are under renovation for offices and housing. There is excellent *mooring* immediately south of bridge 140 on the offside, together with an attractive children's playground opposite.

● Burnley
Lancs. All services. A large industrial northern town, which has worked hard to improve its appearance. It was once the world centre for cotton weaving. The excellent shopping centre is only 10 minutes' walk from Finsley Gate Bridge, and if you feel like a swim, a sauna or a solarium, the Thompson Centre (01282 664444) is even closer.
Apollo Cinema Hollywood Park, Manchester Road, Burnley BB11 2EJ (08712 233445; www. apollocinemas.co.uk). Multi-screen cinema not far from the canal.
Barden Mill Barden Lane, Burnley BB12 oDX (01282 420333; www.bardenmillshop.co.uk). Beside bridge 134. A mill shop selling fabrics, clothes, crafts and gifts. Tearoom. Boat trips also available on the 50-seat *nb Marton Emperor* operating *one-and-a-half-hour 'flights' on Sun afternoons, Apr–Sep*. Telephone 01282 870241 for further details or visit www.boattrips.info.
Queen Street Mill Museum Harle Syke, Burnley BB10 2HX (01282 412555; www.lancashire.gov.uk). North east of Burnley Embankment, along Eastern Avenue and Briercliffe Road from the football ground. This is Britain's only working 19th C weaving mill: 300 looms powered by the 500hp steam engine 'Peace'. Virtually unchanged until it closed in 1982, the mill has now found a new lease of life, with some of the former employees back again to work the looms. Mill shop and café. *Open Apr and Oct, Tue–Fri 12.00–17.00; May–Sep, Tue–Sat 12.00–17.00; Mar and Nov Tue–Thu 12.00–16.00. Also B Hol weekends during season.* Charge.
Rourkes Forge Vulcan Works, Accrington Road, Burnley BB11 5QD (01282 422841; www.rourkes.co.uk). Manufacturers of indoor and outdoor decorative ironwork with visitor centre, gift shop and showroom *open Mon–Thu 08.00–17.00*

(16.00 Fri, Sat) and Sun 11.00–17.00. Live demonstrations for groups *Mon–Fri 09.00–15.00 (13.00 Fri).*
Weavers' Triangle Manchester Road, near town centre.The area between bridges 129B and 130B is one of the best-preserved 19th C industrial districts in the country – there are weaving sheds with 'north light' roofs, engine houses, spinning mills and well-preserved terraces of 19th-C houses. An explanatory leaflet and town trail guide are available from: the Tourist Information Centre or the **Visitor Centre**, Burnley Wharf, 85 Manchester Road, Burnley BB11 1JZ (01282 452403; www.weaverstriangle.co.uk). *Open Easter–Sep, Sat–Tue 14.00–16.00; Oct, Sun 14.00–16.00 only.* Free – donations welcome.
Towneley Hall Museum Towneley Park, Burnley BB11 3RQ (01282 424213; www.burnley.gov.uk). On the southern outskirts of Burnley, 1¼ miles south east of the BW yard. Set in extensive parkland with two golf courses (one 9-hole and the other 18-hole) and play area, the grandiose, battlemented house dating from the 14th C was the home of the Towneley family until 1902. It is now an art gallery and museum with rooms lavishly furnished in period style. The grounds also contain a natural history museum and aquarium. *Open Sat–Thu 12.00–17.00. Closed B Hols.* Natural history centre *also open Apr–Sep, Sat.*
Tourist Information Centre Burnley Mechanics, Manchester Road, Burnley BB11 1JA (01282 664421; www.visitburnley.com). *Open Mon–Sat 09.00–17.00.*
● Brierfield
Lancs. PO, tel, stores, garage, bank, station. A small industrial town merging into Burnley at one end and into Nelson at the other. The parish church of St Luke in Colne Road is a Victorian building with an unusually designed clock tower culminating in a steep pyramid roof.

Leeds & Liverpool Canal

Pubs and Restaurants

There are plenty of pubs in Burnley. This is a selection close to the waterway:

🍺 ✕ **Inn on the Wharf** Manchester Road, Burnley BB11 1JG (01282 459951). Beside bridge 130B. A weaver's warehouse featuring the original beams, stonework and flagstone floors now dispensing real ale. Food *L and E Mon–Fri and all day Sat, Sun and B Hols*, ranging from bar snacks to full à la carte menu. A family pub, demanding presentable dress, with supervised, upstairs children's play area. Canalside seating, mooring.

🍺 **Mechanics (Oliver's Bar)** Mechanics Institute, Manchester Road, Burnley BB11 1JA (01282 664400). Town centre bar, part of the local arts centre, open *Thu–Sat evenings* serving real ale and bar food. Children and dogs welcome. Live music *each night*.

🍺 **Sparrow Hawk Hotel** Church Street, Burnley BB11 2DN (01282 421551). South west of bridge 130H. An excellent selection of ever changing guest real ales are dispensed together with Belgian bottled beers. Home-cooked bar food *available daily L and E* and a more extensive menu is served in the upstairs restaurant *E*. There is a café/bar open every *E and all day Sat and Sun*. Children welcome *L* only. Pub games. B & B.

🍺 ✕ **Queen Victoria** Queen Victoria Road, Burnley BB10 3EF (01282 450250). North of bridge 130H. Brewer's Fayre pub and hotel complex serving real ale. Food *available all day*. Indoor and outdoor children's play areas. Canalside seating. Moorings.

🍺 **Reedley Hollows** 305 Barden Lane, Burnley BB10 1JA (01282 425210). 50yds east of bridge 134. Family pub serving real ale and food *L and E (not Mon E)*. Children welcome. Beer garden. Occasional entertainment

🍺 **Waggon & Horses** Colne Road, Brierfield BB9 5RD (01282 613962). Up the road from bridge 139. A beautifully restored pub in Victorian style with an open fire, offering real ale, and food *L and E daily*. Children welcome. Garden.

Boatyards

Ⓑ **Barden Mill** Barden Lane, Burnley BB12 0DX (01282 420333; www.bardenmillshop.co.uk). Pump out, overnight mooring, toilets, café. Watermate Key required.

121

Foulridge

The navigation winds as it follows the hillside; but this ceases at Nelson, where it crosses the valley on a minor aqueduct and begins to climb the pretty Barrowford Locks, having finally seen off the motorway. Immediately to the north of Bridge 141C, on the offside, there is a *canal users recycling point*, complete with its own *mooring*. This is a refreshing stretch, in which the canal leaves the succession of industrial towns. It rises through the seven Barrowford Locks, passing Barrowford Reservoir (in which the summit level's surplus water is stored), and at the beautifully kept top lock reaches the summit level of the whole canal. Soon various feeder streams can be seen, continuously pouring vital water supplies into the navigation. Meanwhile, distant mountainous country frames beautiful old stone farms nearer at hand. Soon everything is blotted out by Foulridge Tunnel; at the other end there is an old wharf (*toilets and showers*) where it is possible to moor to visit the village.

WALKING & CYCLING

To rejoin the canal beyond Foulridge Tunnel follow the waymarked route along minor roads and footpaths, skirting one of the navigation's extensive water supply reservoirs. Further afield, there is a selection of walks leaflets featuring a variety of treks (from 5 to 45 miles) around Pendle Moors whilst 'Bowland by Bike' is a selection of 10 on- and off-road rides around the area. Available from TICs. National Cycle Route 68 uses this section of the towpath.

- **Nelson**

Lancs. All services. Nelson is a conglomerate of a number of small villages that combined in the 19th C to form one industrial town. The centre has been redeveloped with a large covered shopping precinct. One of Nelson's more valuable assets is the easy access to the beautiful Moors and Forest of Pendle, behind which looms Pendle Hill.

- **Barrowford**

Lancs. PO, tel, stores. There are still some attractive terraces of stone cottages in this village, which lie a short walk to the west of the locks. The Toll House, the last intact survivor from the old Marsden (Nelson) to Long Preston turnpike road, together with the 17th-C Park Hill (the birthplace of Roger Bannister, the first 'four minute miler') now houses:

Pendle Heritage Centre Park Hill, Barrowford, Nelson BB9 6JQ (01282 661702; www.pendletourism.com). *Open daily 10.00–17.00 (except Xmas).* Exhibition on Pendle Witches; 18th-C walled garden and woodland walk; cruck barn with animals; parlour shop and tearoom-cum-restaurant. Also Pendle Arts Gallery. Charge. John Wesley preached from the packhorse bridge in the 1770s; there is a fine park by the river containing traces of a mill dating from 1311.

Tourist Information Centre Park Hill, Barrowford, Nelson BB9 6JQ (01282 661701; www.pendlelife.co.uk). *Open Mon, Wed–Fri 09.00–17.00; Tue 10.00–13.00; Sat 10.00–14.30.*

- **Foulridge**

Lancs. PO, tel, stores, takeaway. Attractive around the green, where alleys festooned with washing lines give the place a homely air. In the surrounding countryside are scattered the reservoirs that feed the summit level of the canal. There is a reception centre housing a small museum in the old warehouse on the wharf.

- **Foulridge Tunnel**

1640yds long, with no towpath, this tunnel is, not surprisingly, barred to unapproved boats. The hole in the hill sprang to fame in 1912 when a cow fell into the canal near the tunnel mouth and for some reason decided to struggle through to the other end of the tunnel. The gallant but weary swimmer was revived with alcohol at the Foulridge end. Photographs in the Hole in the Wall pub recall the incident. The tunnel roof drips liberally.

NAVIGATIONAL NOTES

Entrance to Foulridge Tunnel is restricted and controlled by lights. Please obey signs giving instructions.

BOAT TRIPS

M.V. Marton Emperor Canal trips *Easter–Sep, Sun and Tue 14.30.* Also trips through the tunnel to Barrowford run on *last Sun in month end of May–Aug 11.00.* Private charters available throughout year in centrally heated boat. For further details telephone 01282 844033 or visit www.boattrips.info.co.uk. Day boat hire.

Pubs and Restaurants

✗ **Top Lock Ice Creams** (07738 997566) In the old lock-keepers cottage by Barrowford top lock. Light refreshments and ice cream.

🍺 **Old Bridge Inn** Gisburn Road, Barrowford, Nelson BB9 6AJ (01282 613983). Cosy village local serving real ales. Children and dogs welcome. Pub games. Garden. Regular quiz, karaoke and live music.

🍺 ✗ **White Bear** Gisburn Road, Barrowford, Nelson BB9 6EP (01282 440931). Attractive village local serving real ales and food *all day.* Children *over fourteen* welcome if eating. Outside seating. Quiz nights. Barrowford can be accessed via a footpath near the top of Barrowford Locks.

🍺 **Hole in the Wall** 1 Town Gate, Foulridge, Colne BB8 7PL (01282 863568). 250yds east of tunnel, north end. Here is recorded the famous 'cow in the canal' incident. Thirsty boaters, however, are revived with real ale. Children welcome. Beer garden, pool and darts.

🍺 **New Inn** Skipton Old Road, Foulridge, colne BB8 7PD (01282 864068). Carry on past the Hole in the Wall and cross the main road. A popular village pub serving good food and real ales. Traditional home-cooking with weekly specials available *L and E Wed–Sun.* Children welcome *until 21.30;* dogs in snug area only. Outside seating.

Barnoldswick

Meanwhile the navigation continues northward through this very fine countryside to Salterforth, crossing over the little 'Country Brook' between bridges 149 and 150.This is one of the more remote sections of the whole canal and probably the most beautiful. There is also much canal interest, for just south of bridge 153 was the junction, now disappeared, of the Rain Hall Rock Branch, essentially a linear quarry where the limestone was loaded directly from the rock face onto the boats. Walk up the road from the bridge (east) and turn right at the top where it will come into view, straddled by a tall three-arched viaduct. A mile further along one rounds a corner and is confronted by Greenberfield Top Lock (*showers, toilet, camping and an attractive picnic area with refreshments*), which introduces the beginning of the long descent towards Leeds – the feeder from the distant Winterburn Reservoir enters the canal at the top lock. The three locks here were built in 1820 to replace the original flight (the old dry bed of the earlier route can be seen on the towpath side) and are set in beautiful uplands – for the next few miles the canal winds through scenery that is composed of countless individual hillocks, some topped by clumps of trees. Beyond are distant mountains.

Boatyards

Ⓑ **Lower Park Marina** Kelbrook Road, Barnoldswick BB18 5TB (01282 815883; www.pendletourism.com). 🛡 D Pump out, gas, overnight mooring, long-term mooring, narrowboat hire, boat sales, winter storage, cranage, DIY facilities, wet dock, solid fuel, boat repairs, chandlery, gifts, books and maps, telephone, groceries, hot drinks and fresh milk.

● **Salterforth**
Lancs. PO (Mon and Thu), tel, stores. A small village of narrow streets and terraced houses in an upland setting. Children will enjoy the playground north of bridge 151.

● **Barnoldswick**
Lancs. PO, tel, stores, garage, bank. Set back from the canal, the mainstay of this town's existence is the Rolls Royce factory, where experimental work is done on aero engines. The centre of the town is compact and dominated by the modern Holy Trinity Church completed in 1960.
Bancroft Mill Engine Trust Gillians Lane, Barnoldswick BB8 5QU (01282 865626; www.bancroftmill.org.uk). A 600 hp steam engine and its two boilers, once powering the looms of Bancroft Mill, saved for preservation. Regular steaming and weaving demonstrations. Refreshments, shop. *Open every Sat* for static viewing. Charge. *Telephone for details of steaming days.*
Tourist Information Centre Post Office Buildings, Fernlea Avenue, Barnoldswick BB18 5DL (01282 666704; www.pendle.gov.uk/tourism). *Open Mon and Wed-Fri 09.00-17.00, Tue 10.00-13.00 and Sat 10.00-14.30.*
Pennine Way The Pennine Way is a walking route covering 268 miles of Pennine highland from Edale in the south to Kirk Yetholm in the north. Because of the nature of the route much of the Way is rough, hard walking, but it gives a superb view from the mountains. At East Marton the Pennine Way shares the canal towpath for a short distance – you will notice that the stones here abound with fossils.

Pubs and Restaurants

🍺 ✕ **Anchor Inn** Salterforth Lane, Salterforth, Barnoldswick BB18 5TT (01282 813186). Canalside, at bridge 151. An historic village canalside pub serving real ales, where a second building was built on top of the first – hence where you now drink was once the bedrooms. Real ale and wide range of good, traditional pub food served *L and E and all day Sat, Sun*. Built beside the old packhorse road, the downstairs room (and now the cellar) hosts a spectacular display of stalactites. Garden. Good moorings, children's menu and outdoor play area. Regular quiz nights and live music. *Open all day.*

WALKING & CYCLING
At bridge 158 walkers can pick up the Pendle Way, details of which are available from local TICs.

125

Gargrave

Around East Marton, after skirting the isolated church, the surroundings change briefly: the navigation enters a cutting, passes under a double-arched main road bridge and enters a sheltered fold housing a farm, a pub and some moorings. A steep wooded cutting leads the canal back into the rugged moorlands. There is a useful *shop* and *restaurant* at Wilkinsons Farm, together with B & B and *camping*, by bridge 162, which can also be reached via a lane to the side of the Cross Keys. This is another outstanding stretch, in which the navigation continues to snake extravagantly around the splendid green and humpy hills that fill the landscape. The six Bank Newton Locks lower the canal into Upper Airedale, yielding excellent views across the valley to the hills and moors beyond. The River Aire flows in from the north, accompanied by the railway line to Skipton and Leeds from Morecambe, Settle and distant Carlisle.

The canal crosses the river by a substantial stone aqueduct. Meanwhile, yet more locks take the canal round Gargrave; the beauty of the area may be judged by the fact that the Yorkshire Dales National Park borders the navigation along here.

● **Gargrave**
N. Yorks. PO, tel, stores, garage, station. A very attractive and much-visited village. Holding an enviable position near the head of Airedale between the canal and the river, this place is the ideal centre for boat crews to explore the surrounding countryside. The River Aire cuts Gargrave in two, and the bridge over it forms the centre of the village. There is a charming station, and some pretty stone cottages along the green. The church is mostly Victorian, except for the tower, which was built in 1521. There is a coal and firewood merchant beside bridge 171 and the village store *stays open until late.*

Yorkshire Dales National Park Some of England's finest walking country is contained in this area of fine views, deep valleys, open moorland and rugged hills. Designated as a National Park in 1954 the Dales, covering 680 sq miles, are hardly scarred by habitation.

Pubs and Restaurants

X ⏥ **Abbot's Harbour Restaurant** Sawley House, East Marton, Skipton BD23 3LP (01282 843207). Charming canalside restaurant set in a 12th-C building constructed by Cistercian monks who worked the land and provided shelter to travellers between abbeys. Traditional English home-cooked food *available 10.00–14.30 daily*. Children welcome, dogs by arrangement. Outside seating.

⏥ X **Cross Keys Inn** East Marton, Skipton BD23 3LP (01282 844326). Traditional 16th-C inn, overlooking the canal. A range of real ales is available together with a modern English menu served *L and E, daily (all day Sat and Sun)*. Children and dogs welcome. Outside seating. Quiz *Mon*. Moorings. Telephone kiosk nearby.

⏥ X **Anchor Inn** Hellifield Road, Gargrave, Skipton BD23 3NB (01756 749666). By Anchor Lock. Usual Brewers Fayre pub serving food *all day, every day until 22.00*. Large garden with children's play area.

X **The Dalesman** High Street, Gargrave, Skipton BD23 3LX (01756 749250). In the centre of the village and well worth the walk. The original Spare Tyre menu caters for all tastes and all types including breakfasts, sandwiches, toasties and hot and cold platters, all prepared under the watchful eyes of its ex-teaching/ex-boating proprietors. Children welcome. *Open Tue–Sun 09.00–17.00*.

⏥ **Mason's Arms** Marton Road, Gargrave, Skipton BD23 3NL (01756 749304). An attractive old local pub with a bowling green at the rear dispensing real ales and food *L and E, daily*. Children and dogs welcome. *Sun quiz (Sep– Mar only)*. This pub features a beer-drinking horse. B & B (telephone to confirm).

⏥ X **Old Swan** High Street, Gargrave, Skipton BD23 3RB (01756 749232). Imposing village centre pub and restaurant serving real ales and traditional home-cooked food *L and E (all day in spring and summer)*. *Winter* log fires. Children and dogs welcome; children's play area. Garden and pub games. Quiz *Tue*. B & B.

WALKING & CYCLING

The Pennine Cycleway, which is National Cycle Route 68 and runs from Berwick-upon-Tweed to Derby, joins the waterway west of Gargrave and runs west along the towpath as far as Burnley, before heading south to meet the Rochdale Canal at Hebden Bridge.

NAVIGATIONAL NOTES

Locks 41–30 require a Handcuff Key.

Skipton

The canal now turns south east and proceeds down Airedale, a valley which contains it from here right through to Leeds. Upper Airedale is a flat, wide valley defined by tall steep hills. The countryside is open, unploughed and very inviting to walkers, especially with the moorlands stretching away over the top of the hills. In this robust landscape the navigation hugs the hillsides just above the valley floor, enjoying a lock-free pound that is 17 miles long – although the navigator's relief at the absence of locks may be tempered by the abundance of swing bridges. Entering Skipton, which is usually bristling with pleasure boats, the navigator will see the Springs Branch, a little arm packed with moored craft, that leads off past the town centre and soon finds itself in what is virtually a ravine, overlooked by the castle more than 100ft above. (Navigation is limited – *see* Navigational Note, opposite.) At the junction is a boatyard: next door is a restored canal warehouse. On leaving Skipton the canal continues along the hillside down the valley of the River Aire, with the main road just beside and below the navigation. Excellent views are offered up and down this splendid valley and the surrounding countryside. The village of Bradley has an attractive waterfront and the pub is well worth the 1/4 mile uphill walk (take the first turning on the right over the lift bridge) – the *PO stores* are situated beyond the imposing mill building. Visitor moorings are *on the towpath side only.*

Pubs and Restaurants

There is a wide choice of pubs in Skipton. This is just a selection within reach of the canal:

Herriots Hotel Broughton Road, Skipton BD23 1RT (01756 792781; www.herriotsforleisure.co.uk). Canalside, near bridge 176. 'Modern Victorian' decor and home-made food to suit all tastes are on offer *L and E (not Sun E)* in this bar and à la carte restaurant. Children welcome. Conservatory with open fire. Outside seating. B & B.

Rose & Crown Coach Street, Skipton BD23 1LH (01756 793884). By the junction with the Springs Branch. Real ale is served in this town-centre pub. Children welcome and outside seating. Live bands *Sun.*

Royal Shepherd Canal Street, Skipton BD23 1LB (01756 793178). Friendly, welcoming family-run pub (overlooking the Springs Branch) offering home-cooked food *L and E* and a selection of real ales. Dogs and children welcome. Inside there are historic photographs. Garden and play area. Fun quiz with music *Sun.*

Gallery 17 Otley Street, Skipton BD23 1DY (01756 791534). A tasty range of inexpensive, home-cooked traditional English food served in a continental-style establishment. *Open Mon–Sun 09.00–16.00.* There is a tea garden.

Cock & Bottle Swadford Street, Skipton BD23 1RD (01756 794734; www.cockandbottle.co.uk). Exposed stone walls and beamed ceilings make this 18th C coaching inn a congenial pub in which to enjoy a good selection of real ales. *Open all day,* serving excellent value, pub grub *L.* Children welcome. Outside seating. Quiz *Wed* and 'view-in' cellar visible from both the bar and street.

Narrow Boat 38 Victoria Street, Skipton BD23 1JE (01756 797922; www.markettowntaverns.co.uk).

A lively real ale drinkers pub that pays homage to the traditional brewery and to the canal. Furnished with old pews, this hostelry dispenses at least six ever-changing cask ales and a variety of Belgian and German bottled beers. Food *L.* Outside seating and pub games. Jazz *Tue*; folk *Sun.*

Bay Horse Kieghley Road, Snaygill, Bradley, Nr Skipton (01756 797711). Aiming to provide a 'relaxed, informal experience', this chain pub offers real ale and food *daily 12.00–10.00 (Sun 21.30)*. Comprehensive wine selection and log fires in *winter.* Children welcome. Garden and decking overlooking the canal. Moorings.

Henri's Bistro & Bar Keighley Road, Snaygill, Nr Skipton BD22 0AH (01756 796428). Mediterranean style bar with a large dining area, serving continental lagers and beers together with a mix of Italian and Spanish cooking available *daily 12.00–23.00.* Children welcome *until 18.00.* Outside terrace seating.

Rendezvous Keighley Road, Snaygill, Nr Skipton BD23 2TA (01756 700100; www.rendezvous-skipton.com). Hotel with a conservatory restaurant overlooking the canal. A wide variety of food is sevrved *L and E daily.* Children welcome, outside play area and lots of outside seating. B & B. Hotel also contains a leisure club accessible to the public.

Slaters Arms Crag Lane, Bradley BD20 9DE (01535 632179; www.theslatersarmsatbradley.co.uk). Near bridge 182A. 18th-C quality local complete with a warm welcome,inglenook fireplace and log fires in *winter.* Well kept real ales together with an appetizing range of homemade food is available daily *L and E.* Children welcome *until 21.00*; dogs at any time in the tap room if food is not being served. Large garden overlooking the canal and Aire Valley.

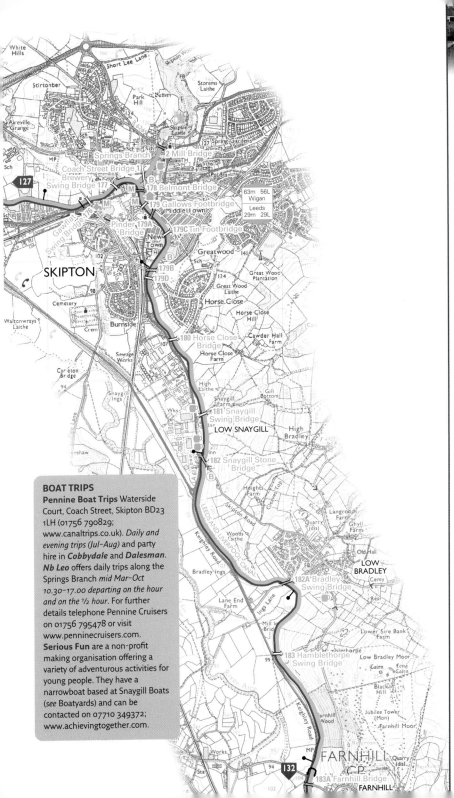

BOAT TRIPS

Pennine Boat Trips Waterside Court, Coach Street, Skipton BD23 1LH (01756 790829; www.canaltrips.co.uk). *Daily and evening trips (Jul–Aug)* and party hire in *Cobbydale* and *Dalesman*. *Nb Leo* offers daily trips along the Springs Branch *mid Mar–Oct 10.30–17.00 departing on the hour and on the 1/2 hour*. For further details telephone Pennine Cruisers on 01756 795478 or visit www.penninecruisers.com.
Serious Fun are a non-profit making organisation offering a variety of adventurous activities for young people. They have a narrowboat based at Snaygill Boats (*see* Boatyards) and can be contacted on 07710 349372; www.achievingtogether.com.

Passing through the swing bridge at Skipton

NAVIGATIONAL NOTES

1 Bridges 173–176, 181, 183–185 and 188–191 require a handcuff key. Bridges 177, 182A and 187 require a Watermate Key. *See* Navigational Notes on pages 137 and 138 for keys required for structures closer to Leeds.

2 Turning in the Springs Branch is restricted and craft over 35ft should be confident that they can reverse out avoiding moored craft. Craft less than 35ft may still have to reverse to find a turning area.

WALKING & CYCLING

British Waterways (01977 554351; enquiries.yorkshire@britishwaterways.co.uk) publishes a Canal Heritage Trail for Skipton aimed at introducing the whole family to the history of the canal. The route takes in ten information posts, nine of which have pictures to take rubbings from – so remember crayons and paper. The walk can be started from any point and takes approximately 1 hour. Details from BW or the Tourist Information Centre.

Boatyards

ⓑ **Pennine Cruisers** The Boat Shop, 19 Coach Street, Skipton BD23 1LH (01756 795478; www.penninecruisers.com). At junction with Springs Branch. 🛥 🛥 🔌 D E Pump out, gas, narrowboat hire, day-hire craft, overnight mooring, long-term mooring, winter storage, dry dock, boat building, boat sales, chandlery, books, maps and gifts, engine repairs.

ⓑ **Snaygill Boats** Skipton Road, Bradley, Nr Skipton BD20 9HA (01756 795150; www.snaygillboats.co.uk). At bridge 182. 🛥 🛥 D E Pump out, gas, narrowboat hire, overnight mooring, long-term mooring, chandlery, dry dock, books, maps and gifts, engine repairs, toilet, shower.

- **Skipton**

N. Yorks. All services (including cinema) and excellent shops. Skipton is probably the most handsome town along the whole Leeds & Liverpool Canal. It is an excellent place for visiting from the canal, for one can moor snugly and safely about one minute's walk away from the centre. It still maintains its importance as a market town, which is referred to in its name: Saxon 'Scip-tun' means sheep-town. The wide High Street is very attractive, lined with mostly Georgian houses, and headed at the northern end by the splendid castle and the well-kept graveyard of the parish church. There is an interesting water mill beside the Springs Branch.

Church of the Holy Trinity High Street, Skipton BD23 1NJ (www.holytrinityskipton.org.uk) Standing opposite the castle, it is a long battlemented church, encircled by large lawns and flourishing gardens. It is in Perpendicular style dating from the 14th C, though it was greatly renovated after suffering serious damage during the Civil War. It has a fine oak roof and a beautifully carved Jacobean font cover.

Craven Museum Town Hall, High Street, Skipton BD23 1AH (01756 706407; www.cravendc.gov.uk). Outstanding local geology and archaeology collection together with a colourful insight into life in the Craven Dales. *Open Apr–Sep Mon, Wed–Sat 10.00–17.00, and Sun 14.00–17.00; Oct–Mar Mon, Wed–Sat 13.30–17.00 and Sun 10.00–16.00.* Free.

Cycle Hire Dave Ferguson Cycles, Albion Yard, Otley Street, Skipton BD23 1FD (01756 795367) and the Bicycle Shop, 3–5 Water Street, Skipton BD23 1PQ (01756 794386).

- **Springs Branch**

A short (770yds) but very unusual branch that leaves the Leeds & Liverpool Canal, passes the centre of Skipton and soon finds itself in what is virtually a ravine, overlooked by the castle that towers 100ft above. The branch is navigable by small craft, and makes an interesting diversion by boat or foot. (The towpath continues past the arm, into Skipton Woods.) It was built by the Earl of Thanet, the owner of Skipton Castle, to carry limestone away from his nearby quarry. It was

extended by 240yds in 1797 from the water-mill bridge through the deep rock cutting, and 120ft-chutes were constructed at the new terminus to drop the rock into the boats from the horse tramway that was laid from the quarry to the castle. The quarry still flourishes, but the canal and tramway have not been used since 1946. Trains and lorries have replaced them. Now a picturesque backwater the Springs Branch acted for many years as a feeder to the Leeds & Liverpool Canal, taking water from Eller Beck, which runs beside it.

Skipton Castle Skipton BD23 1AW (01756 792442; www.skiptoncastle.co.uk). A magnificent Norman castle, with 17th C additions, that dominates Skipton High Street. After a three-year siege during the Civil War, Cromwell's men allowed the restoration of the castle, but ensured that the building could never again be used as a stronghold. The six massive round towers have survived from the 14th C and other notable features are the 50ft-long banqueting hall, a kitchen with roasting and baking hearths, a dungeon and the 'Shell Room', the walls of which are decorated with sea shells. Picnic area, licensed tearooms and shop. *Open daily 10.00–18.00 (16.00 Oct–Feb). Closed Sun until 12.00.* Charge.

Tourist Information Centre Coach Street, Skipton BD23 1LQ (01756 792809; www.skiptononline.co.uk). *Open Mon–Sat 10.00–17.00 and Sun 11.00–15.00.*

Skipton Woods Fine woods leading up the little narrow valley from the Springs Branch. For access, just keep on walking up the towpath of the branch.

Embsay and Bolton Abbey Steam Railway Bolton Abbey Station, Skipton BD23 6AF (01756 710614; www.embsayboltonabbeyrailway.org.uk). Talking timetable (01756 795189). 1 mile north of Skipton off the A59/65 bypass. Bus service from Skipton. A 4-mile round-trip either steam or diesel-hauled. Bookshop, café and picnic site (at all stations). Disabled access at Bolton Abbey Station. *Services throughout year.* Visit website or telephone the talking timetable (01756 795189) for details of upcoming events.

THE SETTLE–CARLISLE RAILWAY

O.S. Nock, the well-known railway writer, described this line (accessible from Skipton station) as 'the only mountain railway in the world built for express trains'. Completed in 1876, at a cost of almost £3.5 million; 72 miles long – including 20 large viaducts, 14 tunnels and no sharp curves and, in common with so many canal projects, some 50% over budget, it very nearly fell to the neo-Beeching axe. It was both one of the most awesome feats of Victorian railway engineering and one of the most fiercely contested closure battles. It is, therefore, fortunate that in the light of today's burgeoning rail freight, common sense finally prevailed, saving the line for a rapidly growing commercial traffic – and our wonder and enjoyment. A regular service connecting the isolated communities along the line (swelled by tourist traffic in the summer months) together with ever-increasing pressure on the West Coast Main Line, will undoubtedly ensure the future of this route.

Silsden

There is a fine wooded stretch north of Kildwick; then one curves sharply round the outcrop on which crouches Farnhill Hall, a mellow stone building. The intriguing village of Kildwick has some well-restored canalside buildings now used as private residences. There are good moorings here prior to quieter country: the main road and the railway cut the valley corner while the canal takes the longer route round to Silsden. Overlooking Airedale, the green hills are very steep and beautifully wooded in places. The distant rows of chimneys, factories and terraced houses across the valley comprise Keighley; most of its industrial and suburban tentacles are quickly passed by the canal, although the constant succession of little swing bridges regularly impedes a boat's progress. This type of swing bridge is prone to intermittent stiffness due to the elements, and all require a handcuff key. There are a *PO* and *stores* south of bridge 197, and an attractive mooring by woods, to the east of bridge 195.

Pubs and Restaurants

🍺 **White Lion Hotel** Priestbank Road, Kildwick BD20 9BH (01535 632265). 17th-C coaching inn near the canal: a sign on the towpath shows the way! Real ales and food *daily L and E*. Children welcome. Dogs welcome in bar area. South-facing garden offers sun and views.

🍺 **Bridge Inn** Keighley Road, Silsden BD20 0EA (01535 653144). Cosy canalside local which predates the waterway, serving a good selection of real ales. Children welcome. Regular entertainment. Moorings. Pub games. B & B.

🍺 **King's Arms** Bolton Road, Silsden BD20 0JY (01535 653216). Friendly, welcoming pub serving real ales and food *L Mon–Fri*. Children welcome, garden. Folk and acoustic jam night *Tue*.

🍺 **Brewery Arms** 17 Long Croft, Keighley BD21 5AL (01535 603102). Serious real ale establishment with a choice of beers to wash down pie and pease which

are always available. Alternative fare is also served. Children and dogs welcome. Pub games and outside seating. *Open all day*.

🍺 **Boltmaker's Arms** 117 East Parade, Keighley BD21 5HX (01535 661936). Intimate, one-roomed pub dispensing real ale and at least 50 whiskies. Sandwiches are available *all day*, *every day*. Children welcome. Pub games.

🍺 **Globe Inn** 2 Parkwood Street, Keighley BD21 4QR (01535 610802). Well worth the walk and an excuse to view the K&WV Railway close up. This genuine, friendly local offers excellent real ale free from the distractions of any machines together with bar meals *L (meals E can be booked in advance)*. Open fires *in winter*; pub games and regular *weekend* entertainment.

There are plenty of other pubs in Keighley.

Boatyards

ⓑ **Silsden Boats** Canal Wharf, Elliot Street, Silsden, nr Keighley BD20 0DE (01535 653675; www.silsdenboats.co.uk). 🚿 🔧 D Pump out, gas, narrowboat hire, overnight mooring, slipway, engine repairs, books, maps and gifts, toilets.

- **Kildwick**
  W. Yorks. Tel. An interesting and unusual village spilling down the hillside. The streets are extremely steep; one of them goes under the canal through a narrow skewed aqueduct. There is a *part-time PO* in the Institute on Main Street, Farnhill on the opposite side of the canal.
- **Silsden**
  W. Yorks. PO, tel, stores, garage, bank, station nearby. A well-contained, stone-built industrial town spreading uphill from the canal. In addition to its proximity to the Yorkshire Dales National Park, it offers plenty of shops near the canal. The canalside warehouses are attractive; there is also an old corn mill dated 1677.
- **Keighley**
  W. Yorks. All services. Compared with some other industrial centres in the area, Keighley is a clean and pleasant town. It boasts a large new shopping centre, much modern housing and some handsome older stone terraces. The oldest part is around the parish church of St Andrew, a large Perpendicular building whose main attraction is its shady churchyard.

Cliffe Castle
Spring Gardens Lane, Keighley BD20 6LH (01535 618231; www.visitbradford.com). Once the home of the Butterfield family, it has been completely restored and now houses the museum and art gallery. Local exhibits illustrate the archaeology, natural history and industrial history of the area. There are reconstructed craft workshops and a textile room. Picturesque grounds where band concerts are held. *Open Tue–Sat 10.00–17.00, Sun 12.00–17.00. Closed Mon (except B Hols), Good Friday and Christmas. Free.*

Keighley & Worth Valley Railway Keighley Station, Keighley BD21 4HP (01535 645214; www.kwvr.co.uk). Talking timetable *24hrs* (01535 647777). Privately preserved by volunteers of the Keighley & Worth Valley Railway Preservation Society, the line runs for 5 miles from the British Rail station at Keighley up to Haworth, the home of the Brontë family, and Oxenhope. British Railways closed the line in 1961, but the Society eventually succeeded in reopening it in 1968 with a regular service of steam trains. In the mornings, the service is operated by diesel railbuses, but in the afternoons magnificent steam engines puff their way along the track. In the goods yard at Haworth the Society has a splendid collection of steam engines and carriages, mostly ancient. The line was made famous by the film *The Railway Children. Open every weekend, most school holidays and throughout the summer.*

Tourist Information Centre 2/4 West Lane, Howarth BD22 8EF (01535 642329; www.visitbradford.com/bronte-country/). *Open daily Apr–Oct 09.30–17.30; Nov–Mar 09.30–17.00.*

Bingley and Shipley

The impressive Bingley Five-Rise staircase locks (*see* page 137) mark the end of the long level pound from Gargrave, and from here to Leeds there are no more views of a sweeping, uncluttered river valley. Just a few hundred yards south of the five locks are the three-rise staircase locks, which bring one steeply down into Bingley. The canal was moved sideways, over a distance of 400yds, in 1994 to allow the construction of a new road. Offside visitor moorings have been provided adjacent to the Damart mill. The waterway bisects this town, but one can see little of the place from the water. Leaving Bingley, trees lead to Dowley Gap and the two staircase locks. At the foot of the locks the towpath changes sides and the navigation crosses the River Aire via a massive stone aqueduct. Woods escort the canal along to the single Hirst Lock; from here one moves past the big mills at Saltaire and right through Shipley. There is a useful *fresh fruit and vegetable shop beside Bridge 197A*.

BOAT TRIPS

Apollo Canal Cruises Shipley Wharf, Wharf Street, Shipley BD17 7DW have a water bus operating a scheduled service *up to twice daily in summer*. They also offer *lunchtime and supper* cruises *throughout the year* aboard their restaurant boat **Water Prince** and waterbus **Apollo**. For further details telephone 01274 595914 or visit www.apollocanalcruises.co.uk.

Pubs and Restaurants

Marquis of Granby Hospital Road, Riddlesden BD20 5EP (01535 607164). At swing bridge 197A. Real ales are served at this long-established canalside pub. Children welcome *until 20.00*. Beer garden and moorings outside. *PO and stores* south of bridge 197.

Brown Cow Ireland Bridge, Bingley BD16 2QX (01274 569482). ¼ mile west of bridge 202. An excellent selection of real ales and good quality home-cooked food at pub prices served *L and E Mon–Sat and Sun L*. Children and dogs welcome. Garden and ghost. Live music *weekends*.

Ferrands Arms Queen Street, Bingley BD16 2JS (01274 563949; www.ferrandsarms.co.uk). 250yds south of bridge 202. Lively pub with a late night licence (*until midnight Thu–Sat*) dispensing real ales and food *all day until 19.00, every day*. Children welcome *until 20.00. Thu* karaoke. Sport tv.

✕ **Five Rise Locks – Café & Store** Beck Lane, Bingley BD16 5EZ (01274 562221). An inexpensive selection of hot and cold, freshly made sandwiches and home-made soup available *until 14.30.* Home-made cakes and gateaux, tea and coffee available *all day. Open Apr–Sep, daily 10.00–17.30; similar opening times during winter school holidays otherwise weekends only Oct–Mar.* Shop sells canal memorabilia, souvenirs, books, etc.

Fishermen's Inn Wagon Lane, Bingley BD16 1TS (01274 561697).

Canalside, above Dowley Gap locks. A comfortable pub serving real ales and home-made food *L and E (not Sun E).* Children welcome *until 21.30.* Extensive patio area with views over the Aire Valley.

Boathouse Inn ✕ Victoria Road, Saltaire BD18 3LA (01274 590408). Between river and canal at bridge 207A. Flying in the face of a century and a quarter of local tradition this is the first licensed premises in Saltaire, and it dispenses real ale. Food *L and E Mon–Sat and 12.00–18.00 Sun.* Children welcome. Quiz and folk music *Wed*. Children welcome in the restaurant. Riverside terrace and beer garden.

There are a wide range of pubs in Shipley: several excellent examples being south of the canal between the town and Saltaire.

Noble Comb Salts Mill Road, Shipley BD17 7JR (01274 585770). Beside Bridge 207C. Spacious family pub serving traditional pub food *daily 12.00–10.00 (21.30 Sun).* Children welcome. Outside seating. Moorings.

✕ **The Cut Waterside Restaurant** Wharf Street, Shipley BD17 7DW (01274 59444). Well-thought off, small and intimate candle-lit restaurant. Outside seating next to canal in summer. *Open for L and E, Wed–Fri 12.00–14.30 and 18.00–23.00, and Sat E 18.00–23.00.*

Bull Hotel 76 Briggate, Shipley HD6 1EF (01274 583925). South of bridge 207D. A pub with its own pigeon loft serving real ale and good cheer. Children and dogs welcome. Pool, darts and dominoes.

Leeds & Liverpool Canal

Bingley and Shipley

135

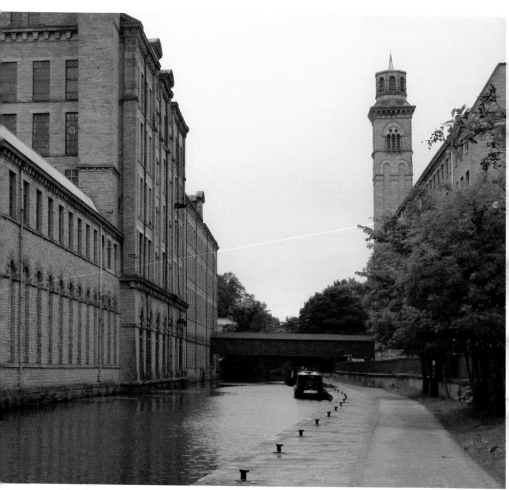

Salts Mill at Saltaire (see page 137)

● **Baildon**
W. Yorks. All services. 1½ miles north of Shipley. A
very old industrial town huddled on a hilltop on the
edge of Baildon Moor. Stretching from Baildon to
Bingley is the Glen, a wooded valley that curves
below the heights of the moor. A splendid scenic
tramway carrying two tramcars connects the coach
road to the higher parts of Baildon Moor – *in summer
a frequent service operates, but in winter it is arranged
only to suit the needs of residents at the upper level.*
Shipley
W. Yorks. All services. A dark stone town built on a
generous scale and based on textile and engineering
industries. There are powerful- looking mills to be
seen, as well as the town hall and a suitably
battlemented Salvation Army citadel. Shipley is lucky
enough to be on the edge of Baildon Moor and
Shipley Glen. The 3-mile-long Bradford Canal used to
join the Leeds & Liverpool in Shipley, by bridge 208,

but this has all been filled in for years. There is a pub
and restaurant beside bridge 207C together with a
useful canalside supermarket between bridges 207D
and 208. There are public moorings at Ashley Lane –
near bridge 207B – with town centre shopping a
relaxed 5 minutes' walk away.
● **Saltaire**
W. Yorks. PO, stores, station. An estate village that
owes its existence to the Utopian dream of Sir Titus
Salt, a wealthy Victorian mill owner. He was so
appalled by the working and living conditions of his
workers in Bradford that he decided to build the ideal
industrial settlement. This he did in 1850 on the
banks of the canal and the River Aire – hence the
name Saltaire. He provided every amenity including
high standard housing, but no pub – for he was a
great opponent of strong drink. The village has
changed little since those days (save the recent
addition of a pub!); everything is carefully laid out

and the terraced houses are attractive in an orderly sort of way. There is an Italianate church near the canal, and a large park beside the river. Admirers of David Hockney's work should visit the art gallery.

Museum of Victorian Reed Organs and Harmoniums Victoria Hall, Victoria Road, Saltaire BD18 4PS (07976 535980). Specialise in harmoniums. *Open Sun–Thu 11.00–16.00; closed Dec and Jan. Please telephone before visiting lest the proprietor has been called out on an urgent musical consultation.* Charge.

Salt's Mill Saltaire BD18 3LB (01274 531163; www.saltsmill.org.uk). The 1853 Gallery showing David Hockney's work, further galleries and a local history exhibition; an inexpensive diner and a café, and three floors of shops. *Open Mon–Fri 10.00–17.30, and Sat,Sun 10.00–18.00 except Xmas.*

Tourist Information Centre 2 Victoria Road, Saltaire BD18 3LA (01274 77499). *Open daily 10.00–17.00.*

● **Bingley**
W. Yorks. All services. An industrial town now known nationally as a centre for thermal underwear. Standing at the south east end of the town, amidst several old cottages, is the large parish church of Holy Trinity, with its massive spire conspicuous from the canal.

Bingley Five-Rise Locks A very famous and impressive feature of the canal system built in 1774 in 'staircase' formation. They are all joined together rather than being separated by pounds of 'neutral' water. The top gates of the lowest lock are the bottom gates of the lock above, and so on. This means it is not possible to empty a lock unless the one below is itself empty. The rapid elevation thus resulting is quite daunting. The BW Sanitary Station is housed in a handsome old stable, where towing horses were once rested.

East Riddlesden Hall Bradford Road, Keightly BD20 5EL (01535 607075; www.nationaltrust.org.uk). NT. Just south of swing bridge 197A. A 17th-C stone manor house complete with tithe barn. Fine collection of Yorkshire oak furniture, textiles, pewter, paintings and armour. The house is set in mature grounds with beech trees, ducks and a pond and the Starkie Wing provides a striking backdrop to a garden planted with lavender, flowers and a fragrant herb border. Also an orchard garden with wild flowers, bulbs, perennials and, of course, apple blossom. *Open mid Mar–Jun and Sep–Oct, Tue–Wed and Sat–Sun, 12.00–17.00; Jul–Aug, Sat–Wed, 12.00–17.00* Shop, picnic area and tearoom (*open as per house except 12.00 on Sat*). Events. Charge.

NAVIGATIONAL NOTES

1 Bridges 188–196 require a Handcuff key, although Bridges 189–91 are usually left open. Bridges 197, 197A, 198A and 199 need a Watermate key. Bridge 209 needs a Watermate key and a windlass.

2 Locks 29–14 and 12–4 require a Handcuff key. Locks 13 and 2 require a Handcuff key and are security locked outside opening hours – *see* note 3. Lock 1 requires a Watermate key.

3 Opening times for Bingley Five-Rise and Three-Rise Locks: mid Mar–mid Apr and Oct 08.15–17.00; mid Apr–Sep 08.15–18.00. They may be used only under the supervision of the lock keeper. To confirm times contact BW 0113 281 6800; enquiries.yorkshire@britishwaterways.co.uk.

Boatyards

ⓑ **Puffer Parts** Excelsior Works, Riddlesden, Keighley BD21 4HB (01535 605703; www.pufferparts.co.uk). 75yds south east of bridge 197A. An extensive and varied supply of sensibly priced chandlery (also mail order). Books, maps and gifts. General assistance available to the boater.

ⓑ **Hainsworth Boatyard** Fairfax Road, Bingley BD16 4DR (01274 565925; www. boattransporter.co.uk). 200yds above the five-rise. 🚽 🔧 D Pump out, gas, overnight and long-term mooring, winter storage, slipway, chandlery, solid fuel, boat sales and repairs, engine repairs, toilets. National boat transporters. *24hr emergency call out.*

ⓑ **Apollo Canal Cruises** Wharf Street, Shipley BD17 7DW (01274 595914; www. apollocanalcruises.co.uk). 🚽 🚽 🔧 D Pump out, gas, day-hire craft, overnight and long-term mooring, toilets, showers, café, telephone, gifts.

Apperley Bridge

This section sees the end of the wide open moorlands that frame the scenery further upstream: from now on, industry and housing begin to feature more as one approaches the outskirts of Leeds. The navigation, however, is thankfully sequestered from these intrusions into the landscape. Leaving Shipley, the adjacent railway cuts through a 500ft-high hill in two mile-long tunnels. The canal goes all the way round this delightfully wooded hill, tenaciously following the Aire Valley. Halfway round the long curve are Field Locks. Beyond the main railway bridge is a British Waterways maintenance yard at the head of Dobson Locks and housed in a former canal warehouse. There are also *showers, toilets and a pump out* here. Temporarily traversing a built-up area, the navigation emerges yet again onto a wooded hillside overlooking the still rural and charming valley that contains the River Aire.

NAVIGATIONAL NOTES

Bridge 214 needs a Watermate key. Bridges 215–219 require a Handcuff key. Bridge 215 is usually padlocked open to the canal.

● **Rodley**
W. Yorks. PO, tel, stores. Rodley has long been associated with the woollen industry with fulling mills and scribbling mills powered by the swift-flowing waters of the River Aire. It is still a useful village with two pubs, several shops and good visitor moorings.

Pubs and Restaurants

🍺 **Shoulder of Mutton** Otley Road, Baildon BD17 7QW (01274 584071). ¼ mile east of bridge 210. Real ales and food available daily *L and E daily*. Garden with swings. Regular live music.

🍺 **Woolpack** Main Street, Esholt, Shipley BD17 7QZ (01274 582425). As featured in the TV series *Emmerdale*. From bridge 211 follow the footpath to the main road, turn right, then take the turning to the right signposted Esholt. Real ale together with *snacks L (not Sun)* served in this well-known pub. Children's room and garden. Quiz *Thu*.

🍺 **Railway Inn** Calverley Bridge, Rodley LS13 1NR (0113 257 6603). Beside bridge 216A. Traditional canalside pub serving real ale and food *L and E*. Children welcome, and dogs welcome outside. Children's play area, moorings and outside seating. Quiz *Wed*.

🍺 **Rodley Barge** Town Street, Rodley LS131HP (0113 257 4606). Unpretentious canalside pub by bridge 217 serving real ale. Inexpensive home-cooked bar meals available *L Mon–Fri, although weekend L food can be pre-booked*. Children (*until 19.00*) and dogs welcome. Canalside garden and moorings. Quiz nights.

🍺 ✕ **Owl Hotel** Town Street, Rodley LS131LB (0113 256 5242). A friendly, family-run pub majoring on live entertainment and serving real ale and a wide variety of food *L and E, daily*. Children and dogs (outside restaurant) welcome. Secure garden.

Boatyards

ⓑ **Calder Valley Marine** Apperley Bridge, Bradford BD10 0UR (01924 467976; www.cvmarine.co.uk). 🚿 D Pump out, gas, overnight mooring, long-term mooring, engine sales and repairs, boat sales and repairs, chandlery, toilets, showers, coffee shop.

ⓑ **Swiftcraft** The Boathouse, Parkin Lane, Apperley Bridge, Bradford BD10 0NF (01274 611786). By bridge 214B. D Gas, overnight mooring, engine repairs, chandlery, long-term mooring. DIY facilities.

ⓑ **Rodley Boat Centre** Canal Wharf, Canal Road, Rodley, Leeds LS13 1LP (0113 257 6132). By bridge 216A. 🚽🚿🛒D E Pump out, overnight mooring, long-term mooring, winter storage, slipway, chandlery, books and maps, boat repairs, boat sales, engine sales and repairs (including outboards), generators and electrics, gifts. *24hr emergency call out.*

Leeds

This is a section full of contrasts; and it probably represents the most pleasant way of entering the city of Leeds. Although the area becomes more and more built up as one travels eastward, the canal remains unaffected by it, maintaining its privileged position on the wooded south side of the narrowing Aire Valley. Leaving the ruined Kirkstall Abbey on the other side of the river, the navigation passes the old Mackeson brewery, now imaginatively converted to student accommodation, and borders for a while the steeply sloping edges of an extensive park. The site of the old Kirkstall Power Station is reached, with its own private canal 'lay-by': until the mid 1960s, scores of barges used to come up to fuel this establishment every week; now both dock and power station have disappeared. Beyond, by bridge 225, is the Leeds Industrial Museum. The route of the Aire & Calder to Castleford and Wakefield is continued on page 16.

Pubs and Restaurants

● **Abbey Inn** 99 Pollard Lane, Newlay, Leeds LS13 1EQ (0113 258 1248; www.theabbey-inn.co.uk). 50yds downhill from bridge 221. CAMRA Community Pub of the Year. Small friendly country pub – once used by the nearby Abbey as a morgue – but now serving real ales and excellent food *L and E* (15.00–19.00) to a somewhat less moribund clientele. Children welcome *until 19.00 unless still eating*. Outside seating. Regular live music and quiz evenings.

● **Old Bridge Inn** Kirkstall, Leeds LS5 3BW (0113 274 9508). 100yds east of bridge 222. Real ales and food available *L and E Mon–Sat and Sun 12.00–17.00*. This welcoming old pub is open all day and in past times is reputed to have served as

both mortuary to the monks at nearby Kirkstall Abbey and, more recently, the police cells. Riverside seating beside a very attractive cast iron bridge over the Aire. Children welcome *until 19.30*; dogs in the garden on a lead. Quiz *Tue*.

● **Old Vic** 17 Whitecote Hill, Bramley, Leeds LS13 3LB (0113 256 1207). South of the canal, almost equidistant from bridges 218 or 221, although a steep climb from the latter. A traditional and friendly local serving an excellent range of real ales that more than justify the walk. Once a vicarage, this comfortable pub offers open fires *in winter* and freedom from machines. Pub games and a quiz *Thu*. *Open all day Sat; from 16.00 Mon–Thu and 14.00 Fri*. There is a *PO, stores, off-licence* and *takeaway* nearby.

Leeds

W. Yorks. All services. See also page 18.

Leeds Industrial Museum Armley Mills, Leeds LS12 2QF (0113 263 7861; www.leeds.gov.uk/armleymills). Access from bridge 225A . There have been corn and fulling mills on this site since at least 1559, with the present building dating from 1805. When built it was the most advanced in the country and it now houses a superb range of real-life exhibits demonstrating the local textile, heavy engineering, tanning and printing trades. There are working cranes, locomotives and waterwheels, and a cinema of the 1920s. *Jack* the locomotive runs on 'steaming up' days. Shop and picnic area. Disabled access. The little stone bridge over the canal here dates from around 1770. *Open Tue–Sat 10.00–17.00 and Sun 13.00–17.00. Small charge.*

Kirkstall Abbey Kirkstall LS5 3EH (0113 230 5492; www.leeds.gov.uk/kirkstallAbbey/). The large elegant ruins of a Cistercian abbey founded in the 12th C. The remaining walls narrowly escaped demolition in the late 19th C, but are now carefully preserved, surrounded by a small, attractive park. *Open daily during daylight hours. Free*

Abbey House Museum Abbey Walk, Kirkstall LS5 3EH (0113 230 5492; www.leeds.gov.uk/abbeyHouse/). This splendid folk museum illustrates the life and work of the people of Yorkshire during the last 300 years. As well as exhibiting toys, costumes and pottery, it houses three streets of fully furnished 19th-C shops, cottages and workshops. *Open Tue–Fri and Sun 10.00–17.00; Sat 12.00–17.00. Last admission 16.00. Small charge.*

Tourist Information Centre The Arcade, Leeds City Station, Leeds LS1 4DT (0113 242 5242; www.leeds.gov.uk). *Open Mon–Sat 09.00–17.30, Sun 10.00–16.00.*

NAVIGATIONAL NOTES

In the interests of safety and water conservation Newlay, Forge and Kirkstall Locks cannot be operated outside the hours *08.15–18.00 mid-Mar-Oct* when BW staff will be in attendance to provide assistance as required. However, please note that when travelling east the latest departure time from Newlay Top lock is *15.00* in order to arrive in Leeds Canal Basin by *18.00*. The latest departure time from Leeds, when travelling west, in order to clear Newlay Top Lock by *18.00*, is *15.00*. To confirm times and the availability of assistance contact BW on 0113 281 6800. Uninterrupted passage between Granary Wharf and Newlay is advised.

Boatyards

ⓑ **Fallwood Marina**
Pollard Lane, Leeds LS13 1ER
(0113 258 1074; www.fallwood-marina.co.uk). By bridge 221. 🛒 🛒 ⚓ D
Overnight and long-term mooring, winter storage, crane, gas, slipway, boat and engine sales and repairs, boat building, boat sales, showers, toilets.

ⓑ **Aire Valley Marina** Redcote Lane, Kirkstall, Leeds LS4 2AL (0113 279 8997; fionadunham@hotmail.com). 🛒 🛒 ⚓ D Pump out, gas, overnight mooring, long-term mooring, winter storage, slipway, crane, boat sales and repairs, DIY facilities, toilets, showers, laundrette.

141

MACCLESFIELD CANAL

MAXIMUM DIMENSIONS

Length: 70' 0"
Beam: 7' 0"
Headroom: 7' 0"

MILEAGE

HARDINGS WOOD JUNCTION
(Trent & Mersey Canal) *to:*
Congleton Wharf: 5¾ miles
Bosley Top Lock: 11½ miles
Macclesfield: 17 miles
Bollington: 20 miles

MARPLE JUNCTION
(Peak Forest Canal): 27¾ miles

Locks: 13

MANAGER

Hardings Wood Junction to bridge 2:
01606 723800; enquiries.wbc**@
britishwaterways.co.uk

Bridge 2 to Marple Junction:
01942 405700; enquiries.northwest@
britishwaterways.co.uk

**walesandbordercounties

With the completion of the Trent & Mersey Canal in 1777, demand was created for an alternative canal link between the Midlands and Manchester, and a direct line through the manufacturing town of Macclesfield was an obvious choice. But it was not until 1825 that Thomas Telford was asked by promoters of the canal to survey a line linking the Peak Forest Canal and the Trent & Mersey Canal. The 28-mile line he suggested was the canal that was built, from Marple to just north of Kidsgrove, although Telford did not supervise the construction, leaving to go and build the Birmingham & Liverpool Junction Canal (now the Shropshire Union). William Crosley was the canal's engineer.

The canal, which runs along the side of a tall ridge of hills west of the Pennines, does, however, bear the distinctive hallmarks of Telford's engineering. Like the Shropshire Union, the Macclesfield is a 'cut and fill' canal, following as straight a course as possible, and featuring a many great cuttings and embankments. Apart from the stop lock at Hall Green, where a 1ft rise was insisted upon as a water preservation measure by the Trent & Mersey Canal Company – to whose Hall Green Branch the Macclesfield Canal connected at the stop lock, all the locks are grouped into one flight of 12 at Bosley. The canal is fed from nearby reservoirs, at Bosley and Sutton.

In spite of intense competition from neighbouring railways and the Trent & Mersey Canal, the Macclesfield carried a good trade for many years. Much of this was coal, along with cotton from the big mills established along its northern reaches. Following its purchase in 1846 by the Great Central Railway Company, the canal began a slow, but steady, decline. The Macclesfield Canal today is an extremely interesting cruising waterway, and forms part of the popular 100-mile Cheshire Ring canal circuit. Look out for the original, and very large, stone milestones showing distances from Hall Green stop lock (the original end of the canal) and Marple. These were removed during World War II in fear of helping invading forces. They have been lovingly restored to their former glory by the Macclesfield Canal Society.

Bingley Five Rise Locks (see page 137)

Hardings Wood

The junction of the Macclesfield Canal with the Trent & Mersey Canal is exciting and unusual. The Macclesfield leaves the Trent & Mersey on the south side at Hardings Wood Junction, then crosses it on Poole Aqueduct after the T & M has fallen through two locks. The Macclesfield Canal then crosses Red Bull Aqueduct to begin its journey to Marple. It is thus a busy area, with canalside pubs,

British Waterways moorings and plenty of boats contributing to an interesting canal scene. Leaving Hardings Wood, the Macclesfield Canal passes through a stop lock in the cutting at Hall Green, to enter glorious open countryside at Kent Green. To the east, Mow Cop crowns the ridge of tall hills that stretches parallel to the navigation for miles to come. You can take a good walk to the top, on footpaths to the east from bridge 85. Beyond this point, the canal loses itself in splendid countryside for several miles as it approaches Congleton.

Boatyards

Ⓑ **Red Bull Services** Red Bull Basin, Congleton Road South, Church Lawton, Stoke-on-Trent ST7 3AJ (01782 779033). Slipway, engine repairs, blackening, boat repairs and welding.

continued in Book 4

- **Little Moreton Hall**
Congleton CW12 4SD (01260 272018;
www.nationaltrust.org.uk). NT. Just 3/4 mile west
of the canal by footpath from bridge 86 (beware
nettles and brambles!). This fabulous moated
house is arguably the finest example of black and
white timbered architecture in the UK, and is
well worth the walk from the canal. It was built
between 1559 and 1580 with carved gables and
ornate windows, and has scarcely changed since.
It contains a fine collection of oak furniture and
pewter. *Open late Mar–Oct, Wed–Sun and B Hols
11.30–17.00; early Nov– late Dec, weekends only
11.30–17.00 or dusk.* Charge. Restaurant.
- **Mow Cop**
(www.mowcop.info). NT. Walk east from bridge
85. A hill nearly 1100ft above sea level, which
gives a magnificent view across the Cheshire
Plain, beyond Stoke and into Wales, which looks
particularly good at night. On top of the hill is
Mow Cop Castle, an imitation ruin built in 1754 by
Randle Wilbraham, a local squire. It was on this
spot that Hugh Bourne, a wheelwright, climbed
to the summit to create the Primitive Methodists
in 1807. Their first meeting lasted 14 hours, and
was an endeavour to create a simpler form of
religion. The memorial church was erected in
1862 on the site of this meeting. A hundred years
later 70,000 disciples climbed to the top to
worship on what had become, for them, a Holy
Mountain. Bourne died at the age of 80, having
seen over 5000 Methodist chapels founded. Coal
from collieries to the east of Mow Cop was carried
down to the canal by a tramway known as 'The
Brake'.
- **Kent Green**
Ches. Tel, stores.

NAVIGATIONAL NOTES

The Macclesfield Canal is generally quite shallow, and mooring is usually only possible at recognised sites.

WALKING & CYCLING
The towpath is in good condition throughout the length of this canal. Ambitious walkers will want to walk to the top of Mow Cop, which is best accessed from bridge 85. From the top you can follow a section of The Gritstone Trail north towards the Old Man of Mow, a 65ft-tall gritstone pillar left as the rock around it was quarried away. Just before a radio mast turn downhill as waymarked to pass through Roe Park Woods, then bear right to reach the lane leading to Ackers railway crossing and the canal. The Staffordshire Way leaves Mow Cop to head towards Kinver, on the Staffordshire & Worcestershire Canal.

Pubs and Restaurants

Blue Bell Canalside, at Hardings Wood
Junction, Kidsgrove ST7 1EG (01782 774052;
www.bluebellkidsgrove.co.uk). Friendly, quiet,
one-bar local which has no juke box, pool table or
gaming machines, but there are four separate
drinking areas. Winner of many CAMRA awards, it
serves real ale, plus a range of specialist bottled
beers, including many from Belgium, plus real
cider and perry. Note the trapdoor in the lounge
ceiling. Snacks are available *at weekends*. Dogs
welcome. Well-behaved children welcome *until
21.00. Open Tue-Fri 19.30-23.00, Sat 13.00-16.00
and 19.00-23.00, Sun 12.00-22.30.* Occasional
entertainment. *Closed Mon.*

Canal Tavern Hardingswood Road, Kidsgrove
ST7 1EF (01782 775382). Canalside by bridge 133.
Food is served *L and E*, and there is a large garden.
Children are welcome *until 19.30.* Karaoke at
weekends.

✕ Red Bull Hotel Congleton Road South,
Church Lawton, Stoke-on-Trent ST7 3AJ (01782
782600). By lock 43 on the Trent & Mersey. A
popular pub, close to Hardings Wood Junction,
serving real ale and bar meals *L and E*, along with
good wine. Children welcome. Canalside seating
area. Quiz nights *Tue.*

Bleeding Wolf Hotel 121 Congleton Road
North, Scholar Green, Stoke-on-Trent ST7 3BQ
(01782 782272). Near bridge 94. A large and lively
thatched country pub with a conservatory,
offering real ale and food (including a carvery) *L
and E (not Mon E).* Children welcome in the
lounge. Large garden and children's play area.
PO, tel, garage and stores nearby.

Travellers Rest 175 Congleton Road North,
Scholar Green, Stoke-on-Trent ST7 3HA (01782
782359). Traditional country pub serving real ale,
together with food *L and E, daily.* Children
welcome and there is outside seating.

Rising Sun Station Road, Scholar Green,
Stoke-on-Trent ST7 3JT (01782 776235). Near the
canal. A friendly and welcoming pub offering real
ale, and excellent home-cooked food, including
steak and ale pie, curry and chilli dishes, *L and E
(not Mon L).* Children welcome. Patio.

Congleton

The canal continues north east, crossing Watery Lane Aqueduct. To the east the ever-present range of hills is a reminder that the Pennine Chain lies just beyond. Passing a golf course, the embanked wharf which overlooks Congleton soon appears, with an aqueduct over the road that runs down into the town. The handsome warehouse at the wharf has now been converted into apartments. There is a useful parade of *shops* a short distance south east (uphill) of bridge 75. Beautifully elegant 'roving' bridges, 76 and 77, follow. These are known locally as 'snake bridges' and, in the days of horse-drawn boats, changed the towpath from one side to the other without having to un-hitch the horse. Past Congleton railway station, the canal is carried on a high embankment – a common feature of the Macclesfield – across a narrow valley, affording a good view westward of the tall and elegant railway viaduct crossing the same valley. Meanwhile the looming fell known as the Cloud, over 1000ft high and topped with remains of ancient earthworks, is given a wide berth as the navigation continues on its lonely lock-free course through this very fine landscape. There is a good walk to the top of the Cloud along footpaths east of bridge 71. The canal then continues its lonely course, turning east to cross the River Dane on an embankment – not very impressive from the boat, but superb when viewed from the river – and arrives at the foot of Bosley Locks, in a really delightful setting which is semi-wooded and semi-pastoral. There are good, quiet moorings here.

WALKING & CYCLING

'Crossroads around Congleton' is a 20-mile cycle ride suitable for family cyclists – details from www.cheshire.gov.uk/countryside/cycling, or telephone 01270 764773 – which will take you past Marton Church, the oldest half-timbered church in Europe still in use, and Cheshire's oldest oak tree, estimated to be 600 years old. You can also walk from Congleton to Astbury Mere Country Park, where there is a network of paths all worthy of exploration. Call in at the visitor centre, telephone 01260 297237 or email astbury@cheshire.gov.uk

Astbury
Ches. Tel, stores. About 1 mile north west of bridges 79 and 80. A pretty village set just off the A34. St Mary's Church is amazing: its light interior and wide aisles are complemented by generous battlements along the roof and a tower standing quite separate from the body of the church.
Astbury Meadow Garden Centre Newcastle Road, Astbury, Congleton CW12 4RL (01260 276466; www.klondyke.co.uk). Just along the main road from the village . Lots of plants, and nice tearooms. Open Apr-Oct and Dec, Mon-Sat 09.00-18.00; Nov, Jan-Mar, Mon-Sat 09.00-17.00; also Sun all year 10.00-17.00.

Congleton
Ches. All services. A compact and busy market town.
Tourist Information Centre Town Hall, High Street, Congleton CW12 1BN (01260 271095; www.congleton.gov.uk). Open Apr-Sep Mon-Sat 09.00-17.00, Oct-Mar Mon-Fri 09.00-17.00, Sat 09.00-13.00. Closed Sun.

Bosley Locks
Effectively the only locks on all the 27 miles of the Macclesfield Canal, these handsome constructions are deep, raising the canal level by fully 118ft to well over 500ft above sea level. Each lock has a pair of mitred top gates instead of the more usual single one, and are a good example of Telford's practice of grouping locks together in flights; here there are 12 within just one mile.

Pubs and Restaurants

Egerton Arms Astbury CW12 4RQ (01260 273946; www.egertonarms.com). A handsome and justly popular village pub built c.1560 opposite the 11th-C church, serving real ale. Home-cooked food is available in both the bar and restaurant L and E, daily. Children, with well-behaved parents, are welcome until 21.00, and there is a large garden with a play area. B & B.

Wharf Inn 121 Canal Road, Congleton CW12 3AP (01260 272809). Near Congleton Wharf. Real ale in a very pleasant red-brick locals pub, decorated with flowers in the summer. Food L and E, daily. Children are welcome, and there is a children's playground in the garden. Large-screen TV.

Moss Inn 140 Canal Road, Congleton CW12 3AT (01260 273583). South of Congleton Wharf. A warm and friendly family-run pub, serving real ale. Food is served L and E, daily. Large safe garden with a children's play area.

Queen's Head Hotel Park Lane, Congleton CW12 3DE (01260 272546; www.queensheadhotel.org.uk). Canalside at bridge 75. A traditional and friendly pub offering a good choice of real ale, often from local breweries, along with food L and E daily. Large garden with play equipment. Children welcome until 21.00. Dogs welcome, Pub games and occasional entertainment. Moorings. B & B. Grocers and off-licence close by.

Railway Station Hotel Biddulph Road; Congleton CW12 3JS (01260 272567). Near Congleton station, by bridge 75. A large family pub offering food L and E daily. Seats overlooking a bowling green. Quiz Mon.

Church House Inn Church Lane, Sutton Lane Ends SK11 0DS (01260 252436). Traditional local's pub. Real ales. Homemade meals served L and E, daily (all day Sat and Sun). Children welcome and there is a beer garden. Curry night Wed.

Robin Hood Buxton Road, Buglawton, Congleton CW12 3PE (01260 273616; www.robinhood-pub.co.uk). South west of bridge 61. A choice of real ale is served in this very friendly and comfortable country pub. Dating from 1787, it was once the Buglawton Court Room and is noted for its ghost sightings. The shelves are liberally sprinkled with local guide books and leaflets. The pub has recently had an extension added which is now the setting for the Court-house Restaurant. Meals, which include Thai curries and home-made soup, are served L and E (not Mon L), and all day at weekends. Large, secure garden.

147

Oakgrove

The Macclesfield Canal completes the climb of Bosley Locks and resumes its lonely journey through open, attractive countryside. The facilities block beside Bridge 54 includes a *shower, toilets and a laundry*. Approaching Oakgrove the foothills and mountains of the Pennines, some over 1200ft high, spill right down to the canal. The swing bridge at Oakgrove was once a notorious obstacle on the canal, often requiring two very strong individuals to prise it open. Thankfully those days have long passed. The navigation now follows the contour of the land as it begins to swing around the hills, passing the large flat expanse of Danes Moss and approaching Macclesfield, now clearly visible to the north. If you choose to moor by Gurnett Aqueduct to visit the pubs nearby, take a look at the plaque on a cottage wall 25yds to the east. It commemorates the training here of James Brindley, the canal builder and civil engineer, between 1733–40 – he was apprenticed to Abraham Bennett. Just beyond the aqueduct, bridge 43 is a superb example of a typical 'snake bridge'.

- **Sutton Lane Ends**
  Ches. Tel stores. This village was the home of Charles Tunnicliffe, 1901–79, the bird artist.
- **Oakgrove** A delightful spot with a pub and a superb backcloth of tall, green hills which are ideal for energetic walks. The lane west of the bridge leads to Gawsworth. Sutton Reservoir is just north.
- **Gawsworth**
  Ches. PO. 2 miles west of Oakgrove. A refreshingly unspoilt village with several small lakes and a lovely 13th-C church, approached by a long avenue of elm trees. Facing the church is the old rectory, a half-timbered house built by Rector Baguley in 1470.
  Gawsworth Hall Church Lane, Gawsworth, Macclesfield SK11 9RN (01260 223456; www.gawsworthhall.com). Close to the church, this is a beautiful black and white manor house, parts of which date from Norman times. It was once the home of Mary Fitton, possibly the Dark Lady of Shakespeare's sonnets. The park encloses a medieval jousting ground, and there is a *summer*

season of open-air theatre. *Open May–mid Jun and Sep, Sun–Wed 14.00–17.00; and mid Jun–Aug daily, 14.00–17.00.* Charge. Fine tea room, selling excellent cake.
  Maggoty's Wood In this pleasant wood just outside the village is the grave of the eccentric fiddler and playwright, Maggoty Johnson. After being totally rejected by London critics he returned to Gawsworth where he died in 1773, having ordered that he should be buried far from the vulgar gentry who did not appreciate his genius.
- **Sutton Reservoir**
  Close to the canal north of bridge 49, this reservoir holds up to 94 million gallons of water. The public are welcome to ramble and picnic here.
  AMF Bowling Brindley Way, Lyme Green Business Park, Macclesfield SK11 0TB (08456 581273; www.amfbowling.co.uk). By bridge 45. Maybe you, or your children, would enjoy some 10-pin bowling. *Open daily 10.00– 24.00.* Charge for bowling only. Fully licensed bar and *food* with pizzas and burgers *all day*, diner *open 11.00–16.00.* Parties welcome.

Pubs and Restaurants

Fools Nook Leek Road, Sutton SK11 0JF (01260 252254). Just east of bridge 49. An inviting old country pub, where wooden beams and comfy settles immediately make you feel at home. Real ale and traditional home-cooked food *L* and *E*, from an extensive menu. Very pleasant courtyard at the rear. Children welcome.

Church House Church Lane, Sutton Lane Ends SK11 0DS (01260 252436). Well worth the ½ mile walk from Gurnett Aqueduct to enjoy this friendly and comfortable village local serving real ale, and

good food *L and E, and all day Sat, Sun.* Children welcome away from the bar, and there is a patio with children's playthings.

Old Kings Head Byrons Lane, Gurnett SK11 0HD (01625 423890). Below the aqueduct. A coaching house and smithy dating from 1695, which was visited by Bonnie Prince Charlie. This comfortable beamy pub serves real ales, and meals in a separate dining area *L and E and all day Sun.* Children welcome. Outside seating.

MACCLESFIELD 151

43 Foden Bank Bridge

Gurnett Aqueduct

GURNETT

44 Leek Old Road Bridge

45 Leek New Road Bridge

LYME GREEN

SUTTON LANE ENDS

46 Danes Moss Bridge

47 Broadhurst Swing Bridge

Danes Moss Landfill Site

Danes Moss

48A Footbridge

OAKGROVE

49 Royal Oak Swing Bridge

50 Mottersheads Bridge

51 Cowley Farm Bridge

52 Crow Holt Bridge

16m 0L
Marple
Junction

Hardings
Wood
11¾m 13L

53 Locketts Bridge

54 Daintrys Road Bridge

54 Daintrys Road Bridge

Bosley Locks 118'0"

147

55 Peckerpool Wood

NAVIGATIONAL NOTES

Royal Oak Swing Bridge is hydraulically operated. You will need a British Waterways key to open it: just follow the instructions on the control box.

Macclesfield

Leaving green and hilly countryside, the navigation enters the outskirts of Macclesfield, where some new housing incorporates a canal crane. A very wide stretch of water is overlooked by a vast and beautifully restored flour mill converted into up-market apartments, marking the site of the original Macclesfield Canal Company. This, the Hovis Mill, was built in the 1820s, and was the birthplace of the famous flour. The word Hovis is derived from the Latin 'hominisunvis' meaning 'power to the man'. Note the archway entrance off the canal, now blocked. The town itself is down the hill; the best place to moor is south of bridge 37, which is also handy for *shops* and *bottled gas*. The tree-lined canal continues northwards to Bollington, passing through glorious open countryside with views of the hills all around, to the Adelphi Mill, once a silk mill and now converted into offices. A 6oft-high embankment and two aqueducts then carry the navigation across the valley towards the huge Clarence Mill, a textile mill now converted into thriving small manufacturing units. High on a hilltop to the south east of the town (directly east of Greens Bridge) is the White Nancy monument, recently renovated. This was erected by the Gaskell family in the 19th C at the northern end of the Kerridge Ridge, probably to commemorate the Battle of Waterloo, and was used by his family as a summerhouse.

Pubs and Restaurants

Dolphin Inn 76 Windmill Street, Macclesfield SK11 7HS (01625 616179). West of bridge 40. A choice of real ale in a friendly local with an open fire. Home-cooked food *L daily (not Sun)*. There are plenty of traditional pub games to play here, and a children's play area in the park opposite. Quiz *Tue. PO box and telephone* nearby.

Navigation Black Road, Macclesfield SK11 7LF (01625 422777). South west of bridge 38. A Victorian local built for the original canal navvies. Real ale, and digital TV. Children welcome. Outside seating.

Puss in Boots 198 Buxton Road, Macclesfield SK10 1NF (01625 423261). Canalside at bridge 37. A comfortable pub with an open fire *in winter*, and serving real ale and food *L and E (Sun 12.30– 18.00)*. Children welcome, garden.

Britannia 260 Hurdsfield Road, Macclesfield SK10 2PN (01625 423954). West of bridge 34. Unspoilt and attractive terraced pub serving real ale. Children welcome. Pub games. *PO, tel, stores and Chinese takeaway* close-by.

Three Crowns 38 Rainow Road, Higher Hurdsfield SK10 2PF (01625 260488). East of bridge 34. A tiny Victorian stone terraced pub with a garden. Real ale.

Dog & Partridge 97 Palmerston Street, Bollington SK10 5JX (01625 572177). West of Bollington Aqueduct and bridge 27. A sociable village pub with an open fire. Real ale. There is a bridewell (prison), built in 1831, at the rear. Garden. Folk music on *Fri*. Children welcome.

Holly Bush 75 Palmerston Street, Bollington SK10 5PW (01625 573073). A traditional 1930s 'brewer's tudor' pub, with an original interior. Real ale, and food *L and E*. Outdoor drinking area.

The Plaice 48 Palmerston Street Bollington SK10 5PX (01625 574333). Originally two cottages, and formerly the Meridian Inn. Now a licensed fish restaurant with fish and chip takeaway. *Open Tue–Sat*.

WALKING & CYCLING
The White Nancy Monument can be reached by walking south from Kerridge Bridge (27) and following the path. Once at the top you will find it an excellent spot for a picnic, and you can walk along the Saddle of Kerridge, enjoying extensive views. The Redway Tavern nearby is handy for a meal and a pint.

BOAT TRIPS
White Nancy **Cruising
Restaurant** A 12-seater
restaurant boat operating
from Bollington Wharf,
Grimshaw Lane, Bollington
SK10 9DR. Book well in
advance on 01625 573100;
www.white-nancy.co.uk.

155

26 Sugar Lane
Bridge

Clarence Mill

26A

Bollington
Aqueduct

27 Kerridge
Bridge

Grimshaw Lane
Aqueduct

BOLLINGTON

Adelphi Mill

28 Greens Bridge

Kerridge

29 Clarke Lane
Bridge

30 Woods Bridge

33 Higherfold Bridge

34 Chapel-en-le-Frith
Bridge

35 Barrack Road
Bridge

Hurdsfield

Smyths Bridge 36
Buxton Road
Wharf

37 Buxton Road Bridge

Hovis Mill

38 Black Road Bridge

Swettenham Wharf
BW Yard

39 Hollands Bridge

40 Leadbeaters Bridge

41 Verdons Bridge

11m 0L
Marple
Junction

Hardings
Wood
16¾m   13L

MACCLESFIELD

149

Ⓑ **Macclesfield Canal Centre** Swettenham Wharf, Brook Street, Macclesfield SK11 7AW (01625 420042; www.maccmarina.com). 🛈 D Pump out, gas, narrowboat hire, day-hire craft, overnight mooring, long-term mooring, winter storage, slipway, boat and engine sales and repairs, toilets, books and maps, solid fuel.

Ⓑ **Peak Forest Cruisers** The Wharf, Buxton Road, Macclesfield SK11 1LZ (01625 424172). Narrowboat hire (two boats available for week or weekend hire),

long-term mooring. *Nearby* 🛈 either side of bridge 37.

Ⓑ **Bollington Wharf** Grimshaw Lane, Bollington SK10 5JB (01625 575811). 🛈 🛈 🛈 D Pump out, gas, overnight and long-term mooring, winter storage, boat building, boat sales.

Ⓑ **Kerridge Dry Dock** The Barn, Oaklands Farm, Kerridge SK10 5AP (01625 574287). Between bridges 28 and 29. Long-term mooring, winter storage, dry dock, boat repairs.

● **Macclesfield**
Ches. All services. Earliest records of a settlement are to be found in the Domesday Book, when the area was detailed as part of the land of Earl Edwin of Mercia. The town grew rapidly until it became the most important town in east Cheshire, being recognised as a borough in 1220. At that time it was the administrative centre for the Macclesfield Forest, and was granted its charter in 1261. Following set-backs resulting from the Battle of Flodden Field in 1513, the town was granted a new charter in 1595, and this was replaced by yet another, granted by Charles II, in 1684. Now the town is an interesting combination of modern industry and old market town, with cobbled streets and a picturesque medieval Market Place, encircled by busy modern roads. There are several fine classical buildings, making the most of the local stone, and detailed in the fine Town Trail leaflet available at the Tourist Information Centre. In the 18th C the town was one of the leading silk producing centres, but now there are only two small manufacturers left. One interesting feature of the town is the Unitarian Chapel in King Edward Street, approached through a narrow passage and guarded by a lovely wrought-iron gate: it is dated 1689 and is 'for William and Mary's subjects dissenting from the Church of England'.

St Michael's Church Market Place, Macclesfield SK10 1HW (01625 421984; www.stmichaels-macclesfield.com). Very little remains of the original structure founded in 1278 by Queen Eleanor and then known as All Hallows, although the Savage Chapel, the oldest stone building in the town, survives. The church still contains many fine monuments.

Silk Industry Museum & Paradise Mill Park Lane, Macclesfield SK11 6TJ (01625 612045; www.macclesfield.silk.museum). Built 1820-60, this handloom silk-weaving mill finally closed down in 1981. Here you can see Jacquard handlooms in action, authentic room settings and an exhibition of a whole wealth of material connected with one of

Macclesfield's major industries. *Open Apr-Oct, Tue-Sun, 13.00-17.00; Nov-Mar, Tue-Sat, 13.00-16.00.* Charge.

Silk Museum Heritage Centre Galleries Roe Street, Macclesfield SK11 6UT (01625 613210; www.macclesfield.silk.museum). The first museum in the country devoted entirely to the study of the silk industry: audio-visuals, costume, textiles, room settings and even parachutes. Visit also the Heritage Centre in the old 1813 Sunday School building. *Open Mon-Sat and B Hols 11.00-17.00, Sun 13.00-17.00.* Charge. Tearoom and shop.

West Park Museum Prestbury Road, Macclesfield SK10 3BJ (01625 619831; www.macclesfield.silk.museum). Opened in 1898, and situated in a park containing the largest bowling green in Europe, the collections include fine and decorative art, local history and Egyptian antiquities, plus a section devoted to Charles Tunnicliffe (1901-79), the famous bird artist. *Open Easter-Oct, Tue-Sun and B Hols, 13.30-16.30 (closed Mon, G Fri, and at 16.00 in winter).* Free.

Macclesfield Leisure Centre Priory Lane, Macclesfield SK10 4AF (01625 615602; www.macclesfield.gov.uk). Three swimming pools, six squash courts and a host of other facilities.

Tourist Information Centre Town Hall, Market Place, Macclesfield SK10 1DX (01625 504114; www.macclesfield.gov.uk). Extremely helpful. *Open Mon-Thu 08.45-17.00 (Fri 16.30), Sat 08.45-13.00. Closed Sun.*

● **Bollington**
Ches. PO, tel, stores, garage, bank. There is a good view of this stone-built town from the huge canal embankment which cuts across it. From here it is only 1 mile to the boundary of the Peak District National Park. The white tower on the ridge south of the town is called White Nancy.

Bollington Leisure Centre Heath Road, Bollington SK10 5EX (01625 574774; www.bollingtonleisure.co.uk). Squash courts, a swimming pool and other facilities.

WALKING & CYCLING

'Dave's Hikes' is a series of excellent walks around Macclesfield, and none are too long. You will find details at: www.communityonline.co.uk/daveshikes.asp. The Middlewood Way (see also www.macclesfield.gov.uk) is a level 10-mile footpath and cycleway (part of Route 55 of the National Cycle Network) along the course of the old Macclesfield, Bollington and Marple Railway. It runs between Macclesfield and Marple. For much of its length it closely follows the Macclesfield Canal and there are several options for circular walks. The railway was opened for passenger traffic in 1869, just 38 years after the Macclesfield Canal was completed, and for goods on 1 March 1870. Cotton, silk, coal and passengers were carried, but the railway always struggled to make a profit. It was finally closed in January 1970 and converted for recreational use in 1985. Dr David Bellamy performed the opening ceremony and then, having proclaimed it 'tewiffic', removed his socks and shoes and waded into a nearby pond.

BIRD LIFE

The *Great Tit* is a common woodland and garden species, appreciably larger than the blue tit alongside which it is often seen at bird feeders. The great tit has bold black and white markings on its head and a black bib forming a line running down its chest, broader in the male than the female. The underparts are otherwise yellow and upperparts mainly greenish. Juveniles have sombre plumage with no white on the head. Their song is extremely variable but a striking 'teecha teecha teecha' is rendered by most males. In summer the birds feed mainly on insects.

A snake bridge at Congleton (see page 146)

Higher Poynton

This isolated stretch is typical of the Macclesfield Canal and in its beautifully quiet, rural isolation it represents much of the charm that most canals possess. Winding northwards along the summit level at over 500ft above the sea, the navigation generally follows the contours of this upland country, but crosses several valleys on embankments with fine aqueducts. There is a pleasant *picnic area* south of Hag Footbridge (16), good *moorings* by the Miners Arms, bridge 18, and between bridges 20 and 19, and a fine shady, wooded section between bridges 22 and 21. There are few centres of population near the canal, just the odd pub here or there, and the countryside is quite unspoilt. Around Higher Poynton the canal becomes wider, the result of ancient subsidence from a coal mine, which necessitated the continual raising of the canal banks and bridges to hold the water in the sinking canal. Be sure to adhere to the main channel here. An old branch near bridge 15 used to lead to the mine; now it is used by a boatyard.

● **Higher Poynton**
Ches. Tel, stores, garage. Considered by some to be the most pleasant moorings on the canal, where the wide water supports large families of ducks, geese and swans. There is a recreation field adjacent, and a handy pub.
Anson Museum Anson Road, Poynton SK12 1TD (01625 874426; www.enginemuseum.org). A working display of early internal-combustion engines, with emphasis on those made in the Manchester area. Tearoom. *Open Apr–Oct, Fri–Sun, 10.00–17.00.*
Lyme Park Disley, Stockport SK12 2NR (01663 766492; www.nationaltrust.org.uk). NT. Two miles east of Higher Poynton. Pedestrian entrance at West Parkgate, ¼ mile south east of bridge 17 or footpath from bridge 15. In the centre of a 1400-acre park containing deer is this magnificent Italianate palace which was transformed from a Tudor house by the Venetian architect Leoni. Some of the original Elizabethan interiors can still be seen. There are Mortlake tapestries, a large collection of English clocks, Grinling Gibbons wood carvings, countless works of art, and four Chippendale chairs claimed to be covered with material from a cloak worn by King Charles I at his execution. The Victorian garden has a sunken parterre, an Edwardian rose garden, a reflection lake, a ravine garden, a Wyatt conservatory and an 18th-C hunting tower. The house featured in a BBC adaptation of *Pride and Prejudice* as 'Pemberley'. Children's playground. Refreshments available. *Open end Mar–Oct, Fri–Tue 13.00–17.00 (closed Wed–Thu); park open Apr–Oct, daily 08.00–20.30 and Nov–Mar, daily 08.00–18.00; garden open Mar and Nov–Feb, Sat and Sun, 12.00–15.00; and Apr–Oct, daily 11.00–17.00.* Charge. Restaurant, shops.

Pubs and Restaurants

◗ ✕ **Windmill Inn** Holehouse Lane, Whiteley Green SK10 5SJ (01625 574222; www.thewindmill.info). 250yds west of bridge 25. Dating from the 15th C, when it was recorded as a farm house, it became a pub in 1674. Real ale is served, along with food which is available *L and E*. Children are welcome away from the bar, and there is a garden. Regular special events. There is an useful post box in the wall. Handy for the Middlewood Way path.
◗ **Miners Arms** Wood Lane North, Four Lane Ends, Adlington SK10 4PF (01625 872731). Near bridge 18. A big, bustling, lively and thriving country pub which is pleasantly family orientated, having extensive gardens and amusements for children. Real ale is served, along with a good choice of food and a children's menu *all day, every day*. Quiz *Sun*.
✕ ⌾ **Lyme View Café** Wood Lane East, Adlington SK10 4PH (01625 850985). You will receive a warm, friendly and relaxed welcome here for coffee, tea and meals. The food is predominantly home-made, tasty and wholesome. Also cycle hire. *Open Tue–Sun and B Hols 09.30–18.00.*
◗ **Boar's Head** Shrigley Road North, Higher Poynton SK12 1TE (01625 876676). Down the hill from bridge 15. An imposing red-brick pub with a short menu of good pub food *L and E*. Real ale is served. Children are welcome, and there is a garden with a children's play area. Moorings.

WALKING & CYCLING
The Gritstone Trail passes through Lyme Park and continues up onto the moors, passing White Nancy (*see* page 150). The Middlewood Way (*see* page 153) continues to the west of the canal. Details of some interesting walks around Higher Poynton and the canal can be found at www.simonholtmarketing.com/PDFs/Green%20Walks%202.pdf

Boatyards

Ⓑ **Lyme View Marina** Adlington Basin, Adlington SK10 4PH (01625 858176). D Pump out, gas, day-boat hire, long-term mooring, slipway, solid fuel.

Ⓑ **Braidbar Boats** Lyme Road, Higher Poynton, Stockport SK12 1TH (01625 873471; www.braidbarboats.co.uk). Near bridge 15. Narrowboat hire, boat building, boat sales and repairs, engine repairs, boat building, wet dock.

Ⓑ **The Trading Post** Lyme Road, Higher Poynton, Stockport SK12 1TH (01625 872277; www.canaltradingpost.com). Near bridge 15. ♿ ♿ D Pump out, gas, day-boat hire, chandlery, books and maps, gifts, café, solid fuel.

Ⓑ **Classic Maritime Diesels** Lyme Road, Higher Poynton, Stockport SK12 1TH (07712 052635). Near bridge 15. Specialists in diesels. Major overhauls and rebuilds, parts made.

BOAT TRIPS

Mary Sunley A 12-berth craft, suitable for those with special needs, available for charter from Lyme View Marina, Adlington SK10 4PH. Telephone 01625 428301, *Mon-Fri 10.00-14.00*, for details.

Maldwyn This is a licensed 42-seater boat, based just south of bridge 15, which does *one-hour trips regularly each Sat during the summer between 11.00-16.00*, and is available for charter *all the year round*. Telephone 07741 092705 for details.

155

Marple Junction

Another massive embankment and a tall aqueduct, this time over a railway, are crossed on the way into High Lane. The canal proceeds northwards in a cutting through High Lane, passing the junction with the short High Lane Arm – well protected and now used as a club mooring site – and a children's play park. There are *moorings* between the arm and bridge 11, with *shops* close by. Beyond the town is a restored mill; then open country intervenes, offering views westward of Stockport and the southern outskirts of Manchester. There is a useful *shop*, the Doodfield Stores, down the hill from bridge 6. At bridge 3 there are *two grocers and a fish & chip shop*. Goyt Mill appears, thankfully restored and now housing workshops, heralding the start of Marple, a busy boating centre much enjoyed by the citizens of Manchester. The area of the junction with the Peak Forest Canal is delightful: an old turnover bridge, mellow wharf buildings and the nearby flight of Marple Locks are framed by the distant mountainous country across the Goyt Valley. The canal here is 500ft above sea level.

Boatyards

(B) **British Waterways Marple Yard** Marple Junction, on the Macclesfield Canal (0161 427 1079).
🗑 🚽 ⚓ Overnight mooring.

● **High Lane**
Gt Manchester. PO, tel, stores, garage, station, fish & chips. More of a spread than a village, but there are good moorings and it is useful for supplies. High Lane is effectively at the south east corner of the Manchester conurbation, and is quite indistinguishable from its neighbours. The very long Disley Railway Tunnel passes deep underneath.
● **Marple**
Gt Manchester. All services. A typical residential town, serving as a dormitory base for Stockport and Manchester. Elements of the old village can still be seen, buried amongst the suburbia, but much the most attractive part is by the canal. The rugged Ludworth Moor is not far away, where 'Robin Hood's Picking Rods' still stand, the supposed remains of a Celtic Druid's temple.
● **Marple Locks**
The 16 locks at Marple were not built until 1804,

four years after the rest of the Peak Forest canal was opened. The 1-mile gap thus left was bridged by a tramway, while the Canal Company sought the cash to pay for the construction of a flight of locks. This was obviously a most unsatisfactory state of affairs, since limestone from Doveholes had to be shifted from wagon to boat at Buxworth Basin, from boat to wagon at Marple Junction, and back into boat again at the bottom of the tramway. Not surprisingly, a container system was developed – using iron boxes with a 2-ton payload – to ease the triple transhipment. However, this was no long-term solution, and when the necessary £27,000 was forthcoming the company authorised construction of the flight of locks. Today they stand comparison with any flight on the network. Note especially Samuel Oldknow's superb warehouse by lock 9, opposite the lock keeper's house, now tastefully converted to offices.

Pubs and Restaurants

🍺 **Bull's Head** Buxton Road, High Lane SK6 8BH (01663 762070) At bridge 11. A lovely comfy, cosy, friendly, locals' pub with an open fire, settles and bookshelves. Real ale and excellent food *L Fri-Sun*. Children welcome, canalside terrace.

🍺 ✕ **Ring O'Bells** 130 Church Lane, Marple SK6 7AY (0161 427 2300; www.ring-o-bells.com). By bridge 2. An award-winning, comfortable and friendly traditional pub serving real ale and good freshly prepared bar and à la carte meals *L, and E (not Mon-Wed or Sun)*. Children welcome. Garden and canalside patio. Charity quiz night *Wed*.

WALKING & CYCLING

There are excellent walks in the Marple area, where stunning scenery combines with the often unexpected remains of early industry. Gordon Mills has written an excellent series of six inexpensive guides for the local community council which take you on some of the finest walks this area has to offer: Marple Dale; The Roman Bridge & Lakes; Marple Locks & Brabyns Park; Chadkirk; From Way to Cut and Donkey Wood. No walk is longer than 4 miles, and each is fully described, with maps and old photographs. You can obtain them from Marple Library or local bookshops, and find details at www.marple-uk.com/Guides.htm. Mr Mills is quite happy for you to download the walks, in exchange for a donation to the British Heart Foundation.

Boating at Macclesfield (see page 152)

KEEPING THINGS ON THE LEVEL

The Macclesfield Canal adheres to a mainly level course, with all the locks (aside from the stop lock at Hall Green) in a single group at Bosley. Had the visionary scheme proposed by J. F Pownall, in his work *The Projected Grand Contour Canal to Connect with Estuaries and Canals in England* (1942), come to fruition, the Macclesfield would have formed a part of his grand plan:

'Through the heart of England there runs a *natural canal line*, as I shall term it. This is a line so naturally favourable for canal construction that a canal can follow it easily for miles at a time whilst remaining throughout at the same level. The old canal surveyors saw this line. . . A canal following this contour would therefore proceed right through the country solely on one level. . . it (also) proceeds in direct reaches for long-distances at a time. . . The natural canal line creates the remarkable possibility, never before known, of having a canal go through the length of the country and serve the great industrial areas without any variation from one level.

(There) are very great advantages. The Grand Contour Canal (would be) uniformly level at 310ft above sea level to serve London, Bristol, Southampton, Birmingham, Manchester, Leeds and Newcastle. All the existing canals would be branches from it. The waterway would be large enough to accommodate coastal vessels of a fair size. The Grand Contour Canal would become the primary water distributor of the country. Along the canal there will be formed a special layer in the bed. . . in this layer pipelines for the transport of commercial liquids and gases would be embedded.

Precisely because it expresses a natural feature, the Contour Canal will lie unobtrusively on the land and will have a characteristic scenery of its own.' *Precisely.*

PEAK FOREST AND ASHTON CANALS

MAXIMUM DIMENSIONS	MILEAGE
Length: 70'	**PEAK FOREST CANAL**
Beam: 7'	*WHALEY BRIDGE to:*
Headroom: 6'	Marple Junction: 6½ miles
	Dukinfield Junction: 14½ miles
MANAGER	Locks: 16
01942 405700;	
enquiries.northwest@	**ASHTON CANAL**
britishwaterways.co.uk	*DUCKINFIELD JUNCTION to:*
	Ducie Street Junction: 6½ miles
	Locks: 18

THE PEAK FOREST CANAL

This canal runs from Whaley Bridge and Buxworth through Marple to the Ashton Canal at Dukinfield Junction. Authorised by Act of Parliament in 1794, it was aimed at providing an outlet for the great limestone deposits at Doveholes, south east of Whaley Bridge. However, since Doveholes is over 1000ft above sea level, the canal was terminated at Buxworth (Bugsworth as it was then known), and the line was continued up to the quarries by a 6½-mile tramway. The canal was completed by 1800 except for the flight of locks at Marple, which were not built until 1804. A second, temporary, tramway bridged this gap in the meantime. Bugsworth soon became a busy interchange point where the wagons bringing the stone down from Doveholes tipped their load either into canal boats or into lime-kilns. This traffic, and the boats bringing coal *up* the canal for firing the kilns, accounted for the greatest proportion of the canal company's revenue.

The Peak Forest was also boosted by the opening of the Macclesfield Canal to Marple top lock in 1831, making it part of a new through route from Manchester to the Potteries. The Cromford & High Peak Railway was opened in 1831, joining up Whaley Bridge with the Cromford Canal on the far side of the Peak District.

By the early 1840s the Peak Forest Canal was suffering from competition from the Trent & Mersey Canal Company and two new railways. It was leased in perpetuity to the Sheffield, Ashton-under-Lyne & Manchester Railway, later the Great Central. In 1922 the Bugsworth traffic finished, while (through) traffic on the 'lower' Peak Forest Canal had disappeared by World War II. Along with the Ashton, full navigation was restored in 1974 and now the splendid Buxworth line is also open.

THE ASHTON CANAL

Authorised in 1792 and opened shortly afterwards, the Ashton was a strong rival of the Rochdale Canal – with which it connects in Manchester. The two canals were constructed simultaneously, partly to tap the big coal-producing area around Oldham. The Ashton also opened a new trade route from Manchester to the textile mills of Ashton, while the Rochdale served as a broad canal link over the Pennines between the Mersey and the rivers of Yorkshire. In 1831 completion of the narrow Macclesfield Canal made the Ashton part of a through route from Manchester to the Potteries.

The 1830s saw the peak of the Ashton Canal's prosperity. The canal company sold out to the forerunner of the Great Central Railway Company in 1846, who continued to maintain and operate the canal. Traffic declined in the present century and by 1962 it was unnavigable. A determined effort by the Peak Forest Canal Society, the IWA, local councils and the BWB (as was) resulted in its reopening in 1974.

Upper Peak Forest

The former Whaley Bridge Branch, now the main line of the Peak Forest Canal, terminates in a small basin at the north end of the town. There is a building here of great interest to industrial archaeologists: it covers a dock and was built in 1832 at this, the junction of the Peak Forest Canal and the Cromford & High Peak Railway. Here transshipment between canal boat and railway wagon could take place under cover. The former railway's Whaley Bridge inclined plane (now a footpath) rises to the south of this historic building. South of bridge 34 the canal splits: the original main line turns east across the Goyt on an aqueduct to Buxworth (its name changed from the supposedly less desirable Bugsworth) with its fascinating basin complex overlooked by a fine pub. There is a handy *supermarket* which can be accessed from bridge 37A. The Peak Forest Canal leads off to the north west; and it rapidly becomes apparent that this is a navigation set in a robust, handsome landscape. Clinging desperately to a wooded hill-side overlooking the steep, wide Goyt Valley, it winds its precarious way to New Mills. The trains that traverse the opposite side of the valley look like tiny models on the distant hills. The A6 road and the railway are always close to the navigation, but they detract not at all from its isolation. There are charming stations at New Mills, Furness Vale and Whaley Bridge: from these one may take a magnificent railway trip past two canal-feeding reservoirs and over the hills to the summit, 1200ft above sea level, then down to the old Roman town of Buxton, now unfortunately the end of the line. The canal continues north west along the hill-side towards New Mills. It is an enchanting stretch, passing plenty of woods, pastures and grazing horses. As you approach New Mills you will notice the smell of sweets in the air – Matlows, the makers of 'Swizzles', have their factory here. Near Disley, another railway pops out of the long Disley Tunnel, way below the canal; while yet another line appears above and beside the canal, from High Lane. Thus around New Mills the valley contains three very picturesque railways. One of the pleasant features of this terrain is the easy co-existence of woods, fields and a canal on the one hand, and a certain amount of industry on the other. There are good moorings at bridge 24, where a public footpath gives easy access to Strines.

BOAT TRIPS
nb Judith Mary II Victoria Works, Woodside Street, New Mills, High Peak SK22 3HF (01663 734737; www.trafalgarmarineservices.co.uk). A long-established and fully equipped 70ft, 42-seater narrowboat available for private charter *all year*. Fully licensed. Also *Phoenix* a 40ft day boat, sailing from Whaley Bridge. As well as the two hire boats, Trafalgar Marine Services manufacture fenders, ropes and other accessories which are sold online.

NAVIGATIONAL NOTES

1 You will need an anti-vandal key for the locks and swing-bridges on the Ashton Canal. Bridge 1 on the Peak Forest also requires an anti-vandal key.
2 A BW key is required to operate bridge 30.
3 Bridges 22 and 24 are windlass operated.

WALKING & CYCLING

The towpath is in good condition throughout. Peter Roger's Guide gives details of some walks and bicycle rides from Whaley Bridge – details at users. breathemail.net/peter.rogers/whaley.htm. Details of local walks exploring Bugsworth (as was) Basin and the parish paths can be obtained from: PFCC, 41 Tatton Street, Knutsford, Cheshire, WA16 6AE or at users.iclway.co.uk/don.baines/maps& guides.htm. The Millennium Walkway, which starts by the Heritage Centre in New Mills (see page 162) gives access to previously inaccessible parts of the gorge near New Mills. You can also obtain a series of leaflets from the centre giving full details of The Torrs Industrial Trail, The Bridges Trail, The Sett Valley Trail and The Waterside Way. The Goyt Way, which has an interpretation board at the canal terminus, and the Mid-Shires Way (from Buckinghamshire!) both pass through here.

Boatyards

ⓑ **T W Marina**
Station Road, Furness Vale SK23 7QA (01663 745757; www. twmarine.co.uk). At bridge 31. Ⓓ Pump out, long term mooring, winter storage, boat sales, engine sales and repairs, chandlery, dry dock.

ⓑ **New Mills Marina**
Hibbert Street, New Mills SK22 3SS (01663 741310; www.newmillsmarina. co.uk). By bridge 28. Ⓓ Pump out, gas, boat hire, overnight and long term mooring, winter storage, slipway, boat and engine sales and repairs, boat building, chandlery, laundrette, toilets, showers. DIY facilities. *Emergency call out.* Public telephone nearby.

● **Whaley Bridge**

Derbs. PO, tel, stores, garage, station, laundrette, fish & chips, banks. Built on a steep hill at the end of the canal, with good views across the Goyt valley, this is now a quiet and pleasant place, a new bypass having removed much of the traffic. The beautiful nearby hills are, however, more noteworthy than the town.

Cromford & High Peak Railway In the early 1820s a physical connection was planned between the Peak Forest Canal at Whaley Bridge and the Cromford Canal, way over to the south east on the other side of the Peak District, using a junction canal. However a waterway would have been impracticable through such mountainous terrain, and so a railway was constructed. Known as the Cromford & High Peak Railway, it was opened throughout in 1831, and was 33 miles long. With a summit level over 1200ft above sea level, this extraordinary standard-gauge goods line was interesting chiefly for its numerous slopes and inclined planes, up which the wagons were hauled by either stationary or tenacious locomotive steam engines (the steepest gradient on the line was 1 in 7). The C & HPR closed in 1967; now much of the route has been turned into a public footpath and bridleway. Around Whaley Bridge one may still see the remains of the short inclined plane (now a footpath) which brought the goods down the hill, then through the town to the wharf at the terminus of the Peak Forest Canal.

Toddbrook Reservoir Just south of Whaley Bridge. A very pleasant area for picnicking and walking. Private sailing club; fishing rights on this BW reservoir are exercised by an angling club (day tickets available).

● **Buxworth**

Derbs. Tel, stores. The main feature in Buxworth is the fascinating old terminal basin system. This used to be a tremendously busy complex, and is of great interest to industrial archaeologists. The canal line to Bugsworth (as it was then known) was built to bring the canal as near as possible to the great limestone quarries at Doveholes, a plate tramway being constructed in 1799 via Chapel Milton to complete the connection. Known as the Peak Forest Tramway, this little line, 6½ miles long, brought the

stone down the hills to Bugsworth, where it was transshipped into waiting canal boats. Throughout the history of the line, the wagons on the tramway were drawn exclusively by horse-power – except for a 500yd inclined plane in Chapel-en-le-Frith, where the trucks were attached to a continuous rope so that the descending trucks pulled empty ones up the 1 in 7½ slope. The tramway was closed by 1926, and the sidings and basins at Buxworth became disused and overgrown, but are now fully restored and open to navigation. They should not be missed!

● **Furness Vale**

Derbs. PO, tel, stores, station. A main road (A6) village, useful for supplies.

● **New Mills**

Derbs. PO, tel, stores, garage, banks, laundrette, stations. A mostly stone-built town on the Cheshire/Derbyshire border; its industries include textile printing, engineering and engraving. A boatyard occupies old canal buildings to the east of bridge 28.

New Mills Heritage Centre Rock Mill Lane, New Mills, High Peak SK22 3BN (01663 746904, www. newmillsheritage.com). North of Thornsett Road Bridge (28). Located by the path leading down into the Torrs Gorge, next to the bus station. A splendid centre where you can see a display illustrating the history of the town, with a superb model. There is also a mock mine tunnel. Local books and walk details can be purchased in the shop, and there is also a café. The Millennium Walkway starts here. *Open Tue–Fri 11.00–16.00, Sat and Sun 10.30–16.30 (16.00 in winter).*

● **Disley**

Ches. PO, tel, stores, garage, station. On the south bank of the canal. The centre of the village is quite pretty, spoilt slightly by the A6 traffic. The village is up the hill, south west of bridge 26. The attractive church stands among trees above the little village square. It was greatly renovated in the last century, but the ancient tower with the griffin leering down at passers-by dates from the 16th C. Vehicular and pedestrian access to Lyme Park (*see page 154*) is from the A6 near Disley, 1½ miles south west of bridge 26.

● **Strines**

Gt Manchester. PO, tel, stores, station. A useful place for supplies.

Pubs and Restaurants

 Railway 33–35 Market Street, Whaley Bridge SK23 7AA (01663 732245). Real ale in a fine straightforward pub. Children welcome.

 Goyt Inn 8 Bridge Street, Whaley Bridge SK23 7LR (01663 732840). An attractive pub with an open fire and a garden, close to the canal basin and shops. Real ale is served along with food *L (E by request)*. Children are welcome, and there is a garden. Quiz *Wed*, karaoke *Thu*.

 Navigation 6 Johnson Street, Whaley Bridge SK23 7LU (01663 732308). Near the canal terminus, this small traditional pub has a narrowboat theme, with some original canal artwork. Have a look on the notice board for pictures of visitor's boats. Real ale and food *L (E by request)*. Children welcome *until 19.00*. Garden, and *weekend* entertainment and quizzes.

 ✕ **Navigation** Buxworth, High Peak SK23 7NE (01663 732072; www.navigationinn.co.uk). By the canal terminus, this is a superbly situated pub overlooking the old basins, beautifully decorated with some fine canal memorabilia, and with real fires *in winter*. It was built around 1794, and was once run by Pat Phoenix, *Coronation Street's* Elsie Tanner. A choice of real ale, along with restaurant and bar meals available *L and E, daily*. Garden with a playground. Children welcome *until 21.00*. Pool table and darts. Occasional live bands. B & B.

 ✕ **Dog & Partridge** Bridgemont, Whaley Bridge SK237PB (01663 732284). Near the junction to Buxworth Basin. A local pub, with open fires, serving a choice of real ales. Good food is served *L and E and all day Sat and Sun*. Children welcome away from the bar, and there is a garden. Regular entertainment.

 The Crossings Station Road, Furness Vale SK23 7QS (01663 743642). By the level crossing, up the hill from bridge 31. A friendly pub serving real ale. Children welcome, garden.

✕ ♀ **Imperial Palace** Buxton Road, Furness Vale SK23 7PH (01663 745777). Cantonese restaurant *open 17.30–late*.

 The Soldier Dick 150 Buxton Road, Furness Vale SK23 7PH (01663 743868). Traditional English pub serving real ales and bar meals *L and E, daily*. Children welcome away from the bar and there is outside seating. A leaflet available locally explains the name.

 ✕ **Beehive** Albion Road, New Mills SK22 3EY (01663 742087). Just along the lane opposite New Mills Wharf, by bridge 28. A welcoming stone-built pub. Usually there is a choice of real ale available, including some from small local breweries. Meals are served upstairs in the Indian restaurant *E only*. Children are welcome, and there is outside seating. Fish and chips opposite.

Beswick Locks (see page 168)

Marple Aqueduct

The canal, accompanied by the River Goyt beyond the road to the east, reaches Marple Junction, where the Macclesfield Canal leaves to the south west by the attractive buildings of Marple Yard. The 16 Marple Locks then carry the Peak Forest Canal down 214ft towards Manchester. The locks themselves, which are spaced out over 1 mile, have an unrivalled setting in an excellent combination of built-up area, parkland, tall trees and steep hillside; the River Goyt is now hidden down in the wooded valley to the east. Look out for the interesting Possett Bridge, where there is a small tunnel for the towpath (and horse) and an even smaller one for the boatman, leading down to the lock. At the foot of the locks, where the River Goyt is crossed, there is the superb spectacle of a major canal

WALKING & CYCLING

There are excellent walks in the Marple area, where stunning scenery combines with the often unexpected remains of early industry. Gordon Mills has a written an excellent series of six inexpensive guides for the local community council which take you on some of the finest walks this area has to offer: Marple Dale; The Roman Bridge & Lakes; Marple Locks & Brabyns Park; Chadkirk; From Way to Cut and Donkey Wood. No walk is longer than 4 miles, and each is fully described, with maps and old photographs. You can obtain them from Marple Library or local bookshops, and find details at: www.marple-uk.com/Guides.htm. Mr Mills is quite happy for you to download the walks, in exchange for a donation to the British Heart Foundation.

aqueduct with an even bigger railway viaduct alongside. West of here a narrow stretch was once Rose Hill Tunnel, long since opened out. The canal then traverses a wooded hillside before diving into Hyde Bank Tunnel, 308yds long. The towpath is diverted over the hill, passing a farm. On the other side, a couple of minor aqueducts lead the canal northwards, away from the Goyt Valley and past Romiley, Bredbury and Woodley, where there is a narrow 176yd-long tunnel, this time with the towpath continuing through it. There is a swimming pool close to the canal at bridge 14.

NAVIGATIONAL NOTES

1 There is no mooring on the Marple flight since water levels in the pounds can fall dramatically when the locks are in use.
2 Hyde Bank Tunnel, although appearing wide, does not have sufficient clearance for two boats to pass. Make sure it is clear before you enter.

● **Marple**
Gt Manchester. All services. Once a famous hat-making centre, the town is most interesting by the canal. The town centre can be accessed from bridge 18.

● **Marple Locks**
The 16 locks at Marple were not built until 1804, four years after the rest of the navigation was opened. The 1-mile gap thus left was bridged by a tramway, while the Canal Company sought the cash to pay for the construction of a flight of locks. This was obviously a most unsatisfactory state of affairs, since the limestone from Doveholes had to be shifted from wagon to boat at Bugsworth Basin, from boat to wagon at Marple Junction, and back into boat again at the bottom of the tramway. Not surprisingly, a container system was developed – using iron boxes with a 2-ton payload – to ease the triple transshipment. However, this was no long-term solution, and when the necessary £27,000 was forthcoming the company authorised construction of the flight of locks. Today they stand comparison with any flight on the network. Note

especially Samuel Oldknow's superb warehouse, by lock 9, now tastefully converted to offices.

● **Marple Aqueduct**
Deservedly scheduled as an ancient monument, this three-arched aqueduct over the River Goyt is a very fine structure, in an exquisite setting almost 100ft above the river. Designed by Benjamin Outram, its construction utilises circular pierced shoulders above each arch to reduce the weight of the rubble filling whilst providing a decorative feature. Contrast and interest are further added by the use of two different colours of gritstone in the parapets and ledges.

● **Romiley**
Gt Manchester. All services. A useful place for supplies.

Boatyards

ⓑ **British Waterways Marple Yard** Marple Junction, on the Macclesfield Canal (0161 427 1079). 🛢 🚰 🚿 Overnight mooring.

Pubs and Restaurants

💬 ✕ **Ring O'Bells** 130 Church Lane, Marple SK6 7AY (0161 427 2300; www.ring-o-bells.com). By bridge 2. A very comfortable and friendly traditional pub serving real ale and good freshly prepared bar and à la carte meals *L and E (not Mon)*. Children welcome *until 19.30*. Garden and canalside patio. Charity quiz night *Wed*.

💬 ✕ **Pineapple Inn** 45 Market Street, Marple SK6 7AA (0161 427 3935; www.marple-uk.com/pubguide/). Walk towards the town centre from bridge 2. A friendly locals' pub serving real ale. Children are welcome *until 19.00*. Beer garden.

💬 ✕ **Navigation** By lock 13, Stockport Road, Marple SK6 6BD (0161 427 2270; www.marple-uk.com/pubguide). Useful for 'lock wheelers' (remember, there is no mooring on the flight!)

A large comfortable pub serving real ale. Food *L and E daily*. Children welcome, and there is seating outside in the courtyard. Regular live music and quiz nights.

💬 **Duke of York Hotel** Stockport Road, Romiley SK6 3AN (0161 430 2806; www.dukeofyorkromiley.co.uk). East of bridge 14. A choice of real ale and cider in an unspoilt 18th-C pub. Mediterranean menu is served *all day*. Children are welcome, and there is outside seating. Quiz *Mon* and live music *Tue*. Moorings.

💬 **Friendship Inn** 77 Stockport Road, Romiley SK6 3AA (0161 494 2183). East of bridge 14. Bowling green. Real ale. Home-made food served *L and E, daily* and children are welcome *until early evening*.

The canal continues northward through a landscape which becomes less rural, but increasingly interesting. Bridge 6 is a pretty roving bridge, grown wider over the years. To the north, beyond the M62 motorway, the industrial tentacles of Hyde – Greater Manchester – ensnare the canal traveller, but the approach to Dukinfield Junction and Portland Basin is still very pleasant. The towpath is tidy, with plenty of grass, trees and seats. A lift bridge, a canal arm, an aqueduct over the River Tame and a stone roving bridge provide plenty of canal interest as you approach the junction, where the Ashton canal heads south-west into Manchester, and the Huddersfield Narrow canal starts its journey east across the Pennines (*see page 65*) to Huddersfield. Portland Basin was constructed to allow boats to make the sharp turn here, and was nicknamed the 'weavers rest', since so many weavers had reputedly drowned themselves here during hard times, such as the famine of 1860 and the depression of the 1930s. The warehouse which faces you across the junction, built in 1834, has been well restored. The Ashton Canal takes you into Manchester proper: this is still a fine, solid industrial section of waterway, still with a few steaming factories, tall chimneys and a good clear towpath. If you pass Dukinfield Junction in *mid-July*, you may see the colourful Tameside Canals Festival, which has been running successfully for many years now.

● Ashton-under-Lyne

Gt Manchester. All services. Walk north west from Portland Basin and you will find the church of St Michael, which was begun by Sir John de Assheton in the early 15th C and completed by his great grandson before 1516. The church is large, with a tall west tower rebuilt by Crowther in 1886–8. Particularly notable is the stained glass, depicting the Life of St Helena and dating from the 15th–16th C. A market was granted to the town in 1284, but by 1801 the population still numbered only 4800. It then expanded rapidly, due to the growth of cotton weaving in the area, and by 1851 totalled over 30,000.

Portland Basin Social & Industrial History Museum Portland Place, Ashton-under-Lyne OL7 oQA (0161 343 2878; www.tameside.gov.uk). This museum is housed in a superb reconstruction of a canal warehouse dating from 1834, at the junction of the Ashton, Peak Forest and Huddersfield canals. It tells the rich story of Tameside's social, political and industrial history, drawing upon many different facets of local life. The museum features a 1920s street, working models, computer interactives, sound and film. The original waterwheel is restored to working order on the wharfside. Displays include topics such as glassmaking, textiles, hatting, printing, canals, coalmining, Chartism, education and politics. *Open all year, Tue–Sun and B Hols 10.00–17.00.* Free. Shop, café.

Astley Cheetham Art Gallery Trinity Street, Stalybridge SK15 2BN (0161 343 2878; www.tameside.gov. uk). Above Stalybridge Library, this gallery was built as a gift to the town in 1901. Exhibition programme of sculpture, textiles, painting and drawings, featuring work by prominent local artists and community groups. *Open Mon–Wed and Fri 10.00–12.30 and 13.00–17.00, Sat 09.00–12.30 and 13.00–17.00 (closed Thu and Sun).* Free.

> #### WALKING & CYCLING
> Pasture and fine woodland are a feature of Haughton Dale Nature Reserve, to the west of the canal near Hyde. Paths follow the River Tame here. Details from: Park Bridge Heritage Centre, The Stable, Park Bridge, Ashton-under-Lyne OL6 6D (0161 330 9613; jwww.tameside.gov.uk /parkbridge). *Open daily.*

Boatyards

ⓑ **Portland Basin Marina** Lower Alma Street, Dukinfield SK16 4SQ (0161 330 3133; www.penninewaterways.co.uk) 🛖 🚽 ⚓ D Pump out, gas, overnight and long-term mooring, winter storage, slipway, crane, 100-year-old dry dock, day boat hire, boat building and fitting, engine repairs, chandlery, toilets, showers, books and maps, gifts, solid fuel, DIY facilities. Laundrette and supermarket close-by. *Emergency call out.*

Pubs and Restaurants

🍺 **Cheshire Ring Hotel** Manchester Road, Hyde SK14 2BJ (0161 368 1826). A few yards east of bridge 6. A friendly family pub, the oldest pub in Hyde, and handy for snacks and sandwiches *L*. Children are welcome *until 20.30. Shops and station nearby.*

🍺 ✕ **Globe Hotel** Globe Square, Dukinfield SK16 4RF (0161 330 5561). By bridge 2. A comfortable and friendly family-run hotel with satellite TV and serving real ale. Food in the restaurant *L and E, daily.* Children welcome. Patio seating. Quiz *Thu.* Accommodation available (*bed only, no breakfast*).

🍺 **Feathers** 62 High Street, Stalybridge SK15 1SE (0161 338 6403). A corner local serving real ale. Children are welcome *until 18.30.* Various artistes and music *weekends.* There is a useful fish and chip shop next door.

🍺 **Station Buffet** Platform One, Stalybridge Station, Rassbottom Street, Stalybridge SK15 1RF (0161 303 0007; www.buffetbar. freewebspace.com). A very fine refurbishment of the Victorian buffet, incorporating the stationmaster's house and ladies' waiting room. Having won many awards, it now serves real ale from a variety of breweries, along with real cider and bottled Belgian beers. Excellent food is served all day, and children are welcome. *Opens 09.30 for coffee.* Quiz *Mon,* folk night *Sat.* A short walk north of the canal.

🍺 **Wharf Tavern** Caroline Street, Stalybridge SK15 1PD (0161 338 2662). Bar snacks are served in this friendly pub, which has had the same landlord since 1949. Large patio leading down to the canal. Moorings.

BOAT TRIPS
Huddersfield Canal Society
Stillwaters is a 46-seater which operates from Portland Basin all year round for party bookings. Public trips (*30 mins*) at the weekend *between 11.00-17.00.* Telephone 0161 339 1332 for details, or visit www.huddersfieldcanal.com.

Droylsden

From start to finish, the Ashton Canal passes through a densely built-up area in which the canal is conspicuous as a welcome relief from the townscape which flanks it. Its clear water, excellent towpath, functional but dignified old bridges and the peace that generally surrounds it make it a haven for local school children, anglers, walkers and idlers, indeed for anyone who enjoys an environment that is quite separate from and unrelated to ordinary daily life. The rare pleasure, afforded only by an English canal, of stepping out of a city suburb into the peaceful and unpretentious atmosphere of the 18th C is once again, with continued restoration work, becoming available to all. At Fairfield Junction the top lock of the 18 which climb from Ducie Street Junction is encountered. It is a picturesque canal scene here with traditional buildings, including a shed dated 1833 standing over a canal arm, giving the area a quiet dignity. Descending the locks, you may wish to look out for the remains of several old canal arms: one of the more important was the 5-mile Stockport Branch, leaving from Clayton Junction, just below lock 11. The canal then falls through the remaining locks into Manchester. The surroundings are brightened by the well-cared-for Beswick flight of four locks, standing next to the new Stadium, where you can see the wonderful 'B of the Bang' sculpture, an explosion of spikes designed by Thomas Heathwick, to mark the success of the Commonwealth Games held here in 2002. Large-scale redevelopment has been completed at Paradise Wharf and Piccadilly Village, making this final stretch unusually gentrified, with smart flats, basins and a crane. The Rochdale Canal, joined here, stretches from Ducie Street Junction for 33 miles over the Pennines to join the Calder & Hebble Navigation, and is once again open to through navigation (*see page 179*) after many years of campaigning. The bottom mile or so of the Rochdale Canal remained navigable, from the junction with the Ashton Canal at Ducie Street down to Castlefield and its meeting with the Bridgewater Canal, and provided a vital link between the Bridgewater and Ashton Canals in the 100-mile Cheshire Ring cruising route.

NAVIGATIONAL NOTES

1 You will need a handcuff lock key for the locks on this and the Peak Forest Canal.
2 BW advise you to cruise the Ashton canal early in the morning, and avoid school holidays if possible. Moor only at recognised sites in this area, and do not offer anyone you do not know a ride on your boat. Keep the front doors locked.
3 Bridge 21 is very low.
4 Passage through locks 1–18 should be commenced *before 10.00.*

THE CHESHIRE RING – THEN AND NOW

This route has remained one of the most popular cruising circuits for many years now – a one-week trip encompassing parts of the Trent & Mersey, the Bridgewater, the Ashton, the Peak Forest and Macclesfield canals, passing through a wide and exciting variety of canalscape. Part of the journey includes a passage through central Manchester, a pleasant experience these days, but it was not always so . . .

The problem used to be timing your passage through the city so that the 'Rochdale Nine' locks were open, and your subsequent overnight mooring was a safe one! Local children preyed upon you as you tackled the Ancoats, Beswick and Clayton flights, leaping across the locks from one side to the other, begging lifts, and 'picking up' *anything* you might have left lying around . . .

The lock machinery was stiff, water supply uncertain, and the things which fouled your propeller defied description . . .

It is, thankfully, VERY different now, and the city passage is very attractive, interesting and enjoyable. Just take the usual precautions.

Pubs and Restaurants

◗ **The Pearl Restaurant Bar and Lounge** 119 Manchester Road, Audenshaw M34 5PY (0161 301 5680). Brightly decorated, upmarket Asian restaurant.
◗ **Strawberry Duck** Crabtree Lane, Clayton M11 4GU (0161 223 4415). Canalside at lock 13. A traditional two-room pub, over 100 years old, serving home-cooked food *L*, and real ale. Children welcome *until 18.00.* Canalside garden.
◗ **Bridge Inn** Clayton Lane, Manchester M11 4SS

(0161 223 8076). Near bridge 11. Traditional local's pub serving food *L and E, daily*. Children welcome and there is outside seating overlooking the canal.
◗ **Jolly Angler** Ducie Street, Manchester M1 2JW (0161 236 5307). Near the junction. A small, plain and friendly pub. Real ale. Café nearby. Regular Irish music sessions *Thu and Sat*, folk on *Sun* and ad hoc sessions whenever enough customers are willing. Children welcome. Moorings nearby, but don't leave your boat here overnight.

● **Fairfield**

PO, tel stores. Gt Manchester. Immediately south of Fairfield Junction is a group of neat and tidy buildings around a fine chapel. This is an original Moravian settlement, established in 1785 by Benjamin Latrobe and consisting of tidy rows of cottages built in brick, intended to house the members of a self-contained community.

Velodrome Stuart Street, Manchester M11 4DQ (0161 223 2244; www.manchestervelodrome.com). Part of Sport City. Access from the bridge, west of bridge 9, and in view from bridge 8, when climbing the locks. This is the National Cycling Centre, where the track is widely regarded as one of the finest and fastest in the world. There is a full programme of exciting cycle races staged in this magnificent stadium, which recently hosted the track events of the Commonwealth Games 2002. *See also* Walking & Cycling.

City of Manchester Stadium Rowsley Street, Manchester M11 3FF (0161 438 7650; www.mcfc.co.uk). Part of Sport City. A wonderful 48,000 capacity stadium used for the 2002 Commonwealth Games. The foundation stone was laid by Tony Blair on the 17th of December 1999, and the stadium was built at a cost of £90 million.

● **Manchester**

All services. One of Britain's finest Victorian cities, a monument to 19th-C commerce and the textile boom, its size increasing remorselessly with the building of the canals, and later railways. Unfortunately virtually no early buildings survived the city's rapid growth, although there is an incredible wealth of Victorian architecture still to be seen, in spite of redevelopment. The town hall and surrounding streets are a particularly rich area. St Peter's Square, by the town hall, was the site of the 'Peterloo Massacre' in 1819, when a meeting demanding political reform was brutally dispersed by troops carrying drawn sabres. Eleven people were killed and many more were injured. The Free Trade Hall, once the home of the Hallé Orchestra, is a little further along the road. Built in 1856, it was badly damaged in World War II, but was subsequently re-built to its original Palladian design. There is theatre, ballet and cinema, art galleries, and a wealth of interesting buildings, Victorian shopping arcades, many pubs with a choice of good beer and a variety of restaurants just a short walk from the canal. Sporting facilities are excellent, partly as a consequence of Manchester being the venue for the 2002 Commonwealth Games. The new developments at Salford Quays, on the Manchester Ship Canal, are quite breathtaking.

Tourist Information Centre Town Hall Extension, Lloyd Street, St Peter's Square, Manchester M60 2LA (0161 234 3157; www.manchester.gov.uk). To the north of Oxford Street Bridge. *Open Mon–Sat 10.00–17.15 (Sun and B Hols 16.30).*

WALKING & CYCLING

Keen cyclists might like to visit the magnificent Velodrome (*see* above) for a 'Taster Session' where, for a very modest fee, you can hire a track bike and a helmet and ride the steeply banked circuit for an hour. Telephone 0161 223 2244 for details and times.

In Manchester

ROCHDALE CANAL

MAXIMUM DIMENSIONS

Length: 72' 0''
Beam: 14' 2" (Locks 40, 41 & 47: 13' 6'')
Headroom: 7' 6" (7' 1" under the M62 culvert)
Draught: 2' 6" (recommended by BW as some
sections of the western side of the canal are only
dredged to 3' 3")

MILEAGE

MANCHESTER to:
Failsworth: 5 miles
Castleton: 11½ miles
Littleborough: 16½ miles
Todmorden: 22 miles
Hebden Bridge: 26½ miles
SOWERBY BRIDGE: 32 miles

MANAGER

01942 405700;;
enquiries.northwest@britishwaterways.co.uk

British Waterways produces a set of navigational
notes, available from the Waterway Unit office
listed above or downloadable from
www.waterscape.com/boatersguides, covering the
safe use of the Rochdale Canal.

The Rochdale Canal is one of three Pennine canal crossings. It was authorised by an Act of
Parliament in 1794 and completed exactly ten years later. With wide locks it was able to
handle barges, Humber keels and even small coasters, the latter sometimes trading
between the Continent and Irish ports, using the River Mersey and the Irwell Navigation at
the eastern end. However, the Achilles' heel of the waterway lay in its requirement for a
copious supply of water at the summit pound, together with the sheer physical effort
required to operate the three locks per mile that are averaged over the canal's relatively
short length.

The boom years for the canal were in the 1820s and 1830s before the inevitable railway
competition began to make an impression. Passenger carrying packet boats (Manchester
to Rochdale: 13 miles and 41 locks in 7 hours) and fast, light-goods-carrying fly boats (20
tons transported from Manchester to Todmorden in 12 hours) were both successful
enterprises in the early 1800s.

In 1887 the canal's fortunes appeared to take an upturn when the canal company bought
its own boats. Traffic included cotton, grain, coal, wool, cement, salt and timber, and
whilst end to end carriage steadily declined, shorter journeys continued to thrive. At the
outbreak of World War I the canal company was still ordering new craft (powered by 25hp
inverted compound steam engines) which were capable, loaded, of pulling a further two
laden dumb barges. However, in 1921, as competition from the roads took its toll, the fleet
ceased operation and traffic became spasmodic. The last loaded boat to trade over the
canal's entire length was *nb Alice*, in April 1937, carrying 20 tons of wire from Manchester
to Sowerby Bridge. The navigation was officially closed by an Act in 1952, except for the
stretch connecting the Bridgewater and Ashton canals in Manchester. Restoration was
commenced nearly 30 years ago and the canal society had not only succeeded in
protecting nearly all its original line, but also re-opened 16 miles of the eastern end. It has
also, in conjunction with the local authority-based Canal Trust, inspired the construction
of Tuel Lane Lock and Tunnel.

Subsequently British Waterways and its partners have completed restoration at a cost of
£23 million, rebuilding locks, bridges and tunnels and completing many new structures.
This investment has only been possible because of projected benefits to the local
community over a number of years, totalling in the region of £200 million.

171

Departing from Dale Street Basin, the canal begins its unremitting climb into the Pennines flanked by a series of not unattractive, although somewhat unusual, stone-filled gabions. Attractively painted cast iron bridges (note how the colour scheme suddenly changes) regularly span the navigation as it heaves its way up past a series of abandoned, but still impressive, cotton mills. Moving steadily onwards and upwards the waterway is accompanied by a mix of urban housing, parkland and industry; the redeveloped Victoria Mill at Miles Platting is a most impressive example. Passing Newton Heath with its canalside *market* and handy *shops*, the canal soon reaches Failsworth where there is a collection of fine mill buildings, many now in their second or third incarnations. The section of the waterway west of the A62 bridge had been built over and part of a supermarket had to be demolished during restoration; the remaining portion together with a *PO, banks and a chemist* still lies to the north beside the new footbridge. Beyond Failsworth, and several more solid mill buildings, development starts to step back from the navigation as it enters a pleasantly tree-lined section. Between here and Littleborough, the line of the canal has been designated an SSSI in recognition of its importance as a site for certain rare aquatic plants, particularly floating water plantain (*Luronium natans*). The staked-out rectangles along sections of the waterway are 'in-channel reserves' designed to protect the plant's tendrils of floating oval leaves and delicate three-petalled white flowers.The white-clawed crayfish has also adopted the canal, living in the well-oxygenated water of the lock by-washes where they remain hidden from the prying eyes of their natural predators such as herons and mink.

Pubs and Restaurants

✕ **Cyberia** 12 Oxford Street, Manchester M1 5AN (0161 661 1106). Internet café. Try also **Internet Café** at Debenhams, Market Street M1 1PF (0161 832 8666) and **Internet Exchange** in Coffee Republic 1–3 Piccadilly M2 3BB (0161 718 5402).

✕ ⌷ **Moon** Jackson's Warehouse, Tariff Street, Manchester M1 2FJ (0161 228 2677). Modern and trendy bar. Food available *all day*. Extensive outdoor, waterside seating. Funk, soul and house DJ's *Fri, Sat*.

▸ **Spanking Roger** Sawley Road, Miles Platting, Manchester M40 8DB (0161 205 7627). Food available *L* and *E, daily* in this friendly city local. Children welcome. Games room and satellite TV.

▸ **White Lion** Old Church Street, Newton Heath, Manchester M40 2JF (0161 681 4294). Cosy, welcoming local serving bar snacks *all day*. No children or dogs. DJ and live music *Fri, Sat and Sun*.

▸ **Black Horse Inn** Oldham Road, Failsworth, Manchester M35 0HB (0161 624 2921). On corner of A62 and Ashley Road West. Basic city local with pub games. Children welcome. *Open all day*.

▸ **Foresters Arms** Oldham Road, Failsworth, Manchester M35 0EN (0161 370 3581). Pub games. *Open all day*.

▸ **Brown Cow** Oldham Road, Failsworth, Manchester M35 0AN (061 688 0528). Real ales and pub grub *L* and *E*, daily. Satellite TV and pub games. Regular live entertainment. *Open all day*.

▸ **Mare & Foal** Ashton Road West, Failsworth, Manchester M35 0ES (0161 681 3112). A large, bright and airy pub serving real ales and food *L Mon-Fri*. Children welcome. Beer garden, darts and pool. *Open all day*.

▸ ✕ **Millgate** Ashton Road West, Failsworth, Manchester M35 0ES (0161 688 4910). Real ales and food available *all day, every day (12.00-20.30)* in this family pub. Children welcome. Beer garden and children's play area. Occasional entertainment. *Open all day*.

NAVIGATIONAL NOTES

See Navigational Notes on page 174.

1 Passage between Locks 83-65 in both directions is limited to four boats per day *Mon-Sat* (booked in advance) and will commence promptly at *08.30*. Any boats arriving late for bookings will be re-scheduled to the next available date. Locks at each end of the flight will be locked at *16.00*. The recommended mooring – if travelling from lock 83 – is the visitor moorings in Dale Street Basin, on the offside above Lock 84; if starting from Lock 65, The Rose of Lancaster pub below Lock 63. It should be noted that it is 1 hour's cruising from here to Lock 65. For bookings contact 01942 405700; enquiries.northwest@britishwaterways.co.uk.

2 No booking is required to travel the Rochdale 9-Locks 92-84 – but passage must be completed by *16.00* as this flight is locked at night.

3 *See also* Navigational Notes on page 169.

WALKING & CYCLING

The entire towpath from Manchester to Sowerby Bridge is in a good state of repair, much of it at the western end reinstated after the extensive restoration work. A great number of guided walks and tours are on offer within the Manchester area, with something to suit all persuasions; details from the Tourist Information Centre (*see* page 168).

● **Manchester**.
All services. One of Britain's finest Victorian cities, a monument to 19th-C commerce and the textile boom, its size increasing remorselessly with the building of the canals, and later the railways. Unfortunately virtually no early buildings survived the city's rapid growth, although there is an incredible wealth of Victorian architecture surviving, in spite of redevelopment. The town hall and surrounding streets are a particularly rich area (north of Oxford Street Bridge). St Peter's Square, by the town hall, was the site of the 'Peterloo Massacre' in 1819, when a meeting demanding political reform was brutally dispersed by troops carrying drawn sabres. Eleven people were killed and many more were injured. The Free Trade Hall, once the home of the Hallé Orchestra, is a little further along the road. Built in 1856, it was badly damaged in World War II, but was subsequently re-built to its original Palladian design. There is theatre, ballet and cinema, art galleries, and a wealth of interesting buildings, Victorian shopping arcades, many pubs with a choice of good beer and a variety of restaurants just a short walk from the canal. Sporting facilities are excellent, partly as a consequence of Manchester being the venue for the 2002 Commonwealth Games. The new developments at Salford Quays, on the Manchester Ship Canal, are quite breathtaking.
Bridgewater Hall Lower Mosley Street, Manchester M2 3WS (0161 907 9000; www.bridgewater- hall.co.uk). A visually striking hall – built beside the Rochdale Canal coal wharves and its junction with the Manchester & Salford Junction Canal (its name was almost as long as the waterway itself) – and home to the Hallé Orchestra, BBC Philharmonic, Manchester Camerata and an impressive pipe organ. The auditorium seats over 2000 for classical concerts, celebrity recitals, jazz

and rhythm and blues music. Conducted tours of the auditorium and backstage can be pre-booked. Telephone for programme details.
Gallery of Costume Platt Hall, Wilmslow Road, Rusholme, Manchester M14 5LL (0161 224 5217; www.manchestergalleries.org.uk). Housed in the Georgian mansion of a Manchester textile merchant, this is one of the largest collections of costume and accessories in Britain. The collection includes clothes worn from the 17th C to the present day, ranging from rare items, through the everyday dress of local working people to contemporary designer wear. Over 23,000 items are displayed on rotation. Shop. *Open Mon-Fri and last Sat in the month 10.00-17.00*. Free.
East Lancashire Railway Bolton Street Station, Bury BL9 0EY (0161 764 7790; www.east-lancs-rly. co.uk). An award-winning restored railway offering a mainly steam-hauled service along the picturesque Irwell Valley. Shop and refreshments. Trains operate *at weekends and B Hols throughout the year and May-Sep Wed-Fri. Charge*.
24 Hour Museum Guide Visit www.24hourmuseum.org.uk/cityheritage to plan your day out and gain a unique perspective on the heritage of English cities. Non-commercial and free to use.
Granada Studios Water Street, Manchester M60 9EA (0161 833 0880). Close to the Museum of Science and Industry. An extremely popular attraction, where you can visit Coronation Street, 'Baker Street', '10 Downing Street', The Giants Room, 3D shows, Motion Master cinema and many other highlights. Restaurants and shops. Disabled facilities. *Opening times vary: open daily Jul-Aug, plus most days during the summer season; open less often during the winter. You are advised to telephone for details. Admission for tours 09.45-15.00, closes at 17.00. Charge.*

Library Theatre Central Library, St Peter's Square, Manchester M2 5PD (0161 236 7110; www.librarytheatre.com). Intimate theatre space in the basement of the Central Library. Telephone for programme details or visit their website.

Manchester Airport-Aviation Viewing Park Sunbank Lane, Altrincham WA15 8XQ (0161 489 3932; www.manchesterairport.co.uk). The chance to get a close-up of Concorde G-BOAC together with a selection of other aircraft and unrivalled views of the operational runways at Manchester Airport. Shop, snack bar and picnic area. *Open 08.30-dusk.* Charge.

Manchester Art Gallery Mosley Street, Manchester M2 3JL (0161 235 8888; www.manchestergalleries.org.uk). Outstanding collection of 19th-C Pre-Raphaelite paintings; works from 18th-C masters (Gainsborough, Reynolds and Stubbs); contemporary art and sculpture; fine examples of Dutch and Italian painting and an internationally renowned collection of decorative art (ceramics, metalwork, furniture and textiles). Also the Clore Interactive Gallery for 5-12 year olds and their families. Shop and Gallery Restaurant. *Open Tue-Sat 10.00-17.00 and B Hol Mon.* Free.

Manchester Cathedral Victoria Street, Manchester M3 1SX (0161 833 2220; www.manchestercathedral.org). Founded as a Chantry College in 1421, it became the cathedral for the newly formed diocese in 1847. 16th-C misericords render a humorous depiction of medieval life; carving in the choir stalls and canopies is exquisite as is the choir screen and the six bays that make up the nave, which are the widest of any church in England.

Manchester City Football Club Sportcity, Manchester M11 3FF (0870 062 1894; www.mcfc.co.uk). Much the same as Manchester United really except the *opening times are Mon 11.30-16.30; Tue-Sat 09.30-16.30 and Sun 11.00-15.00.*

Manchester Jewish Museum 190 Cheetham Hill Road, Manchester M8 8LW (0161 834 9879; www.manchesterjewishmuseum.com). Beautifully restored, Grade II listed building opened in 1874 and now a museum but retaining the basic layout of a synagogue. Striking architecture, stained glass and the former Ladies Gallery containing the Permanent Exhibition which tells the 200-year old story of Manchester Jewry. Heritage Trails take place *monthly Mar-Oct.* Shop. Open *Mon-Thu 10.30-16.00 and Sun 10.30-17.00.* Charge.

Manchester Museum University of Manchester, Oxford Road, Manchester M13 9PL (0161 275 2634; www.museum.manchester.ac.uk). This university museum helps to uncover the mysteries of Ancient Egypt, discover the world of neotropical frogs, tease out the intricacies of the human body and encourage you to marvel at the dinosaurs and other prehistoric beasts. Stunning displays and interactive exhibits.

Shop and café. *Open Tue-Sat 10.00-17.00, Sun, Mon and B Hols 11.00- 16.00.* Free.

Manchester United Football Club Sir Matt Busby Way, Old Trafford, Manchester M16 0RA (0870 442 1994; www.manutd.com). Museum charting the history of the club from 1878 to the present day, hall of fame and the trophy room. The tour visits the player's dressing rooms, takes in Sir Alex's dugout and lets you run down the players tunnel to the imaginary roar of the crowd. Shop and café. *Open 09.30-17.00.* Charge

Markets Piccadilly Gardens, Manchester (0161 234 7357; www.manchester.gov.uk/markets). Flower Market *Thu-Sat 10.00- 18.00;* French Market *once a month (usually 3rd week) Thu-Sat 10.00-18.00;* Farmers' Market *once a month (usually 2nd week) Fri-Sat 08.30-17.00.* Fashion Market, Tib Street *Sat 10.00-17.00.*

Museum of Science and Industry Liverpool Road, off Deansgate, Manchester M3 4FP (0161 832 2244; www.msim.org.uk). Located on the site of the world's first passenger railway station, this exciting hands-on museum has 14 galleries covering everything from steam to space, transport to textiles, and includes a working steam train, a reconstructed Victorian sewer (complete with smells!) and an interactive science centre. *Open daily 10.00-17.00.* Free. Coffee shop.

Palace Theatre and Opera House Oxford Street, Manchester M1 6FT (0870 401 6000). Two of the most prestigious theatres in the Northwest, hosting the best in musicals, drama, opera and comedy.

Royal Exchange Theatre St Ann's Square, Manchester M2 7DH (0161 833 9833; www.royalexchangetheatre.co.uk). Theatre-in-the-round set in the recently restored Royal Exchange Centre. Telephone for programme details.

Smithills Hall Smithills Dean Road, Bolton BL1 7NP (01204 332377; www.boltonmuseums.org.uk). Some of the finest examples of Medieval, Tudor and Victorian Architecture in the region exhibited in a Grade I listed building. Shop and refreshments. Guided tours. *Open Tue-Sat 11.00-16.15 and Sun 14.00-16.15.* Charge.

Travel Metroshuttle is a free city centre bus-contact Traveline for details of this and all public transport information on 0870 608 2 608 *open 07.00-20.00 (08.00 weekends).* For Metrolink Trams contact 0161 205 2000; www.metrolink.co.uk and for train travel 08457 48 49 50.

Urbis Cathedral Gardens Manchester M4 3BG (0161 907 9099; www.urbis.org.uk). New interactive museum devoted to urban living, beginning with a sky glide in The Glass Elevator with the city as a backdrop, thence through four cascading themed 'involvements' entitled Arrive, Change, Order and Explore. *Open Tue-Sun 10.00-18.00.* Café *(open 10.00-17.00)* and shop. Free. Last admission 1½ hours before closing.

Whitworth Art Gallery University of Manchester, Oxford Road, Manchester M15 6ER (0161 275 7450; www.whitworth.manchester.ac.uk). Home to internationally renowned collections of British watercolours, textiles and wallpapers. Also an impressive range of paintings, drawings, sculptures and prints. Exhibitions and events throughout the year. Gallery Bistro (0161 275 7497) serving drinks, home-made cakes and light lunches *Mon–Sat 10.00–16.30 and Sun 14.00–16.30*. Specialist art bookshop (0161 275 7498). Gallery *open Mon–Sat 10.00–17.00 and Sun 14.00–17.00*. Free.

Tourist Information Centre Town Hall Extension, St Peter's Square, Manchester M60 2LA (0161 234 3157; www.manchester.gov.uk). *Open daily Mon–Sat 10.00–17.30, Sun and B Hol Mon 11.00–16.00*.

● **Rochdale Canal Corridor Regeneration** The £24m restoration of the waterway, part of which runs through Oldham and Rochdale, is seen as a core programme of restoration acting as a catalyst for areas and communities within the canal corridor. A study commissioned by British Waterways and the two local authorities came up with proposals which include a range of accessible canalside developments where people can live and work, a series of visitor attractions, a waterside network of safe green spaces and walking routes together with good maintenance and management marketed by a cross-section of public and private groups. The Rochdale Canal Strategy will also help to create a further 15,000 jobs, the construction or re-use of 627,000 sq yds of office, leisure and shopping floorspace as well as reclamation and recovery of 1484 acres of land. A comprehensive brief has been developed to maximise the potential the navigation has to offer the local community in terms of economic regeneration, leisure, transport, tourism and movement. Hopefully this holistic approach will ultimately succeed in eliminating many of the social problems that beset the area and, in their turn, detract from the boater's enjoyment of this historic section of newly restored waterway.

● **Ancoats Mills** (www.heritageworks.co.uk) Not far out of Ducie Street Basin the canal passes, on the off side, a collection of fine old cotton spinning mills. These are of national importance and include some of the earliest mills built in Manchester. Murray's Mills were constructed between 1798 and 1804 and Old Mill – built 1798 – is the city's oldest surviving mill and is of a non-fireproof design. Of slightly later construction is Sedgewick Mill (1818–20), while Paragon and Royal Mills were the last of a whole series of buildings on this site, being completed in 1912. They ceased production around 1960.

● **Newton Heath**
Gt Manchester. PO, tel, stores, butcher, baker, bank, takeaway, station. A satellite to Failsworth, once engaged in cotton spinning and weaving and now a useful place to stop outside the city.

● **Failsworth**
Gt Manchester. PO, tel, stores, banks, stores, garage, takeaways, station. Virtually the most southerly outpost of the cotton industry in Rochdale and close to the crescent-shaped Lancashire coalfield, exploited around Ashton-under-Lyne.

Newton Heath Lock

Slattocks

This stretch is a mix of industry and housing, with the navigation sometimes part buried in a leafy cutting. There is only one lock in this 3-mile stretch. Beyond Mills Hill there is an abrupt and welcome change as, on crossing the infant River Irk, the waterway bends around to confront a stone bridge and lock in a delightfully rural setting. As it gains height the navigation has partially looped back on itself and at Higher Boarshaw the locks are interspersed with two striking examples of the Manchester & Leeds Railway's bridges. Above the second bridge, as the waterway rounds a slight bend, the Pennines first come into full view and although still distant, herald the challenge yet to come – for which the compact flight of the six Slattocks Locks provides a telling overture!

● **Slattocks**
Gt Manchester. PO, tel, stores, takeaway, garage. A long, narrow village. It is reputed to derive its name from a Northern-style amalgamation of the two words 'South Locks'.

Pubs and Restaurants

◖ **Boat and Horses** Broadway, Chadderton, Oldham OL9 8AU (0161 681 2363). Busy pub serving real ale and food *all day, every day 12.00–21.30*. Beer garden. Moorings.
◖ **Railway & Linnet** Grimshaw Lane, Chadderton, Oldham M24 1GQ (0161 655 3889). Immediately west of Grimshaw Vertical Lift Bridge. Friendly local twixt canal and railway serving real ale.
◖ **Rose of Lancaster** 7 Haigh Lane, Chadderton, Oldham OL1 2TQ (0161 624 3031). Real ales. Food *available all day, every day 12.00–21.30*. Children welcome. Beer garden and terraced seating overlooking the canal. Quiz *Tue*. Moorings.
◖ **Hopwood Arms** Rochdale Road, Middleton M24 2RA (01706 359807). Village pub at Slattocks Top Lock serving real ale and food *L and E*. Children welcome. Outside seating.

Boatyards

See Bridgewater Canal page 37.

Rochdale

Above the locks there are fine open views as the waterway bends first towards the railway then swings back to duck under the motorway, in what was a road crossing over a farm lane. No provision was made for the canal, then derelict, when the M62 was constructed and to build one retrospectively, when the navigation was restored, would have been prohibitively expensive. The ingenious solution devised was to commandeer an existing culvert, divert the line of the waterway through it, relocate lock 53 south of the motorway to correct the levels, and provide an alternative approach to the farm. Above Castleton, the canal heads into Rochdale but skirts the town itself which used to be served by an arm below Moss Locks, now derelict. The main line maintains a discrete distance and retains its Pennine vistas, stretching out ahead in a wide arc. Passing through a shallow cutting in open moorland, the navigation arrives at the charming cluster of buildings at Clegg Hall: early 19th-C weavers' cottages, an old mill from the same era and the gaunt and newly renovated hall peeping out from behind the trees. Beyond, the waterway negotiates a series of new bridges – replacing previous infilling – and passing Little Clegg, a chemical works and Smithy Bridge station, arrives in Littleborough accompanied by the railway.

NAVIGATIONAL NOTES

1 The M62 culvert is only 14' 7'' wide with a maximum draught of 3' 3'' and an air draught of 7' 1''. All craft should proceed with extreme caution. Wide boats wishing to use this culvert must give 24 hrs notice (01942 405700; enquiries.northwest@britishwaterways.co.uk) as a floating towpath has been installed.
2 The new section under the A627M is made up of new narrow channel, a passing place and a 121yd tunnel. As there are short sightlines throughout, boaters should proceed with caution. The channel and tunnel are only 16' 6'' wide so wide boats must give way in the passing place between the two.
3 The new channel west of Well i'th Lane Bridge (approximately ½ mile east of the A627M Tunnel) is 20' wide but there is a tight curve at the eastern end. Care should be taken, especially by wide boats.

Pubs and Restaurants

There are plenty of pubs at Castleton, and an excellent selection of pubs and restaurants in Rochdale, so it is worth walking up into the town.

🍺 **Blue Pits Inn** 842 Manchester Inn, Castleton OL11 2SP (01706 632151). Real ale, pub games and open fires *in winter*. Fun quiz *Mon*.

🍺 **Crown & Shuttle** 170 Rochdale Road, Firgrove OL16 3BU (01706 648259). South east of Wallhead Bridge. A small upstairs military museum, three comfortable rooms downstairs and real ale makes this friendly and traditional local well worth the walk. Outside seating, open fires *in winter* and pub games *all the year round*. *Open all day.*

BOAT TRIPS
The *Lady Alice* operates trips on Hollingworth Lake *Apr–Oct, 12.00–17.00*. Also rowing boats for hire. Telephone 01706 370499 for further details.

- **Castleton**
  Gt Manchester. PO, tel, stores, off-licence, takeaway, laundrette, station. A cotton-spinning town and once home to Tweedales & Smalley, a textile machinery manufacturer that specialised in the production of ring spinning machines. The works is now used by Woolworths as a distribution centre. The Arrow Mill, standing beside the canal with its somewhat truncated chimney, is a fine example of a cotton mill built in 1908.

- **Rochdale**
  Gt Manchester. All services. Home of the Co-operative Movement and birthplace of Gracie Fields, this is also another cotton-spinning town

par excellence, although by the 18th C Rochdale was the flannel capital of Britain – a centre for the production of coarse and plain weave flannel. Lord Byron became Lord of the Manor of Rochdale in 1808 and, while residing at Hopwood Hall, Middleton, wrote a large part of *Childe Harolde*.

Touchstone Rochdale The Esplanade, Rochdale OL16 1AQ (01706 864986; www.rochdale.gov.uk). Four art galleries, museum, heritage gallery, tourist information centre and café. *Open Mon–Fri 10.00–17.15.*

Rochdale Pioneers Museum 31 Toad Lane, Rochdale OL12 0NU (01706 524920; www.museum.co-op.ac.uk). Best accessed from Hunter's Lane, south side of St Mary's Gate. The Rochdale Society of Equitable Pioneers held their first meeting here on 15 August 1844 and 31 Toad Lane went on to become the world's first viable Co-operative shop. *Open Tue–Sat 10.00–16.00 and Sun 14.00–16.00.*

St Chad's Parish Church Sparrow Hill, Rochdale OL16 1QT (01706 645014). There has been a church overlooking the town, perched on this site, for over 1,000 years and parts of the present tower date back to Saxon times, although there have been several different buildings over the centuries. There is a striking Burne-Jones stained-glass window in the tower and further glass by William Morris. The town stocks, dating from 1688, are within the church curtilage.

Corgi Heritage Centre 53 York Street, Heywood, Rochdale OL10 4NR (01706 365812; www.corgi-heritage. co. uk). The chance to discover the fascinating history of Corgi die-cast model vehicles from a manufacturer established before World War II. Archive collections offer the visitor a long walk down memory lane. *Open Mon–Fri, 09.00–17.30 and Sat 09.00–17.00.* Free. On main bus route from Rochdale to Bury.

Tourist Information Centre Touchstones, the Esplanade, Rochdale OL16 1AQ (01706 864928; www.rochdale. gov.uk). *Open Mon–Sat 10.00–16.00.* Also at The Clock Tower, Town Hall, Rochdale OL16 1AB (01706 356592; www.rochdale. gov.uk). *Open Mon–Sat 10.00–16.00.* Both centres offer details of a *Rochdale and Co-operation Town* trail.

- **Milnrow**
  Gt Manchester. PO, tel, stores, takeaway, station. Very much a centre for stone quarrying, open-cast and shaft mining, lying on the south east end of the crescent-shaped Lancashire coalfield. At Tunshill Farm there is a bank of old coking kilns and the remains of a fulling mill, with evidence of a paved pack-horse track and numerous local paths. Also six beehive coking ovens nearby.
  Ellenroad Engine House Elizabethan Way, Newhey, Rochdale OL16 4LG (01706 881952; www.ellenroad. org.uk). Home of the world's largest working steam mill engine and the Whitelees beam engine. The engine house is *open and in steam on 1st Sun in each month. Telephone or visit website for further details.* Charge. Regular bus service from Rochdale terminus and Newhey railway station is nearby.

Summit

Leaving Littleborough, the canal climbs steadily upwards past the strung-out Courtaulds factory, leaving the industrial chimneys of Rochdale far behind. The transition between sheltered valley bottom, with its compact, functional towns, and the open moorland that the waterway now heads towards, is fairly abrupt. Above West Summit Lock two contrasting, though striking features planted on the landscape are the Steanor Bottom Toll House (at the intersection of two roads to the west) and the 763yd span of the high-voltage line totally straddling the valley here. The typical moorland of the area is an acid peat overlying gritstone, poor draining and therefore agriculturally unproductive. At Longlees Lock the remote summit pound finishes. This was once the site of both a chemical and a brick works. Now reverted to coarse grasses, rushes and mosses, this section of the waterway is a haven to birdlife that can include meadow pipit, snipe, sandpiper, wheatear, dunlin, curlew and redshank. The descent into Todmorden is as scenically exhilarating as it is physically exhausting and the extended views, both in front and behind, steadily give way to the valley's intimacy.

- ### Littleborough
  Lancs. All services. Laundrette. A bustling little town, busy with visitors in summer though, strangely, without a market. Opposite the solid stone parish church is the excellent Coach House Heritage Centre – a local initiative to provide tourist information established in a grade II listed building. Just round the corner, in Victoria Street, are a good butcher and baker.
  Coach House Heritage Centre Lodge Street, Littleborough OL15 9AE (01706 378481; www.rochdaleonline.co.uk). *Open summer, Tue–Fri and Sun 14.00–17.00, Sat 11.00–17.00; winter closes at 16.30.* Exhibits and gifts.

- ### Summit
  Lancs. PO, tel, stores. Once a bustling woollen weaving community, the village has played an important part in three very different forms of transport. It sits beside the summit level of the canal, a place of sustenance to the thirsty boater and source of the much-needed water supply for locks descending east and west. The railway burrows underneath in a tunnel 2869yds long – the longest rail tunnel in the world when built in 1839. Some 23 million bricks were used in its construction. In 1984 a petroleum-carrying goods train caught fire and burnt uncontrollably in the tunnel for several weeks, smoke and flames belching from the ventilation shafts. It took £4 million and six months to re-open the tunnel to traffic.
  Steanor Bottom Toll House
  Just to the north of the village and built in 1824 at the junction of the old and new routes to Littleborough.

● **Walsden**

W. Yorks. PO, tel, stores, garage, takeaways, station. Meaning 'Valley of the Welsh' this textile village, just outside Todmorden, offers the boater all the important forms of sustenance.

NAVIGATIONAL NOTES

1 Passage over The Summit is limited to four boats per day (booked *24hrs in advance*) and will *commence daily at 08.30* from Lock 37 *and shortly afterwards* from Lock 36. Boats arriving *after 08.30* will be re-scheduled to the next available date. Boats booked for passage the next day should moor below Locks 36 and 37. For bookings contact 01942 405700; enquiries.northwest@ britishwaterways.co.uk. Boaters ringing at the *weekend* to book a *Sun or Mon (inc B Hol)* passage should telephone the lock keeper on 07733 124596 who operates a call-back service for passage bookings only.

2 There is strictly no mooring between Locks 44–38.

Pubs and Restaurants

Wheatsheaf Church Street, Littleborough OL15 8AB (01706 377695). A comfortable, family pub serving real ale. Children and dogs welcome. Garden. Disco *Fri and Sat.* Moorings.

Royal Oak Church Street, Littleborough OL15 8AB (01706 371346). Small town pub serving real ales. Children welcome. Outside seating. Darts and pool.

✗ **Coach House Coffee Shop** Lodge Street, Littleborough OL15 9AE (01706 378481). Inexpensive home-made snacks and cakes, teas and coffees served in this friendly annexe to the Heritage Centre. *Open daily 10.30–16.30.*

Falcon Inn Church Street, Littleborough OL15 9AA (01706 378640). Bar meals are available *Fri and Sat L* and traditional *Sunday* lunch *is served 12.00–18.00* in this mid-17th-C coaching inn which is now a large, comfortably furnished, family pub with disco on *Fri* and folk group on *Tue*; karaoke *Sat and Sun.* Pool and big screen TV.

Red Lion Hotel 6 Halifax Road, Littleborough OL15 0HB (01706 378195). Once a farmhouse, this very traditional old pub has been been licensed since the 18th C to dispense a wide selection of regular and guest real ales. Also an excellent range of Belgian bottled beers and foreign ales – both bottled and on draught, and real cider. Pub games, open fires *in winter* and no machines. Live music *Sun.* Camping. *Open all day (from 15.00 Mon–Thu).*

✗ **Waterside Bar and Restaurant** 1 Inghams Lane, Littleborough OL15 0AY (01706 376250). Modern bar-restaurant with an exciting menu offering Mediterranean options as well as modern British food. Meals served *L and E.* Children welcome; beautiful garden with decking overlooking the canal. Exciting regular theme nights.

✗ **Summit Inn** Summit OL15 9QX (01706 378011). Canalside at West Summit Lock 37. Real ale and a wide range of interesting bar food (generous portions) *available L and E, daily. Sunday* carvery. Children welcome, garden. Pub games. Telephone for details of special, pre-booked, ethnic menus.

✗ **Bird i'th Hand** Rochdale Road, Todmorden OL14 6UH (01706 378145). Between Walsden and Summit, near Warland Upper Lock 35. Food-orientated establishment offering anything from snacks to a gourmet meal *L and E, daily* in a warm, cosy three-roomed pub. Dating from 1823, this coaching house (once owned by a pigeon fancier) now serves real ale. Children welcome, and quiz *Wed.*

✗ **Waggon and Horses** Rochdale Road, Walsden OL14 7UA (01706 813318). A pub that welcomes boaters and families with an extremely inexpensive menu served *L and E (no food Mon).* Children welcome. Quiz *Tue*, singer *Fri.*

✗ **Border Rose** Rochdale Road, Walsden OL14 7UA (01706 812142). Busy, upmarket pub and restaurant serving a wide range of home-made food *L and E Mon–Thu and all day Fri–Sun.* Also real ale. Children welcome. Beer garden and aviary with cockatiels.

✗ **Cross Keys Inn** Rochdale Road, Walsden OL14 6SX (01706 815185). A homely, welcoming establishment serving a wide range of real ale together with traditional, home-cooked food *L and E and all day Sun.* Children welcome: dogs welcome when food is not being served. Canalside patio and moorings. B & B. *Open all day.*

✗ **Grandma Pollard's Fish & Chips and Home-made Pies** Rochdale Road, Walsden OL14 6SA (01706 815769). Something of an institution in the area, this is a chippy and pie provider of great character. *Open Mon and Tue 09.00–15.30 and Wed–Fri 09.00– 20.00.* Grandma pleads exhaustion as her excuse for remaining *closed over the weekend!*

✗ **Hollins Inn** Hollins Road, Walsden OL14 6QF (01706 815843). 70yds from Hollins Lock. Comfortable, family pub resurrected from the ashes of the original which burnt down in 1978. It now extends a warm welcome to all canal users and offers a variety of real ales. The ghost of a previous licensee is reputed to cause disarray by moving glasses and bottles around on the shelves. However, an excellent selection of reasonably priced à la carte and bar food is still *available L and E (until 20.00 but not Mon E).* Home-made steak and ale pie is a speciality. Children welcome *until 21.30*, as are dogs. Outside seating and bowling green. Quiz *Thu*, live entertainment *Fri and Sat.*

181

Todmorden

Now the descent begins in earnest with 17 locks in less than 3 miles and a spectacular railway crossing for good measure. A sweeping bend leads the waterway into the town with an immense brick retaining wall of massive proportions running all the way around the outside. The 'Great Wall of Todmorden' supports the railway embankment at this point and estimates of the total number of bricks used put the figure at more than 4 million. Beyond the compact town of Todmorden the countryside initially opens out revealing the disused Cross Stone Church, perched high on hills to the north of the navigation. Its badly blackened stonework is a reminder of the concentration of local industry, both past and present. Lobb Mill has finally been re-built (and turned into luxury apartments) while opposite Callis Lock there is a useful, boater-friendly *coal merchant* selling just about everything that is combustible. The waterway is now tucked tightly under a steep hillside covered by ancient deciduous woodland as the canal hugs the narrow valley bottom, interspersed, on the towpath side, with textile mills and dyeworks. The navigation approaches Hebden Bridge descending Stubbing (meaning a cleared area of woodland), Upper and Lower locks and passing gaily painted cottages, washing stretched like bunting across cobbled alleyways.

As so often happens with an aqueduct, the canal user is unaware of its beauty, grandeur or construction. So it is with Black Pit Aqueduct whose four substantial arches squat almost toad-like, close to the bed of the newly-merged rivers Hebble and Calder.

NAVIGATIONAL NOTES

1 Copperas House Bridge 32 is the lowest on the navigation and spans a short pound on which the water level can vary significantly, making the bridge very low at times. Proceed with caution.

2 Immediately below Lobb Mill Lock 17 there is a canoe centre. Approaching boaters are requested to sound their horn.

Boatyards

ⒷⓂobile Boat Repairers Sandworth Street, Todmorden OL14 6NP (01706 810046/07957 869641). Repairs to engines, gearboxes and generators. *24hr emergency call out.*

ⒷPickwell and Arnold Unit 10, Nanholme Mill, Shaw Wood Road, Todmorden OL14 6DB (01706 812411; www.pickwellandarnold.co.uk). Below Shaw

Plains Lock 15. 🏠 🛒 ⛽ D Pump out, gas, engine sales and repairs, boat building and repairs, chandlery, toilets, telephone. *Emergency call out.*

ⒷAble Fuels Lower Underbank, Halifax Road, Charlestown HX7 6PH (01422 842284; www.ablefuels.co.uk). Opposite Callis Mill. Coal, logs, coke, sticks, charcoal, firelighters, stoves. *Open Mon–Fri 10.00–17.30 and Sat 09.00–16.00.*

CHARLESTOWN RAILWAY DISASTER

In 1912 there was a serious derailment on the Charlestown curve when the 14.25 Manchester to Leeds express left the track, having effectively shattered the alignment of the rails at this point. The accident, involving a 2-4-2 radial tank engine, occurred on the stretch of line just before the railway crosses the canal on Whiteley Arches. The inspector, Colonel Druit, found at the subsequent enquiry that while the 45mph line speed at this point was suitable for normal express running, it was too high for tank engines of this type. Indeed, he went on to question the suitability of tank engines per se – with their high centre of gravity and inherent instability – for sustained high-speed traction. The derailed locomotive, together with all its carriages, toppled down the embankment, coming to rest strewn across the grounds of the old Woodman Inn.

- **Todmorden**

W. Yorks. All services. Laundrette. 19th C manufacturing success led to the concentration of wealth in the pockets of a few individuals whose ostentation was often manifested locally in civic and domestic architecture. Todmorden is fortunate, indeed, to have benefited greatly from the philanthropy of the Fielden family, whose legacy of good taste in buildings represents a feast in stone. Their choice of architect, in John Gibson of London, proved most successful. His work both echoes the solid vernacular building from a previous era, while introducing a further wealth of styles, which in turn complement the fine stone railway viaduct that dominates the town's centre. Simple classical building sits side by side with the richly ornate, a striking example of the latter being the elaborately pedimented town hall. Originally built astride the county boundary (moved in a later reorganisation) between Lancashire and Yorkshire, this Italian Renaissance style building is fronted by six sturdy pillars, surmounted by statuary depicting, on the one half, the agriculture and engineering of Yorkshire, while on the other various facets of cotton spinning in Lancashire. In contrast the Unitarian Church, erected by Joshua and Samuel Fielden, again to a design by Gibson, is pure Victorian Gothic revival and a fitting memorial to their father, John Fielden MP. His concern for his fellow man extended to Westminster and industrial reform, being largely responsible for the Ten Hours Act of 1847 which limited the maximum working day to ten hours for any person under 18 and any woman over 18.

Craft Centre Lever Street, Todmorden (01706 818170). Small family-run centre: stalls, workshops and a tearoom.

Free Library Rochdale Road, Todmorden OL14 7LB. Typifies the many individual buildings in the town displaying the skills of the stone mason in conjunction with the philanthropy of local benefactors. The library was a gift from the local Co-operative Society in 1897 and its asymmetry is pleasing in a simple way. It gives a second name to Todmorden Lock beside it, namely Library Lock.

Hippodrome Theatre Halifax Road, Todmorden OL14 5BB (01706 814875). A striking building of its period.

St Mary's Church Rochdale Road, Todmorden OL14 7BS. Built on land given to the town c. 1476 it still retains its 15th C tower. Subsequently much altered, the present Gothic Revival chancel bears little relationship to the original, although it contains a pleasing carved oak screen and attractive stained-glass windows.

Stoodley Pike The original monument was erected in 1815 to commemorate the end of the Napoleonic Wars. However, weakened by lightning, it collapsed 40 years later and was replaced by the present 120ft high structure. Visible from the canal, as you approach the town, it makes the object of a bracing walk, rewarded by stunning views across Calderdale.

Tourist Information Centre 15 Burnley Road, Todmorden OL14 7BU (01706 818181; todmorden@ytbtic.co.uk). *Open Easter–mid Sep, Mon–Sat, 09.30–16.30. Winter Mon–Sat 10.00–16.15.*

ON YOUR TOD

It is said that the only man-made feature distinguishable on the Earth, when viewed from the moon, is the Great Wall of China. Clearly this must be due to its length rather than its – relatively speaking – minuscule width. For a guard detachment, patrolling some of its more remote lengths, it must have been a singularly lonely and, in some cases, solitary occupation. The 'Great Wall of Tod' – the name given to the canalside railway retaining wall before Library Lock – is unlikely to hold quite such long-standing historical significance. Nor will it become a talking point amongst future lunar cosmonauts. Owing its existence to the less than prosaic function of keeping 'railway out of t'cut' it still remains, nonetheless, one of the wonders of a more local world. Building with brick in the Calder Valley, rather than the local gritstone, was largely down to the advent of the railway: a phenomenon repeated throughout many other areas of the country.

BIRD LIFE

The *Nuthatch* is recognised by its rounded, short-tailed appearance and its habit of descending tree trunks head-downwards, a trait unique in Britain to this species. The nuthatch has blue-grey upperparts, a black eyestripe, white cheeks and orange-buff underparts. The chisel-like bill is used to prise insects from tree bark and to hammer open acorns wedged in bark crevices. This woodland species has a falcon-like call. It nests in tree holes, often plastering the entrance with mud to reduce its diameter.

Pubs and Restaurants

Mason's Arms 1 Bacup Road, Gauxholme OL14 7PN (01706 812180). Close to bridge 31. Almost lost under the railway arches, this quaint drinkers' pub dispenses four real ales – two regulars and two rotating guests: local breweries are always well represented. They describe themselves as a 'nice locals' drinking hole serving good quality beer and make reference to the three distinctive tables that have always inhabited the tap room, and were reputed to have been mortuary slabs – *whilst in their present location*. Children welcome *until 20.00*; dogs without restriction. Beer garden with lovely views. Pool, darts, open fires and no machines. *Open all day (from 15.00 Sun–Thu in winter)*. Useful *PO and stores* through railway viaduct and turn left.

Fox and Goose 9 Heptonstall Road, Hebden Bridge HX7 6AZ (01422 842649; www.foxale.co.uk). A serious beer drinker's pub dispensing an excellent (and ever-changing) selection of real ales. A 'conversational establishment' eschewing theme nights. They also serve German and Czech bottled beers and at least 30 malt whiskies. Outside seating. Traditional pub games.

Canal Café 9 Pebble End, Hebden Bridge (01484 845065). Teas, coffees and large portions of appetising home-made fare (cakes, snacks and meals) at very reasonable prices. Beers, wines and ciders. Children welcome (accompanied by an adult if under 14); dogs outside only. Canalside seating. Gifts. *Open daily Easter–Oct; winter weekends and B Hols all year. Late opening in summer.*

Stubbing Wharf King Street, Hebden Bridge HX7 6LU (01422 844107). A range of regular and guest real ales together with real cider dispensed in a comfortable, family pub beside the canal. A wide selection of inexpensive food served in the bar and dining room *L and E, daily*. Outside courtyard seating. Open fires; pub games. Acoustic night *Wed*, quiz *Thu*, storytelling *last Fri of month*. Moorings.

Shannon and Chesapeake 257 Halifax Road, Todmorden (01706 813386). North of canal, between bridges 27 and 28. A small pub with a friendly atmosphere – always with something going on *at the weekends* – serving real ale. Breakfast *Sun 11.00–14.00*. Children and dogs welcome without restriction. Small garden at the rear. Pool.

Rope and Anchor Halifax Road, Todmorden OL14 5QR (01706 816054). North of canal, near bridge 29. Real ale and food available *L and E Mon–Sat and all day Sun*. Children welcome. Pub games. *PO, butcher, grocer and two takeaways opposite.*

Bramsche Continental Bar Rochdale Road, Todmorden OL14 7LA (01706 815117). Close to bridge 30. Bearing the name of Todmorden's twin town, this bar not only serves a wide range of continental lagers and fruit beers but also dispenses a selection of real ales. Children welcome. Beer garden overlooking marina. Moorings. Interesting selection of spirits but no ghosts!

Golden Lion Rochdale Road, Todmorden OL14 6LZ (01706 813532). Close to bridge 30. Variously post office, armoury and drawing office for Stoodley Pike, this 300-year-old coaching house now concentrates on serving real ales and bar food (*always available*). Children welcome. Outside seating. Quiz *Wed*.

White Hart Station Road, Todmorden OL14 8JR (01706 812198). Imposing mock-Tudor building replacing the 1728 original that once housed the local court. Market place and focal point of the town's development, it now dispenses real ale and food *L Wed–Mon*. Children welcome; outside seating.

Slattocks Locks (see page 177)

Rochdale Canal

Todmorden

185

Hebden Bridge

Leaving Hebden Bridge (there is a useful *coal merchant* close to Bridge 16 – 01422 842526), the canal continues its

steady descent through open countryside, passing Walkley's Canalside Mill and heading for Mytholmroyd. There is a slightly incongruous but very striking ape sculpture beside Broadbottom Lock 7. Beyond is the hamlet of Brearley (*pub, telephone box, children's playground and public toilets*) perched on a hill to the north, while the River Calder, still little more than a grubby grey beck, flows to the south. All around the waterway offers views of a tranquil rural scene: one of tiny stone-walled fields reaching up steep hillsides to the nearby horizon. Dotted here and there with crouching stone homesteads, it is a chequer-board landscape of rich pasture grazed, for the most part, by sheep and horses. All too soon the navigation burrows into more shady surroundings and, despite sharing the often narrow defile of the infant Calder Valley with road, rail and river, it manages to preserve a seclusion and an intimacy, hemmed in as it is by woodlands and spanned by solid stone bridges. The Rochdale Canal terminates at Sowerby Bridge where for many years the waterway had lain forlorn, a ribbon of water languishing in a supermarket car park, its contact with the Calder & Hebble Navigation a tantalising 50yds away, severed by infilling beneath a road junction. Today it is again accessible by craft travelling the inland waterways system and offers an unrivalled ascent into the undisturbed uplands of the Pennine chain.

● **Hebden Bridge**
W.Yorks. All services. Developed as a settlement in late medieval times, providing both a meeting point of packhorse routes and a river crossing. However, it was not until the late 19th C, with the advent of steam power, the building of canal and railway, together with the mechanisation and centralisation of the textile industry, that the town attained its present size and layout. Displaying a variety and delicacy of stonework – towers, turrets and pediments at every turn – houses and mills peel off from the market square to straggle haphazardly up steep hillsides. The first bridge to cross the River

Hebden was wooden, dating from 1477 and replaced by the present stone packhorse bridge some 30 years later. This solid structure contrasts with the delicate ironwork of the cast iron Victorian road bridge, sited upstream beside the ornate council offices, which incorporate the original fire station. Double-decker housing and a diversity of religious non-conformism are also characteristic of this strikingly compact mill-town.

Hebden Bridge Alternative Technology Centre
Hebble End Mill, Hebden Bridge HX7 6HJ (01422 842121; www.alternativetechnology.org.uk). Information line 08453 304930. Working from a

strong base within the local community, this charitable organisation – in making sustainability sustainable and simply irresistible – aims to provide inspiration, practical innovation, information and advice. By setting a stimulating and exciting example, it seeks to enable people to improve all aspects of their lives and environment. Permoculture garden, plastic pipe recycling, 'renewables' and shop. *Open daily Mon–Fri 10.00–17.00; Sat 12.00–17.00 and Sun 12.00–16.00. Extended opening on B Hol weekends.*
Hour Glass Art Studio Hebden Bridge (01422 846060; www.hourglass-studio-gallery.co.uk). Contemporary art exhibitions; local original art work; shop selling local jewellery, small paintings and sculpture; educational art. *Open Wed–Sun 11.30–17.30.*
Hardcastle Crags NT, Hollin Hall Office, Hebden Bridge HX7 7AP (01422

844518; www.nationaltrust.org.uk). Large tract of Trust-managed countryside, 1½ miles north of Hebden Bridge, easily accessible by bus. Rich in natural history and famous as the seat of the hairy wood ant. Regular events and guided walks – telephone for details. *Open all year.* Free.
Tourist Information Centre 1 Bridge Gate, Hebden Bridge HX7 8AF (01422 843831; www.calderdale. gov.uk). *Open mid Mar–mid Oct Mon–Fri 09.30–17.30, Sat 10.15–17.00 and Sun 10.30–17.00. Winter Mon–Fri 10.00–17.00, Sat and Sun 10.30–16.15.*
Metro (0113 245 7676; www.wymetro.com). Contact for all local travel information or a selection of free timetables.

● **Heptonstall**
W. Yorks. PO, tel, stores. An extraordinary 'textile village', little changed over the centuries, set high on hills overlooking Hebden Bridge. Walk up the Buttress (beyond the packhorse bridge) or take a bus and visit this settlement barely touched by time. In one small area there is a ruined 15th-C church, its early Victorian replacement and the Octagonal Chapel, one of the oldest continually used Methodist churches in the world, dating from 1764. Also a 16th-C cloth market hall, school museum, a dungeon and David Hartley's (the infamous coiner) grave.

NAVIGATIONAL NOTES

1   Tuel Lane Lock is operated by a resident lock keeper and passage will only be permitted when the lock is manned – *usually 7 days a week, 08.00–16.00; beginning Easter weekend and ending a few days after bonfire night.* The lock keeper can be contacted on 07717 342258/01422 316678. Outside these times *48hrs notice* is required for a *weekday passage and 72hrs at weekends.*

2   Do not enter Tuel Lane Tunnel whilst boats are in the lock, or when the lock is emptying, as turbulence can cause a serious accident.

3   *See* Navigational Notes on page 174 before setting out along the Rochdale Canal.

There is also the grave of Sylvia Plath, American poet and wife of Ted Hughes. The village provides one of the most spectacular viewpoints in Calderdale.

Old Grammar School Museum Church Yard Bottom,Heptonstall, Hebden Bridge HX7 7PL (011484 843738; www.calderdale.gov.uk). Depicts an old school classroom together with varying local history displays. *Open Easter–Oct, weekends and B Hols 13.00–17.00.* Charge.

Cloth Hall Heptonstall. Built between 1545 and 1558 as a market for local handloom weavers to sell their cloth to dealers. It is now a *private* house.

Weavers' Square Church Yard Bottom, Heptonstall HX7 7PL (01422 843738; www.calderdale.gov.uk). A unique museum of stone depicting many types of Yorkshire paving.

● **Mytholmroyd**
W. Yorks, PO, tel, stores, takeaways, hairdressers, station. Since the 11th C the ingredients of a farming and weaving community have existed in the area, confined largely to individual settlements above the marshy valley bottom. The site of the present village was initially a fordable crossing of the River Calder and, with the coming of the canal and the railway, developed as a focus for steam-powered textile production. Initially producers of cotton goods (with the canal as both supplier of raw materials and shipper of finished goods) the mills went on to manufacture worsted in the late 19th C, which in turn stimulated the growth of local dyeworks. Infamous as the base for the activities of David Hartley and the 'Coiners', Mytholmroyd was also the birthplace of Ted Hughes, the late Poet Laureate, and home to the annual Dock Pudding championships – *held in May.*

The Coiners of Cragg Vale Coining was the illicit manufacture of coins, often using metal filed or clipped away from the perimeter of genuine coins. This was melted down and cast into new coins with an appropriate design hammered onto the face and reverse sides. A new rim was then hammered onto the adulterated coin. On 10 November 1769 an excise man, William Dighton, who had been sent to curtail the activities of the Cragg Vale coiners, was murdered in Halifax by members of the gang. Loyalty was not a notable feature within coiner circles and the miscreants were quickly betrayed to the authorities in return for an enticing reward.

Dock Pudding Championships Dock Pudding is made from the weed *Polygonum bistorta* (sweet dock) and is not to be confused with the large coarse cow docks. Mixed with other ingredients and cooked to a variety of secret recipes, the finished product, looking not unlike a slimy, spinach concoction, is entered into a competition and judged on its culinary merits. Believed by many locals to be an essential spring medicine, efficacious in the cure of acne and as a cleanser of the blood.

● **Luddenden Foot**
W. Yorks. PO, tel, stores, off-licence, takeaway, library. Centred around more recent lines of communication in the valley bottom, the village once featured the railway station where Branwell Brontë was booking clerk. Passengers arriving on one of the earliest passenger lines to be opened in Britain, were greeted with the cry of 'Foo-it! Foo-it!' as porters sought to differentiate this upstart settlement from the ancient, textile- producing village, perched on the hillside 1/2 mile above.

Longlees Lock (see page 180)

Pubs and Restaurants

See also Calder & Hebble Navigation, page 55.

🍺 There is a wide choice of pubs to choose from in Hebden Bridge, together with an even wider choice of real ales.

✕ The selection of tearooms, bistros, pizzerias and restaurants is equally copious.

🍺 **White Lion** Bridge Gate, Hebden Bridge HX7 8EX (01422 842197; www.whitelionhotel.net). A friendly and relaxed family pub with many interesting features set in a 17th-C listed building. An excellent selection of real ales and good food, made using fresh local ingredients, served *all day*. Children's room and riverside garden. Open fires *in winter*. B & B. *Open all day every day.*

This pub represents a worthwhile walks or bus ride:

🍺 **Hare & Hounds** Billy Lane, Chiserley Old Town, Hebden Bridge HX7 8TN (01422 842671; www.hare-and-hounds.connectfree.co.uk). Cosy pub serving real ale and tasty bar meals *L and E*, *daily (all day Sat, Sun)*. Children welcome. Beer garden with stunning views over the Calder Valley – close to the Pennine Way. Pub games. Quiz *Sun*. B & B. *Hourly* Halifax service bus no 593 *during day* or minibus H3 and H7 *evenings and weekends*.

✕ **Dusty Miller** Burnely Road, Mytholmroyd HX7 5LH (01422 882247; www.dustymiller.co.uk). Once the regular haunt of the Crag Vale Coiners, its now a restaurant with rooms. B & B.

🍺 **Shoulder of Mutton** New Road, Mytholmroyd HX75DZ (01422 883165). Opposite railway station. Award-winning hostelry that takes its beer and food seriously. An excellent selection of both regular and guest real ales are served; there are three cosy eating areas,

portions are generous and the prices low. Tasty, home-cooked food available *L and E*. Children and dogs welcome. Streamside garden.Tasty, home-cooked food available *L and E (19.00–20.30 except Tue)*. Children and dogs welcome. Streamside garden.

🍺 **White Lion** Burnley Road, Mytholmroyd HX7 5LN (01422 883131). An interesting range of very reasonably priced bar meals and snacks served *L*, *daily*, in comfortable surroundings, by a friendly, welcoming landlady. Real ale, moorings outside, pub games, Quiz *Mon* and live music alternate *Fri*. Children welcome *until 20.00*. Beer garden.

🍺 **Grove Inn** Burnley Road, Brearley, Luddenden Foot HX2 6HS (01422 883235). Cosy, single room pub, beside the main road, serving real ale. Snacks and traditional bar food served *L and E Tue–Sun*. Children welcome; garden. Games room with pool and darts. Quiz night *Thu*. Busy in *summer*.

✕ ♀ **O Sole Mio Restaurante Italiano** Burnley Road, Brearley, Luddenden Foot HX2 6AH (01422 884102). Italian restaurant serving *L and E daily*.

✕ ♀ **Manny's** Station Road, Luddenden Foot (01422 886640). Above Old Brandy Wine. Asian restaurant and takeaway.

🍺 **Old Brandy Wine** Station Road, Luddenden Foot HX2 6AD (01422 886173). Real ales are served in this ex-factory and working-man's club. Discos *Fri and Sat*; karaoke *Sun*. Children welcome *until 21.00*. Outside seating.

🍺 **Puzzle Hall Inn** 21 Hollins Mill Lane, Sowerby Bridge HX6 2QG (01422 835547). South of canal before Sowerby Long Bridge. A wide cross section of customers gather at this 300-year-old hostelry of great character set between river and canal. Real ale and food *L (E Wed only)* are served in this tiny, two-roomed pub where *Wed E* is curry night. Well-behaved children and dogs welcome (but no dogs *Wed E*). Garden. Live jazz *Tue* and various entertainment *Thu and Sat*.

Boatyards

See Calder & Hebble Navigation, page 54.

BOAT TRIPS
Brontë Boats The Marina, Hebden Bridge HX7 8AD (01422 845557; www.bronteboats.co.uk). Cruises throughout the year from Hebden Bridge Marina on the 53-seat *Verdopolis*. On-board facilities include central heating, toilets, and a PA system.

Todmorden (see page 182)

THE BEER NECESSITIES

Take an old ice cream cooler, a scrapyard copper, a home-made cask washer and two locally constructed mash tuns; place them in a canalside mill (once a sweet factory) and what have you got? A family-run brewery – whose proprietor (for many years a joiner) is not short of ingenuity. Always fermenting new ideas for the future, his imagination stretches into the often mind-bending task of naming new brews, tapping into local history with names like 'Luddite' and 'Coiners'. When the ailing sweet factory finally called time on its production it was sold, complete with its old manufacturing equipment. Ideas were already brewing as to how it might be pressed into use for ale production. The family are all adept at meeting new challenges, right down to Sooty the brewery cat. Keeping the mouse population in check is a doddle for a four-legged feline; not so easy if you've had the misfortune to lose a leg in a brush with a car.

TRENT & MERSEY CANAL

MAXIMUM DIMENSIONS

Derwent Mouth to Horninglow Basin, Burton upon Trent
Length: 72' 0"
Beam: 14' 0"
Headroom: 7' 0"
Stenson Lock is very tight for 14ft beam craft and Weston Lock is tight for boats of 72ft length.

Burton upon Trent to south end of Harecastle Tunnel
Length: 72' 0"
Beam: 7' 0"
Headroom: 6' 3"

Harecastle Tunnel
Length: 72' 0"
Beam: 7' 0"
Headroom: 5' 9"

North end of Harecastle Tunnel to Croxton Aqueduct
Length: 72' 0"
Beam: 7' 0"
Headroom: 7' 0"

Croxton Aqueduct to Preston Brook Tunnel
Length: 72' 0"
Beam: 8' 2"
Headroom: 6' 3"

MANAGER:

Derwent Mouth to bridge 71, Colwich: 01827 252000
enquiries.centralshires@britishwaterways.co.uk
Colwich to Trentham (Oldroad Bridge 104):
0121 200 7400
enquiries.westmidlands@britishwaterways.co.uk
Trentham (Oldroad Bridge 104) to Preston Brook:
01606 723800
enquiries.wbc@britishwaterways.co.uk

MILEAGE

DERWENT MOUTH to:
Swarkestone Lock: 7 miles
Willington: 12¼ miles
Horninglow Wharf: 16½ miles
Barton Turn: 21¼ miles
Fradley, junction with Coventry Canal: 26¼ miles
Great Haywood, junction with Staffordshire & Worcestershire Canal: 39 miles
Stone: 48½ miles
Stoke Top Lock, junction with Caldon Canal: 58 miles
Harding's Wood, junction with Macclesfield Canal: 63¾ miles
King's Lock, Middlewich, junction with Middlewich Branch: 76¼ miles
Anderton Lift, for River Weaver: 86½ miles

PRESTON BROOK north end of tunnel and Bridgewater Canal: 93½ miles

Locks: 76

This early canal was originally conceived partly as a roundabout link between the ports of Liverpool and Hull, while passing through the busy area of the Potteries and mid-Cheshire, and terminating either in the River Weaver or in the Mersey. Its construction was promoted by Josiah Wedgwood (1730-95), the famous potter, aided by his friends Thomas Bentley and Erasmus Darwin. In 1766 the Trent & Mersey Canal Act was passed by Parliament, authorising the building of a navigation from the River Trent at Shardlow to Runcorn Gap, where it would join the proposed extension of the Bridgewater Canal from Manchester.

The ageing James Brindley was appointed engineer for the canal. Construction began at once and in 1777 the Trent & Mersey Canal was opened. In the total 93 miles between Derwent Mouth and Preston Brook, the Trent & Mersey gained connection with no fewer than nine other canals or significant branches.

By the 1820s the slowly-sinking tunnel at Harecastle had become a serious bottle-neck, so Thomas Telford recommended building a second tunnel beside the old one. His recommendation was eventually accepted by the company and the new tunnel was completed in under three years, in 1827. Although the Trent & Mersey was taken over in 1845 by the new North Staffordshire Railway Company, the canal flourished until World War I.

Look out for the handsome cast iron mileposts, which actually measure the mileage from Shardlow, not Derwent Mouth. There are 59 originals, from the Rougeley and Dixon foundry in Stone, and 34 replacements, bearing the mark of the Trent & Mersey Canal Society - T & MCS 1977.

Harding's Wood Junction

At the north end of Harecastle Tunnel (2926yds long) the navigation passes Kidsgrove station and a coal yard; there is also a shower in the facilities block beside the north tunnel portal. Beyond is Harding's Wood and the junction with the Macclesfield Canal, which crosses the T & M on Poole Aqueduct. There are *showers, laundry facilities and toilets* at the BW yard at Red Bull. The canal continues to fall through a heavily locked stretch sometimes called 'heartbreak hill' but known to the old boatmen as the 'Cheshire Locks'.

Pubs and Restaurants

🍺 ✕ **The Harecastle Hotel** Liverpool Road, Kidsgrove ST7 1EA (01782 773925). Family pub close to bridge 132. Reasonably priced food *all day until 20.00*, accompanied by their own traditional Mowcop gravy. Real ales. Children welcome. Karaoke and quizzes *Fri and Sat*. B & B.

🍺 **The Blue Bell** 25 Hardingswood, Kidsgrove ST7 1EG (01782 774052; www.bluebellkidsgrove.co.uk). Canalside, at Hardings Wood Junction. Friendly, quiet, one-bar local, winnner of many CAMRA awards. Real ale, plus a range of specialist bottled beers, including many from Belgium, plus real cider and perry. No juke box, pool table or gaming machines. Four separate drinking areas. Note the trapdoor in the lounge ceiling. Well-behaved children welcome *until 21.00*. Snacks are available *at weekends. Open Tue-Fri 19.30-23.00; Sat 13.00-16.30, 19.00-23.00; Sun 12.00-16.30, 19.00-22.30 (all day during summer). Closed Mon.*

🍺 **The Canal Tavern** Hardingswood Road, Kidsgrove ST7 1EF (01782 775382). Canalside by bridge 133. Food served *L and E*. Children welcome *until 19.30*. Large garden. Karaoke at *weekends*.

🍺 ✕ **The Red Bull Hotel** Congleton Road South, Church Lawton ST7 3AJ (01782 782600). By lock 43. Popular pub close to Hardings Wood Junction, serving real ale and bar meals, including fish dishes *L and E*,

along with good wine. Children welcome. Canalside seating area. Quiz night *each Tue*. Moorings.

🍺 **The Broughton Arms** Mill Mead, Rode Heath ST7 3RX 01270 878661). Canalside at Rode Heath. Friendly family pub, with comfortable bars and canalside seating. Range of real ale. Food available in bar and dining area *L and E*. Children welcome away from the bar. Waterside garden with patio heaters. Quiz *Tue*.

✕ ♀ **Lockside 57** The Canal Centre, Hassall Green CW11 4YB (01270 762266; www.lock57.co.uk). A well-restored 18th-C building beside the canal. Appetising range of reasonably priced dishes (vegan by arrangement) served *breakfast, L and E (seasonal). Sunday* roast. Children's menu. Lockside seating. Cyclists and walkers warmly welcomed. *See* also under Boatyards.

🍺 **The Romping Donkey** Hassall Green CW11 4YA (01270 765202). Haunted 17th-C pub serving real ale, and home-made bar meals and snacks *L and E*. Children welcome, and there is a garden.

Two minor aqueducts are encountered, and most of the locks are narrow pairs – the chambers side by side. At Hassall Green there is a *PO, tel and stores* incorporating a canal shop, restaurant and limited boatyard services.

● **Kidsgrove**
Staffs. All services. Originally an iron and coal producing town, Kidsgrove was much helped by the completion of the Trent & Mersey Canal. James Brindley is buried here.
● **Rode Heath**
Cheshire. PO, tel, stores. A useful shopping area right by bridge 140. A butcher's shop at bridge 139.
Rode Heath Rise ST7 3QX Once the site of a salt works, it has now been landscaped and restored as a wildflower meadow. Telephone 01477 534115 for further information.

NAVIGATIONAL NOTES

HARECASTLE TUNNEL Do not enter in an unpowered craft. With the complete removal of the towpath, headroom is no longer the problem it once was. A one-way system operates, so follow the instructions of the tunnel keepers. *For updated tunnel opening times, telephone 01782 785703.*

Boatyards

Ⓑ **Smithsons Solid Fuel and Caravan Centre** Liverpool Road, Kidsgrove ST7 1EA (01782 787887). Near bridge 132. Ⅾ Calor gas, solid fuel, lubricants and caravan fittings which can be used as chandlery. Also bicycles and bicycle spares for sale.
Ⓑ **Canal Centre** Hassall Green, Sandbach CW11 4YB (01270 762266). Ⅾ Gas, groceries, books and maps, coal, short-term mooring, chandlery, toilets. Also PO, general store, off-licence, gifts, licensed restaurant and tearoom, coal.

WALKING & CYCLING
The towpath is in good condition through to Preston Brook and offers the opportunity to sample a varied landscape, ranging from the beauties of the Dane Valley through to the industry indigenous to this long-established salt-producing area.

Wheelock

The canal now descends the Wheelock flight of eight locks, which are the last paired locks one sees when travelling northwards. The countryside continues to be quiet and unspoilt but unspectacular. The pair of locks half-way down the flight is situated in the little settlement of Malkin's Bank, overlooked by terraced houses. The boatman's co-op used to be here, in the small terrace of cottages. The adjoining boatyard now specialises in the restoration of traditional working boats. At the bottom of the flight is the village of Wheelock (*toilets and shower*); west of here the navigation curls round the side of a hill before entering the very long-established salt-producing area that is based on Middlewich. The 'wild' brine pumping and rock-salt mining that has gone on hereabouts has resulted in severe local subsidence; the effect on the canal has been to necessitate the constant raising of the banks as lengths of the canal bed sink. This of course means that the affected lengths tend to be much deeper than ordinary canals. Non-swimmers beware of falling overboard. The navigation now begins to lose the rural character it has enjoyed since Kidsgrove. Falling through yet more locks, the canal is joined by a busy main road (useful for *fish & chips*, west of Kings Lock; and *Chinese takeaway*, west of bridge 166) which accompanies it into an increasingly flat and industrialised landscape, past several salt works and into Middlewich, where a branch of the Shropshire Union leads off westwards towards that canal at Barbridge. The first 100yds or so of this branch is the Wardle Canal, claimed to be the shortest canal in the country.

- **Wheelock**
  Ches. PO, tel, stores, *fish and chips*. Busy little main road village on the canal.
- **Sandbach**
  Ches. PO, tel, stores, *garage, chemist, takeaways, bank, station*. 1½ miles north of Wheelock. An old market town that has maintained its charm despite the steady growth of its salt and chemical industries. After walking from the canal you can refresh yourself with a pint of real ale from any of the seven pubs visible from the seat in the market place.
  Ancient Crosses In the cobbled market place on a massive base stand two superb Saxon crosses, believed to commemorate the conversion of the area to Christianity in the 7th C. They suffered severely in the 17th C when the

Puritans broke them up and scattered the fragments for miles. After years of searching for the parts, George Ormerod succeeded in re-erecting the crosses in 1816, with new stone replacing the missing fragments.
St Mary's Church High Street, Sandbach CW11 1AN. A large, 16th C church with a handsome battlemented tower. The most interesting features of the interior are the 17th C carved roof and the fine chancel screen.
The Old Hall Hotel High Street, Sandback CW11 1AL. An outstanding example of Elizabethan half-timbered architecture, which was formerly the home of the lord of the manor, but is now used as an hotel.

Boatyards

ⓑ **Malkins Bank Canal Services** The Boatyard, Betchton Road, Malkins Bank, Sandbach CW11 4XN (01270 764595). Long-term mooring, slipway, boat building and historic boat restoration, boat repairs. Breakdown service.

ⓑ **The Northwich Boat Company** Moss Bridge Cottage, Moss Lane, Sandbach CW11 3PW (01270 760160; www.thenorthwichboat.com). Also (01270 760770; www.carefreecruising.com) on same site. Boat building and fitting out.

Pubs and Restaurants

🍺 **Nags Head** 504 Crewe Road, Wheelock CW11 3RL (01270 762457). ¼ mile west of bridge 154. Small black and white pub serving real ale and traditional bar meals *L and E (not Sun E)*. Children and dogs welcome. Garden. Pool and traditional pub games. Chinese takeaway opposite.

🍺 **Commercial Hotel** Game Street, Wheelock CW113RR (01270 760122). Near bridge 154. Set in a Georgian house with an old-fashioned and spacious feel this pub serves real ale, real cider and bar meals. *Open all day.* Children and dogs welcome. Beer garden, snooker room, darts and dominoes.

🍺 **Cheshire Cheese** 466 Crewe Road, Wheelock CW11 3RL (01270 760319). Heavily beamed, canalside pub serving real ale and a range of meals and snacks *L and E, daily*. Children and dogs welcome (dogs in the garden). Large beer garden. Moorings.

🍺 **Market Tavern** Market Square, Sandbach CW11 1AT (01270 762099). Opposite the crosses. Lively, old, traditional town pub serving real ale and home-cooked bar food *L Mon–Sat*. Children's menu and beer garden. One of the many real ale pubs in, or close to, the square. Regular live music.

Middlewich

The Trent & Mersey skirts the centre of the town, passing lots of moored narrowboats and through three consecutive narrow locks, arriving at a wide (14ft) lock (which has suffered from subsidence) with a pub beside it. This used to represent the beginning of a wide, almost lock-free navigation right through to Preston Brook, Manchester and Wigan (very convenient for the salt industry when it shipped most of its goods by boat), but Croxton Aqueduct had to be replaced many years ago, and is now a steel structure only 8ft 2in wide. The aqueduct crosses the River Dane, which flows alongside the navigation as both water courses leave industrial Middlewich and move out into fine open country. Initially, this is a stretch of canal as beautiful as any in the country. Often overhung by trees, the navigation winds along the side of a hill as it follows the delightful valley of the River Dane. There are pleasant moorings with picnic tables and barbecue facilities, created by the Broken Cross Boating Club in old clay pits, just north of bridge 176, on the off-side. The parkland on the other side of the valley encompasses Bostock Hall, a school for children with learning difficulties. At Whatcroft Hall (privately owned), the canal circles around to the east, passing under a railway bridge before heading for the industrial outskirts of Northwich and shedding its beauty and solitude once again.

NAVIGATIONAL NOTES

There are several privately owned wide 'lagoons' caused by subsidence along this section of the Trent & Mersey, in some of which repose the hulks of abandoned barges and narrowboats, lately being salvaged. Navigators should be wary of straying off the main line, since the off-side canal bank is often submerged and invisible just below the water level.

Boatyards

Ⓑ **Kings Lock Boatyard** Booth Lane, Middlewich CW10 0JJ (01606 737564). 🚽 D Gas, overnight mooring, long-term mooring, winter storage, slipway, engine sales and repairs, boat repairs, chandlery (including mail order), books, maps, gifts, solid fuel. *Emergency call out.*
Ⓑ **Andersen Boats** Wych House, St Anne's Road, Middlewich CW10 9BQ (01606 833668; www.andersenboats.com) Pump out, gas, narrowboat hire, books and maps. Useful DIY shop nearby.

Ⓑ **Middlewich Narrowboats** Canal Terrace, Middlewich CW10 9BD (01606 832460; www. middlewichboats.co.uk). 🚽 🚽 🚿 D Pump out, gas, narrowboat hire, overnight mooring (*not Fri*), long-term mooring, dry dock, boatbuilding, groceries, chandlery, books and maps, engine repairs, toilets, laundry service, breakdown service, grit blasting, hull and cabinside painting. *Closed Sun.* Useful tool hire shop next door.

Pubs and Restaurants

The Kings Lock 1 Booth Lane, Middlewich CW10 0JJ (01606 833537). Overlooking the lock. Real ales and bar food available *L and E*. Children welcome *until 21.00*. Dogs in bar areas only. Canalside seating. Moorings.

The Cheshire Cheese Lewin Street, Middlewich CW10 9AX (01606 832097). Friendly, traditional establishment serving real ales. Children welcome. Landscaped garden with large patio and marquee. *Weekly* karaoke and occasional live bands. Wide-screen TV.

The Newton Brewery Inn Webbs Lane, Middlewich CW10 9DN (01606 833502). ¼ mile south of Big Lock. Small friendly pub with an attractive garden running down to the towpath. Real ale. Telephone for details of food. Children welcome.

The Boars Head Kinderton Street, Middlewich CW10 0JE (01606 833191; www.theboarsheadhotel.com). Large rambling pub offering real ale and food *L and E, daily*. Pool room. Patio. Live music *Sat*. B & B.

The Big Lock Webbs Lane, Middlewich CW10 9DN (01606 833489). Canalside. Variously a bottle-making factory and canal-horse stables, this pub now serves real ale. Bar snacks and an à la carte menu available *L and E*. Children and dogs welcome. Garden area. Quiz *Mon*.

● **Middlewich**
Ches. PO, tel, stores, chemist, takeaways, bank, garage. A town that since Roman times has been dedicated to salt extraction. Most of the salt produced here goes to various chemical industries. Subsidence from salt extraction has prevented redevelopment for many years, but a big renewal scheme is now in progress. The canalside area is a haven of peace below the busy streets. There is an interesting town trail depicting Roman Middlewich as a Romano-British saltworks settlement in the period 150–250 AD. Interpretation boards can be found on the towpath north of Bridge 172 and beside the Newton Brewery Inn.

St Michael's Church Queen Street, Middlewich CW10 9AR. A handsome medieval church which was a place of refuge for the Royalists during the Civil War. It has a fine interior with richly carved woodwork.

Anderton Lift

The outlying canal settlement of Broken Cross acts as a buffer between the beauty and solitude of the Dane Valley and the industrial ravages around Northwich. Beyond is another length in which salt mining has determined the nature of the scenery. Part of it is heavily industrial, with enormous ICI works dominating the scene;

much of it is devastated but rural (just), some of it is nondescript, and some of it is superb countryside. Donkey engines can still be seen in surrounding fields pumping brine. Leaving the vicinity of Lostock Gralam (*licensed grocer 100yds east of bridge 189 open daily until 22.00*) and the outskirts of Northwich, one passes Marston (*late opening stores and tel*) and Wincham (*PO, tel, stores*). Just west of the village, one travels along a ½-mile stretch of canal that was only cut in 1958, as the old route was about to collapse into – needless to say – underground salt workings. Beyond the woods of Marbury Country Park (attractive short-stay moorings) and before Bridge 198, there is a full range of *facilities* including *toilets, showers and washing machines*, followed by Anderton (*PO, tel, stores*) – the short entrance canal to the famous boat lift down into the Weaver Navigation is on the left. The main line continues westwards, winding along what is now a steep hill and into Barnton Tunnel. There is a useful range of shops, up the hill from the east end of the tunnel, including a laundrette, chemist and butcher. You then emerge onto a hillside overlooking the River Weaver, with a marvellous view straight down the huge Saltersford Locks. Now Saltersford Tunnel is entered: beyond it you are in completely open country again. There are good moorings in the basins to the east of both tunnels.

NAVIGATIONAL NOTES

1 Saltersford Tunnel is crooked, affording only a brief glimpse of the other end. Two boats cannot pass in this or Barnton Tunnel, so make sure they are clear before proceeding.

2 *See* notes on page 200 covering use of the Anderton Boat Lift.

● **Marston**

Ches. Tel. A salt-producing village, suffering badly from its own industry. The numerous gaps in this village are caused by the demolition or collapse of houses affected by subsidence. Waste ground abounds.

The Lion Salt Works Offershaw Lane, Marston CW9 6ES (01606 41823; www. lionsaltworkstrust.co.uk). Beside the canal at bridge 193. The Thompson family established an open pan salt works in Marston in 1842, producing fishery salt, bay salt, crystal salt and lump salt. The salt was pumped as wild brine from 45yds beneath the works and evaporated in a large iron pan. The crystals thus formed were raked into tubs to form blocks, and subsequently dried in brick stove houses, before being exported (with the first part of the journey by canal) to India, Canada and West Africa. The works closed in 1986 but is currently being restored and is well worth visiting.

Open Sun–Thu 13.30–16.30, groups by appointment. Charge. Also information on the attractive countryside of Vale Royal and its rich industrial heritage.

Marbury Country Park Comberbach CW9 6AT (01606 77741; www.cheshire.gov.uk). Two-hundred-acre park occupying the landscaped gardens of the former Marbury Hall and estate, once the home of the Barry and Smith-Barry families. Overlooking Budworth Mere, the house was demolished in 1968 and the much-neglected gardens restored to their former glory by Cheshire County Heritage and Recreation service. The Information Centre (½ mile north of bridge 196) houses a display of Marbury's wildlife and history, including its use as a POW camp during World War II. Visitor's moorings and picnic area.

● **Anderton Lift**

Lift Lane, Anderton CW9 6FW (01606 786777; www.andertonboatlift.co.uk). An amazing and enormous piece of machinery built in 1875 by Leader Williams (later engineer of the Manchester Ship Canal) to connect the Trent & Mersey to the flourishing Weaver Navigation, 50ft below. As built, the lift consisted of two water-filled tanks counterbalancing each other in a vertical slide, resting on massive hydraulic rams. It worked on the very straightforward principle that making the ascending tank slightly lighter – by pumping a little water out – would assist the hydraulic rams (which were operated by a steam engine and pump) in moving both tanks, with boats in them, up or down their respective slide. In 1908 the lift had to have major repairs, so it was modernised at the same time. The troublesome hydraulic rams were done away with; from then on each tank – which contained 250 tons of water – had its own counterweights and was independent of the other tank. Electricity replaced steam as the motive power. One of the most fascinating individual features of the canal system, it draws thousands of sightseers every year. Restoration to full working order is now complete, following the original 1875 hydraulic design, using oil as the motive force rather than the chemically contaminated water that was the cause of the 1908 failure. The more recent counter balance weights, together with their ungainly supporting structure, have been retained to demonstrate the engineering development of the lift.

● **Northwich**

Ches. All services. Regular buses from Barnton. A rather attractive town at the junction of the Rivers Weaver and Dane. (The latter brings large quantities of sand down into the Weaver Navigation, necessitating a heavy expenditure on dredging.) As in every other town in this area, salt has for centuries been responsible for the continued prosperity of Northwich. The Weaver Navigation has of course been another very prominent factor in the town's history, and the building and repairing of barges, narrowboats, and small seagoing ships has been carried on here for over 200 years. Nowadays this industry has been almost forced out of business by foreign competition, and the last private shipyard on the river closed down in 1971. (This yard – Isaac Pimblott's – used to be between Hunt's Locks and Hartford Bridge. Their last contract was for a tug for Aden.) However, the big BW yard in the town continues to thrive; some very large maintenance craft are built and repaired here. The wharves by Town Bridge are empty, and are an excellent temporary mooring site for anyone wishing to visit the place. The town centre is very close; much of it has been completely rebuilt very recently. There is now an extensive shopping precinct. Although the large number of pubs has been whittled down in the rebuilding process, there are still some pleasant old streets. The Weaver and the big swing bridges across it remain a dominant part of the background.

Tourist Information Centre 1 The Arcade, Northwich CW9 5AS (01606 353534; www2.valeroyal.gov.uk). *Open Mon–Fri 09.00–17.00; Sat Apr–Oct 10.00–14.00 and Nov–Mar 09.30–12.30.*

Dock Road Edwardian Pumping Station Weir Street, Northwich CW9 8AB (01257 260157). Intriguing listed building housing unique pumps and gas-powered engines fully restored to working order. Building open and engines working *Easter–Sep Sun and B Hols 14.00–17.00, groups by arrangement.* Charge.

Salt Museum Weaver Hall, London Road, Northwich CW9 8AB (01606 41331; www.saltmuseum.org.uk). The history of the salt industry from Roman times to the present day, housed in the town's former workhouse. Look out for the remarkable model ship, made from salt of course. *Open all year Tue–Fri 10.00–17.00; Sat and Sun 14.00–17.00 (12.00–17.00 during Aug); B Hol Mon 10.00–17.00.* Audio visual introduction. Charge.

BIRD LIFE

The *Kingfisher* is a dazzlingly attractive bird, but its colours often appear muted when the bird is seen sitting in shade or vegetation. It has orange-red underparts and mainly blue upperparts; the electric blue back is seen to the best effect when the bird is observed in low-level flight speeding along a river. It is invariably seen near water and uses overhanging branches to watch for fish. When a feeding opportunity arises, the kingfisher plunges headlong into the water, catching its prey in its bill: the fish is swallowed whole. Kingfishers nest in holes excavated in the river bank.

Boatyards

Ⓑ **Orchard Marina** School Road, Gadbrook Park, Rudheath, Northwich CW9 7RG (01606 42082; www.orchardmarina.com). Beside bridge 182. 🛒 🛥 D Pump out, gas, overnight/long-term mooring, dry dock, boat and engine repairs, boat fitting out, boat and engine sales, DIY facilities, books, maps, solid fuel, toilets, showers, laundrette. *Emergency call out.*

Ⓑ **Colliery Narrowboat Co** Wincham Wharf, Lostock Gralam, Northwich CW9 7NT (01606 44672). Beside bridge 189. 🛒 🛒 🛥 D Pump out, gas, overnight/ long-term mooring, slipway, crane, storage, dry dock, boat building, boat sales, boat and engine repairs, wet dock, DIY facilities, toilets.

Ⓑ **Alvechurch Boat Centres** Anderton Marina, Uplands Road, Anderton CW9 6AQ (01606 79642; www.alvechurch.com). Services are on the canal. 🛒 🛒 🛥 D E Pump out, gas, narrowboat hire, overnight mooring, long-term mooring, slipway, sales, engine sales and repairs, boat painting, covered wet docks for hire, chandlery, gifts, restaurant, telephone, toilets.

Ⓑ **Barnton Wharf** Barnton Road, Northwich CW8 4EP (01606 783320). 🛥 D Pump out, gas, daycraft hire, long-term mooring, boat and engine sales, boat and engine repairs, boat fitting out, solid fuel. *24hr emergency call out.*

Ⓑ **Travelreign** Uplands Road, Anderton CW9 6AQ (07931 323747). 🛥 Overnight and long-term mooring, winter storage, slipway, wet dock.

NAVIGATIONAL NOTES

1 The Anderton Boat Lift is available for use *7 days a week* and pre-booked passage is essential by telephoning 01606 786777. *Open Apr–Sep 09.00–18.00 with reduced operating hours Oct–Mar.*

2 Boaters should differentiate between the holding moorings at the top and bottom of the lift, which are solely for lift use, and the visitor moorings beside Anderton Nature Park on the Weaver. Similar short stay visitor moorings are available on the Trent & Mersey.

Pubs and Restaurants

🍺 **Old Broken Cross** Broken Cross Place, Rudheath, Northwich CW9 7EB (01606 40431). Canalside, at bridge 184. Real ale and food *L and E, all day*. Children and dogs welcome. Monthly entertainment. Small canalside garden. Moorings. *Chemist, grocer, laundrette and other shops are* 1/2 *mile past pub, towards Northwich.*

🍺 ✕ **Wharf** Wincham Wharf, Manchester Road, Lostock Gralam, Northwich CW9 7NT (01606 46099). Canalside by bridge 189. Converted warehouse, reputed to be the oldest on the Trent & Mersey. Real ale is served, together with inexpensive bar meals *L and E (until 19.00 unless by prior arrangement)*. Children welcome. Music, karaoke and quiz nights. Large-screen TV upstairs.

🍺 **Salt Barge** Ollershaw Lane, Marston CW9 6ES (01606 43064). Opposite the Lion Salt Works, beside bridge 193. Deceptively large pub with a friendly atmosphere, neatly divided into cosy areas, and with an inviting family room. Real ales and good food available *L and E, daily*. Children's menu and *Sunday* lunch. Garden. Quiz *Thu* and live music at *weekends*.

✕ ♀ **The Moorings** Anderton Marina, Uplands Road, Anderton CW9 6AJ (01606 79789; www.mooringsrestaurant.co.uk). Canalside seating. Boaters please moor outside the basin. Small, independent restaurant and bar overlooking Anderton Marina and the Trent & Mersey Canal. *Open all day.* Wide variety of food with emphasis on fresh fish and fresh produce, served *L and E (not Mon E or Tue all day)*. Children and dogs welcome. Patio and terrace.

✕ **Anderton Boat Lift Café** Lift Lane, Anderton, Northwich CW9 6FW (01606 786777; www.andertonboatlift.co.uk). Café inside the Lift Operations Centre serving tea, coffee, hot and cold snacks, ice creams, etc. Children welcome. *Open as per the Lift Centre.*

🍺 **Stanley Arms** Old Road, Anderton CW9 6AG (01606 75059; www.stanleyarmsnorthwich.co.uk). Canalside, right opposite the Anderton Lift *(also PO, stores)*. Friendly real ale pub where children are welcome. Bar food served *all day, every day*. Outside seating and children's play area. The landlord keeps a collection of local tourist information leaflets. Excellent 'bottom of garden' moorings.

Dutton

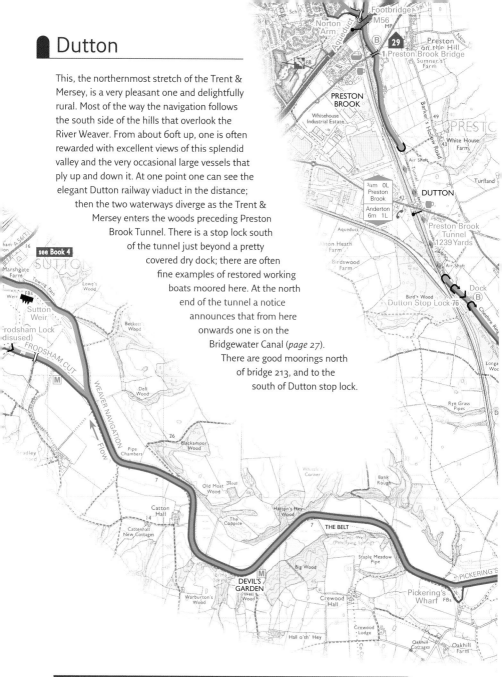

This, the northernmost stretch of the Trent & Mersey, is a very pleasant one and delightfully rural. Most of the way the navigation follows the south side of the hills that overlook the River Weaver. From about 6oft up, one is often rewarded with excellent views of this splendid valley and the very occasional large vessels that ply up and down it. At one point one can see the elegant Dutton railway viaduct in the distance; then the two waterways diverge as the Trent & Mersey enters the woods preceding Preston Brook Tunnel. There is a stop lock south of the tunnel just beyond a pretty covered dry dock; there are often fine examples of restored working boats moored here. At the north end of the tunnel a notice announces that from here onwards one is on the Bridgewater Canal (*page 27*). There are good moorings north of bridge 213, and to the south of Dutton stop lock.

NAVIGATIONAL NOTES

1. Access to Preston Brook Tunnel is restricted to *northbound on the hour to 10 minutes past the hour; southbound on the 1/2 hour to 20 mins to the hour.*
2. North of Preston Brook Tunnel you are on the Bridgewater Canal, which is owned by the Manchester Ship Canal Company. *See page 27.*
3. A British Waterways licence is valid for seven consecutive days on this canal.

Pubs and Restaurants

🍺 ✕ **Leigh Arms** Warrington Road, Little Leigh CW8 4QT (01606 853327). ¼ mile south of bridge 209, overlooking the Weaver and Acton Swing Bridge. Attractive old coaching inn with large restaurant area serving real ales and an extensive menu of home-made food *all day, every day*. Children and dogs welcome. Patio and garden seating, large children's play area. Moorings.

🍺 ✕ **Horns Inn** Warrington Road, Little Leigh CW8 4QT (01606 852192). 200yds south of bridge 209 on the A49, by Acton Swing Bridge. Friendly, roadside pub serving home-made bar food *L and E, daily*. Cosy bars, large garden and children's play area.

🍺 ✕ **Hollybush** Acton Bridge CW8 4QY (01606 853196). ¼ mile north of bridge 209. Listed, timber-framed building, one of the oldest farmhouse pubs in the country, with unique charm and character. Wide range of interesting, home-cooked food served in bar and restaurant *L and E, daily*. Children welcome. Garden with children's play area, including bouncy castle. Traditional pub games. Accommodation.

🍺 **Tunnel Top** Northwich Road, Dutton WA4 4JY (01928 718181). Family pub with friendly atmosphere, serving real ale and excellent food *L and E (not E Mon,Tues, Sun)*. Children and dogs welcome. Large garden.

Boatyards

Ⓑ **Black Prince Holidays** Bartington Wharf, Acton Bridge, Northwich CW8 4QU (01606 852945; www.black-prince.com). 🔧 🛠 D E Pump out, gas, electric boat recharging, narrowboat hire, day-hire craft, long-term mooring, engine repairs, groceries, books and maps, toilets, gifts, coal.

Ⓑ **Dutton Dry Dock** Tunnel End, Dutton WA4 4LA (01928 716701; duttondock@onetel.co.uk). Dry dock, historic boat repairs, boat blacking, boat repairs, engineering and machine shop, vintage engine repairs.

● **Preston Brook**
Tunnel 1239yds long and forbidden to unpowered craft. It is crooked, like Barnton and Saltersford tunnels, and there is no towpath.

● **Dutton**
Ches. Tel, garage. Small settlement on top of Preston Brook Tunnel, at the end of the lane uphill from the south end of the tunnel.

INDEX